Britain and the *Casus Belli*
1822–1902

Britain and the
Casus Belli
1822–1902

A study of Britain's international position
from Canning to Salisbury

by

CHRISTOPHER HOWARD

UNIVERSITY OF LONDON
THE ATHLONE PRESS
1974

Published by
THE ATHLONE PRESS
UNIVERSITY OF LONDON
at 4 Gower Street London WC1

Distributed by Tiptree Book Services Ltd
Tiptree, Essex

U.S.A. and Canada
Humanities Press Inc
New York

© *Christopher Howard* 1974

ISBN 0 485 11149 7

Printed in Great Britain by
WESTERN PRINTING SERVICES LTD
Bristol

TO
E. E.

FOREWORD

In a small book, published some years ago, under the title *Splendid Isolation*, I touched on certain views, long current, concerning Britain's international position and her attitude towards other great powers during the later years of the third Marquis of Salisbury.

In the present book I have carried the discussion of these views back to the time of Canning.

I gladly acknowledge the gracious permission of Her Majesty the Queen to make use of material in the Royal Archives at Windsor Castle.

I am most grateful for the facilities kindly granted me by: His Grace the Duke of Devonshire; His Grace the Duke of Wellington; the Marquis of Salisbury; the Earl of Clarendon; the Earl of Derby; the Earl of Harewood; the Earl of Harrowby; the Earl Spencer; the Viscount Harcourt; General the Lord Robertson of Oakridge; Lady Hermione Cobbold; Sir Charles Buchanan; Mr Oliver Bagot; Col. A. C. Barnes; Mr Mark Bonham-Carter; Mr Lawrence Scott; the Trustees of the Broadlands Archives; the National Trust, the owners of the copyright of the Hughenden Archives; the Proprietors of *The Times*; the Librarian of the University of Birmingham; the Librarian of the National Liberal Club; and the Trustees of the Centre for Military Archives, King's College, London.

Extracts from Crown Copyright Records in the Public Record Office appear by kind permission of the Controller of Her Majesty's Stationery Office; those from documents in the Public Record Office of Northern Ireland by kind permission of the Deputy Keeper.

I should like to express my appreciation of the courtesy extended to me by the Queen's Librarian and by the Registrar of the Royal Archives, Windsor Castle; by the Librarian and Keeper of the Devonshire Collections; the Librarian to the

Duke of Wellington; the Archivist of the Harrowby Manu-
scripts; the Librarians of Balliol College and Christ Church,
Oxford; the Librarian of King's College, London; and the
Archivist of the Hughenden Archives.

I am also much indebted for help, information or advice
given to me on various occasions by Lord Blake; Mr David
Ayerst; Dr F. R. Bridge; Professor J. B. Conacher; Professor
Douglas Dakin; Dr M. L. Dockrill; Dr P. J. Marshall; and Dr
A. E. O'Day.

I wish to express my gratitude to King's College, London,
for generously granting me a year's leave of absence, and to the
University of London for a grant from the Central Research
Fund.

Finally, I should like to acknowledge my debt to those
historians from whose writings and editorial work I have
profited. They are too numerous for me to name them all
individually here. It is, however, fitting that I should make
special mention of the late Dr G. P. Gooch, Sir Harold Temperley, Sir Charles Webster and Dame Lillian Penson.

King's College, London   C.H.D.H.

CONTENTS

A NOTE ON SOURCES

The principal sources for this study are the papers of contemporaries. Outstanding among these are the documents in the Royal Archives at Windsor Castle.

I have consulted the papers of every prime minister of the period under review and those of every foreign secretary of the period to which it is possible to have access. (I have been unable to locate Dudley's papers or to obtain access to those of Malmesbury or Kimberley.) For the whereabouts of the various prime ministers' papers see John Brooke, *The Prime Ministers' Papers 1801–1902* (London, 1968). For that of the foreign secretaries' papers see *The Records of the Foreign Office 1782–1939* (London, 1969), in 'Public Record Office Handbooks'. The papers of the fifteenth Earl of Derby are now in the Liverpool Record Office.

The following collections of papers (for the whereabouts of which see, unless otherwise stated, Brooke, op. cit.) have also yielded significant information:

Sir William à Court, later Baron Heytesbury, Sir John Ardagh (P.R.O.); Herbert Asquith, later Earl of Oxford and Asquith; Sir Charles Bagot; Arthur Balfour, later Earl Balfour; Sir John Bloomfield (P.R.O.); John Bright; James Bryce, later Viscount Bryce; Sir Andrew Buchanan (St Anne's Manor, Sutton Bonington, Loughborough); Sir Henry Campbell-Bannerman; Stratford Canning, later Viscount Stratford de Redcliffe; Joseph Chamberlain; Richard Cobden; Earl Cowley; Richard Cross, later Viscount Cross; George Curzon, later Marquis Curzon of Kedleston; Thomas Delane (Printing House Square); eighth Duke of Devonshire; Sir Charles Dilke; Marquis of Dufferin and Ava; Chichester Fortescue, later Baron Carlingford; first Earl Granville; Sir Edward Grey, later Viscount Grey of Fallodon; Sir Edward Hamilton; Edmund Hammond, later Baron Hammond; Sir William Harcourt; Gathorne Hardy, later Earl of Cranbrook; Sir Michael Hicks Beach, later Earl St Aldwyn (Gloucestershire County Record Office); Sir Frank Lascelles (P.R.O.); Sir Henry Layard; Earl of Lytton; Sir Edward Malet; Sir Robert Morier (Balliol College, Oxford); Sir Augustus Paget; Marquis of Ripon; Lord Odo Russell, later Baron Ampthill (P.R.O.); Field Marshal Sir William Robertson (Centre for Military

Archives, King's College, London); Sir Thomas Sanderson, later
Baron Sanderson (P.R.O.); Dudley Ryder, Viscount Sandon, later
third Earl of Harrowby; Sir Ernest Satow (P.R.O.); C. P. Scott
(University of Manchester); eighth Earl Spencer; J. A. Spender;
Viscount Tenterden (P.R.O.); Sir William White (P.R.O.).

I have also consulted the papers of the Cabinet, Foreign Office,
Admiralty and War Office in the Public Record Office and those of
the India Office in the India Office Library.

Page-references to *Accounts and Papers* relate to the set in the State
Paper Room at the British Museum.

A NOTE ON NOMENCLATURE

Two Earls Granville were concerned in the events of the period. The first earl (1773–1846) was ambassador in Paris from 1824 to 1841. The second earl (1815–91) was three times foreign secretary.

Two Earls of Derby were also concerned. The fourteenth earl (1799–1869) was three times prime minister. His son, Edward Stanley (1826–93), known from 1851 to 1869 as Lord Stanley, the fifteenth earl, was twice foreign secretary.

Sir William à Court (1779–1860) was raised to the peerage as Baron Heytesbury in 1828.

Stratford Canning (1786–1880) was raised to the peerage as Viscount Stratford de Redcliffe in 1852.

Gathorne Hardy (1814–1906) was raised to the peerage as Viscount Cranbrook in 1878.

Chichester Fortescue (1823–98) was raised to the peerage as Baron Carlingford in 1874.

Spencer Compton Cavendish (1833–1908), known as the Marquis of Hartington from 1858 to 1891, succeeded his father as eighth Duke of Devonshire in the latter year.

ABBREVIATIONS

A.P.	*Accounts and Papers*
A.P.P.	*Die Auswärtige Politik Preussens 1858–71*, ed. E. Brandenburg, O. Hoetzsch, H. Oncken, W. Hoppe and A. O. Meyer, 10 vols. to date (Oldenburg, 1933–39)
B.D.	*British Documents on the Origins of the War 1898–1914*, ed. G. P. Gooch and Harold Temperley, 11 vols. (London, 1927–38)
B.F.S.P.	*British and Foreign State Papers*
B.I.H.R.	*Bulletin of the Institute of Historical Research*
B.I.L.A.	*Britain and the Independence of Latin America 1812–1830*, ed. C. K. Webster, 2 vols. (Cambridge, 1938)
B.M.	British Museum
D.C.M.	Arthur Wellesley, Duke of Wellington, *Despatches, Correspondence and Memoranda*, ed. 2nd Duke of Wellington, 8 vols. (London, 1867–80)
D.D.F.	*Documents diplomatiques français 1871–1914*, ed. Ministère des Affaires Etrangères, Commission de Publication des Documents Relatifs aux Origines de la Guerre de 1914, 3 series (Paris, 1929–59)
D.E.W.H.	*The Diary of Sir Edward Walter Hamilton 1880–1885*, ed. Dudley W. R. Bahlman, 2 vols. (Oxford, 1972)
E.H.R.	*English Historical Review*
F.B.F.P.	*Foundations of British Foreign Policy*, ed. Harold Temperley and Lillian M. Penson (Cambridge, 1938)
G.G. 1868–76	*The Political Correspondence of Mr Gladstone and Lord Granville 1868–1876*, ed. Agatha Ramm, 2 vols. (London, 1952)
G.G. 1876–86	*The Political Correspondence of Mr Gladstone and Lord Granville 1876–1886*, ed. Agatha Ramm, 2 vols. (Oxford, 1962)
G.P.	*Die Grosse Politik der Europäischen Kabinette 1871–1914*, ed. J. Lepsius, A. Mendelssohn Bartholdy and F. Thimme, 40 vols. (Berlin, 1922–27)
Hansard	Hansard's *Parliamentary Debates*

H.J.	*Historical Journal*
I.O.L.	India Office Library
J.M.H.	*Journal of Modern History*
L.Q.V.	*The Letters of Queen Victoria*, ed. A. C. Benson, Viscount Esher and G. E. Buckle, 3 series (London, 1907–32)
M.E.T.	*The Map of Europe by Treaty*, ed. Edward Hertslet, 4 vols. (London, 1875–91)
O.D.	*Les origines diplomatiques de la guerre de 1870–71*, ed. Ministère des Affaires Etrangères, 29 vols. (Paris, 1910–32)
P.D.I.	Rose Louise Greaves, *Persia and the Defence of India 1884–1892* (London, 1959)
P.R.O.	Public Record Office
P.S.S.	W. E. Gladstone, *Political Speeches in Scotland*, 2 series (Edinburgh, 1880)
R.A.	Royal Archives
T.R.H.S.	*Transactions of the Royal Historical Society*

CHAPTER I

'Freedom from all
entanglements'

(i)

Is it possible to formulate any general principle that governs,
or ought to govern, the conduct of a country's foreign policy?
At least one British foreign secretary of the nineteenth century
took the view that, so far, at least, as this country was concerned,
it was not. On 31 May 1875 the fifteenth Earl of Derby told the
House of Lords:

I do not believe that it is possible for us to lay down any formula or
any general rule which shall bind us in our foreign policy for all time
and on all occasions. We must deal with the circumstances of each
case as it arises.[1]

On the other hand, the history of the United States offers an
obvious example of a 'formula' or 'general rule' for the conduct
of the country's foreign policy, publicly laid down and frequently
invoked. In 1796, in his Farewell Address, George Washington advised his fellow-countrymen that ' 'tis our true policy to
steer clear of permanent Alliances, with any portion of the
foreign world'.[2] In 1801, in his First Inaugural Address, Thomas
Jefferson explained that one of the 'essential principles' of his
administration would be 'peace, commerce, and honest friendship with all nations, entangling alliances with none'.[3] The
words of both Washington and Jefferson came to form part of
the American treasury of political wisdom. They have been
quoted over and over again. Moreover, so far, at least, as the
United States's relations with Europe during the nineteenth
century are concerned, it would be difficult to point to any
transaction that was obviously at variance with the principle
enunciated by both the first and third presidents.

Britain's international position was and is essentially different from that of the United States. Nevertheless, it is often said to have been, at the end of the nineteenth century, one of freedom from commitments, even of 'isolation'.[4] Moreover, that freedom, or 'isolation', is frequently said to have been the result of an attitude on the part of successive British governments, not very different from that recommended to their fellow-countrymen by Washington and Jefferson. One reads of Britain's 'reluctance to enter into binding commitments';[5] her 'traditional . . . anxiety to avoid commitments';[6] her 'traditional line of non-commitment';[7] her 'time-honoured refusal to enter binding alliances';[8] her 'tradition of eschewing alliances and avoiding guarantees';[9] her 'traditional policy of a free hand';[10] her 'time-honoured principle of isolation'.[11] In the eighth decade of the twentieth century these views retain their popularity. A work published in 1971 refers to Britain's 'traditional policy of avoiding involvement in alliances'.[12]

There is some disagreement among historians as to the geographical area to which this policy—or principle—applied. Some authorities have seen it as applying only to the continent of Europe,[13] others, apparently, as having no geographical limit.[14] There is also disagreement as to the date of its origin. It has been said to go back to 'the age of congresses',[15] even to Waterloo.[16] Another view is that it dates from the time of Canning—that is, presumably, from the period of his second foreign secretaryship.[17] Some historians prefer, understandably, not to specify precisely when it originated. It is often said to have come to an end with Lansdowne's foreign secretaryship, which saw the conclusion, on 30 January 1902, of Britain's alliance with Japan.[18]

A somewhat different explanation of the supposed British attitude, given by some historians, stresses the limitations placed on the power of the British government by the popular and parliamentary nature of the constitution. It was, it is argued, not the government, but public opinion, expressed through the House of Commons, which had the final decision on all important questions, such as the choice between peace and war. What that decision would turn out to be in a particular case was, however, something that there was no means of foreseeing. It was, therefore, actually impossible for any British government, even should it desire to do so, to give a pledge to any other power or powers that would, should a given contingency arise, bind the country to go to war.[19]

(ii)

It should not be thought that these views are merely the invention of academic historians, writing many years after the event. On the contrary, contemporary documents abound with statements similar to those quoted. One foreign secretary after another from the time of Canning onwards expressed the British government's unwillingness to give any pledge that would bind the country, should a given contingency arise at some time in the future, to go to war.[20] In the later years of the Salisbury era it was frequently claimed that Britain was not, in fact, bound by any such pledge,[21] that she enjoyed freedom of action, that her international position was, to quote a highly popular catch-phrase of the period, one of 'splendid isolation'.[22] Moreover, the maintenance of this state of affairs was widely, if not univers-ally, believed to be a matter of long-standing policy, even of principle.

'The policy pursued by England is to be free from all binding engagements', wrote Lord Augustus Loftus, a former ambas-sador, in his *Diplomatic Reminiscences*, published in 1892.[23] In 1896 a Canadian newspaper referred to Britain's 'traditional policy of freedom from all entanglements'.[24] There was much talk of her 'policy of isolation'.[25] For the Liberal *Speaker* this 'isolation' meant 'not that we had nothing in common with other European Powers, but that we did not choose to make entangling engagements'.[26]

'Engagements' is a broad term. It can include, and the *Speaker* may well have intended it to include, guarantees, relating to the independence, neutrality, territorial integrity or institutions of another country, or to some similar matter. Indeed, it would be easy to quote contemporary expressions both of unwillingness to give pledges of this type and of the opinion that to do so would be contrary to an established principle of British foreign policy.[27]

However, the type of engagement that many contemporaries, especially in the Salisbury era, no doubt thought of, as being more particularly precluded, was an alliance, of which there were on the continent at the time a number of conspicuous examples. Much was said and written at the time concerning what was believed to be Britain's systematic and sustained avoidance of such commitments. Joseph Chamberlain, for example, told the House of Commons in 1898 that 'the policy of this country, hitherto well known to all nations of the world, and declared again and again, was that we would not accept any alliance'.[28] There was a great deal in the reports of parliamentary debates, in the press and in the diplomatic correspondence of the period to similar effect.[29]

Indeed, contemporaries sometimes discussed Britain's attitude towards alliances with other powers in terms reminiscent of those employed by the men who, a century earlier, had laid down guiding principles for the conduct of the foreign policy of the United States. Thus, Joseph Chamberlain recorded, also in 1898, having told Hatzfeldt, the German ambassador, that 'the policy of this country for many years had been a policy of isolation—or at least of non-entanglement in alliances', and of having gone on to compare it with 'the policy of the United States since the time of Washington'.[30] A few weeks later Kimberley, speaking in the House of Lords, appealed to 'the principle upon which we have for many years acted with regard to our foreign affairs, of not engaging in what are commonly called entangling alliances with other Powers'.[31] In 1902 an anonymous contributor to the *Quarterly Review* wrote of 'the old principle of avoiding entangling alliances'.[32]

Britain's adherence to this policy—or principle—was believed by many people at the time to be of considerable standing. Joseph Chamberlain claimed that it went back to the time of the Crimean War,[33] Sir William Harcourt to that of what was then known as the 'Great War'—that is, the conflict with France in the revolutionary and Napoleonic era.[34] In general, however, the politicians, diplomats and journalists of the period, although agreeing as to its antiquity, preferred not to specify its date of origin. It was 'traditional', 'old', even 'historic'.[35] The conclusion of the agreement with Japan was widely regarded as marking its abandonment and also that of the freedom of action that had resulted from it.[36]

The view that the nature of the constitution made it actually impossible for any British government to give a pledge that entailed an obligation, should a hypothetical contingency arise at some time in the future, to go to war in support of another power, was also contemporary. Salisbury was the leading exponent of this theory and he had a number of disciples.[37]

(iii)

Interesting as these contemporary expressions of opinion are, they constitute, of course, no sort of proof that Britain really enjoyed freedom of action in her foreign relations, or that this freedom—assuming that it existed—was the result of a policy, or of adherence to a principle, or even of the operation of factors inherent in the British constitution.

Assertions by politicians with only limited knowledge of the activities of the Foreign Office, or by even less well informed journalists, are not reliable sources of information. Even statements by prime ministers or foreign secretaries cannot be accepted uncritically. What a minister says is not necessarily a good guide to what he does. To see in Castlereagh's conduct of affairs at Chaumont, in Vienna, in Paris in November 1815, or at Aix-la-Chapelle three years later, the operation of a 'traditional policy of freedom from all entanglements' would be fanciful. It is also evident that, despite everything that was said to the contrary in the Salisbury era, Britain had long been bound by certain pledges.

However, not everyone looked on these pledges as entailing obligations that were especially onerous. There were few of them that a prime minister or foreign secretary, if he were so minded, could not plausibly explain away.[38] Moreover, for a considerable period, although clearly not as early as 1815, successive British governments did refrain from involving the country in any long-term commitment that would have bound it, should the *casus foederis* have arisen, to go to war on the continent of Europe.[39] The question is whether this abstention was systematic, as so many contemporaries claimed.

In short, the view that a high proportion, if not all, of Castle-reagh's successors, down to the beginning of the twentieth century, acted in the way described by the historians cited in the preceding pages cannot be dismissed as wholly unworthy of serious discussion.

CHAPTER II

'Prospective engagements'

(i)

There has long been in this country a strong feeling of aversion from any kind of continental entanglement. This feeling had already found expression in the eighteenth century.[1] 'Nature has separated us from the continent', a peer told the House of Lords in 1755, '. . . and as no man ought to endeavour to separate whom God Almighty has joined, so no man ought to endeavour to join what God Almighty has separated.'[2] A generation later Jeremy Bentham wrote that it was 'not the interest of Great Britain to have any treaty of alliance, offensive or defensive, with any other power whatever'.[3]

It is easy to cite similar expressions of opinion from the reports of parliamentary debates and from the press of the nineteenth century. Cobden's pronouncements are probably the best known.[4]

It is also easy to quote the prime ministers and foreign secretaries of the period to the effect that any 'exclusive', 'monopolizing', 'separate', 'single' or 'special'—the epithets varied—alliance was unnecessary or undesirable or both. Thus, in an important statement of policy, made in the House of Lords after the formation of his third administration, the fourteenth Earl of Derby laid down that it was the duty of the government of this country 'to keep itself upon terms of goodwill with all surrounding nations, but not to entangle itself with any single or monopolizing alliance with any one of them'.[5] At one time or another Canning, Palmerston, Russell, Gladstone, Granville, the fifteenth Earl of Derby, Salisbury, Rosebery and Kimberley all spoke or wrote to similar effect.[6]

The question is: Should we accept these declarations as reliable guides to their authors' actual conduct of foreign affairs?

In this connexion the term 'alliance' presents certain difficulties.

In the nineteenth century this word was often employed to denote a relationship between powers far less intimate than any to which it would normally be applied today, at least in an official document. Its use as a description of Britain's relationship with another power did not necessarily imply the existence of any obligation on Britain's part to render armed assistance to that power in the event of war. It was, in fact, as Salisbury reminded the House of Lords in 1887, a term that was both 'vague' and 'general'.[7] Of this vagueness and generality the documents of the period afford innumerable illustrations. The same is true, *mutatis mutandis*, of the term 'ally', as Palmerston in 1849 pointed out to the House of Commons.[8]

It was, no doubt, their realization of the imprecision of what was, nevertheless, for purposes of discussion of the country's foreign relations, an indispensable term, that caused some contemporaries to specify at considerable length the kind of alliance that, in their opinion, was open to objection. Harcourt, for example, told his constituents in 1896 that Britain needed no 'formal alliance in the technical sense of the word'.[9] In 1901 Lascelles, the ambassador in Berlin, wrote of the British government's 'traditional policy of avoiding alliances which would bind them for a long period'.[10]

However, the fundamental objection, as more than one politician made clear, was to a pledge that would bind the country to go to war in a hypothetical contingency that might arise in the future, and, therefore, in circumstances, the nature of which it was impossible to foresee. Such a pledge was often termed a 'prospective engagement'.

Thus, in 1825 Canning pointed out, in a dispatch to the minister in Mexico City, that it was not the British government's policy to give any pledge that would 'fetter . . . its decision upon future contingencies and with respect to cases hypothetically proposed'.[11] In 1834 Palmerston wrote to the ambassador in Paris, expressing his objections to 'Treaties which are formed in Contemplation of Indefinite, and indistinctly foreseen Cases'.[12] Seven years later he declined a Russian overture on the ground that it was not usual for this country 'to enter into engagements with reference to cases which have not actually arisen, or which are not immediately in prospect', since Parliament might 'not

approve of an engagement which should bind England pros-
pectively to take up Arms in a contingency which might happen
at an uncertain time, and under circumstances which could not
as yet be foreseen'.[13] In 1859 Russell warned Queen Victoria
that 'there never was a time when it was less expedient to fetter
this country with prospective engagements'.[14] In 1891 Gladstone
declared his opposition to what he, too, termed 'prospective
engagements'.[15]

(ii)

A principle that precluded any pledge that would be binding on
the country in anticipation of a contingency that might arise in
the future left, of course, a door open for a pledge given in
connexion with a situation that already existed. 'We have no
objection to Treaties for a Specific and definite and immediate
object', wrote Palmerston in 1834, in the letter to the British
ambassador in Paris, already quoted.[16] In 1851 Russell explained to Queen Victoria that, although Britain's 'tradi-
tionary policy' was 'not to bind the Crown and country by
engagements', this rule was, nevertheless, subject to exception,
'upon special cause shown, arising out of the circumstances of
the day'.[17]

The most obvious 'special cause' that was liable to arise was a
war, actual or imminent. More than one contemporary showed
his awareness of the need to recognize this qualification to the
general rule. Mountague Bernard, the international jurist, for
example, expressed in 1865 the opinion that 'standing alliances'
had generally been 'unprofitable'. However, he excepted
'specific engagements made with a view to a particular object',
explaining that 'treaties of alliance in contemplation of an
actual or impending war' were in this category.[18] Dilke, speaking in the House of Commons in 1898, although declaring his
opposition to 'permanent, standing alliances, when war is not in
immediate view', acknowledged that 'a policy of alliance when
you have an immediate common object in view of war with
other Powers is one which everybody would favour'.[19] Monson,
the ambassador in Paris, reported a few months later having
assented to the proposition, advanced by Delcassé, that 'the

conclusion of any foreign Alliance would be contrary to the traditional policy of Great Britain', but with the reservation that the rule was 'subject to exception in case of war'.[20]

The fact is that Britain has fought all her successful land wars in Europe in collaboration, for at least part of the time, with a great power or, more often, with several.

A good example of a situation, to which the 'special cause' principle applied, was that created by the approach and out-break of the war over Schleswig and Holstein. Russell's own account of his conduct in this situation deserves, because of the principle that it implies, quotation:

France was invited in clear and explicit tones to join Great Britain in defending Denmark by force of arms. To this proposal the Government of the Emperor replied by a decided refusal. The proposal was again made after the London Conference, and was again refused.[21]

Gladstone, in a speech delivered during his second Midlothian campaign, clearly implied the same principle. He told an audience at West Calder that Palmerston's government, of which he had been a member, made 'a formal offer to France that we should join together in forbidding the German Power to lay violent hands upon Denmark'. The reason, he explained, why this offer was not acted upon was that the Emperor of the French 'most blindly' refused it.[22]

Another example is afforded by the treaties concluded by Granville with Prussia—or, if one prefers, the North German Confederation—and France on, respectively, 9 and 11 August 1870, with the purpose of ensuring respect for the independence and neutrality of Belgium both during the war that had broken out three weeks previously and at the eventual peace settle-ment.[23] The treaties bound each belligerent to cooperate with Britain against any power that violated the neutrality of Belgium. However, they did not commit Britain to take part in any military operations beyond the limits of Belgium's actual territory. Their validity, too, was limited to the duration of the war and the twelve months subsequent to the ratification of the final peace treaty. Their life proved, accordingly, to be brief, although that was something that the cabinet could scarcely have foreseen, when, on 30 July 1870, it authorized Granville to open negotiations with the belligerents. At that time no major battle had as yet been fought. John Bright offered Gladstone his resignation in protest against the decision to negotiate these treaties, but no other member of the cabinet did so.[24]

(iii)

On occasion, too, Britain joined one or more of the other great powers in an undertaking that certainly involved the possibility of using force, but only for a limited purpose, arising out of an already existing situation, without formal declaration of war and, in any case, not against one of the other four great powers.

The treaty with France and Russia, signed in London by Dudley on 6 July 1827 during Canning's brief premiership and intended to bring the six-year-old conflict between the Turks and Greeks to an end, is a case in point. The parties were to offer their mediation to the Porte, with a view to effecting a reconciliation between it and the Greeks. An additional and secret article provided that, if, within the space of one month, either the Turks should reject the proposed armistice, or the Greeks refuse to execute it, the three powers would attempt to prevent any further collision between the two sides, but without actually taking part in the hostilities.[25]

Moreover, the treaty was supplemented, six days later, by a protocol, to which was annexed an 'instruction commune', stating that, if within the space of one month the Porte did not accept the proposed mediation and armistice, the three powers would inform it that they would take such steps as the circumstances of the case required. The measures to be taken were to consist of an immediate 'rapprochement' with the Greeks and the union of the squadrons of the three powers with the object of preventing any Turkish reinforcements from reaching the Greek mainland or islands; the squadrons were to treat the Greeks thenceforward as friends, although without actually taking part in the hostilities between the two contending parties.[26]

Did this transaction constitute a 'prospective engagement'?

The contingency envisaged lay in the future, but not in the distant future. The circumstances in which it might arise should not have been entirely unforeseeable. Moreover, there was no formal declaration of war by either side, the events of 20 October 1827 in the Bay of Navarino being, as Palmerston wrote at the time, 'only a slight act of Remonstrance stuck parenthetically into unbroken Friendship'.[27]

Palmerston, in his turn, certainly entered into a number of engagements 'for a specific, and definite and immediate object'. There was the convention with France of 22 October 1832, providing for joint action to compel the King of the Netherlands to withdraw his forces from Belgium.[28] There was the treaty with France, Portugal and Spain of 22 April 1834, under which Britain promised naval cooperation for the purpose of ensuring the departure from Portugal of Dom Miguel and Don Carlos, the absolutist claimants to the thrones of the two Iberian kingdoms.[29] There were the additional articles of 18 August 1834, concluded after Don Carlos had made his way *via* London to Navarre, under which Britain undertook to furnish the Madrid government with munitions and, if necessary, naval assistance.[30] There was the convention with Austria, Prussia, Russia and the Ottoman Empire, signed in London on 15 July 1840, and aimed at Mehemet Ali.[31] Not one of these transactions involved, of course, an obligation formally to declare war. Nor was any of them directed against a great power.

(iv)

Sometimes all the great powers collaborated in an attempt to solve some problem, often one arising from the disturbed condition of the Ottoman Empire. In course of time such collaboration came to be known as the 'Concert of the Powers', the 'Concert of Europe' or the 'European Concert'.[32] 'The European Concert means that six Powers act together', Salisbury explained at the Guildhall in 1896.[33] Such collaboration could involve the use of force. However, as various declarations by Gladstone,[34] Granville[35] and Salisbury[36] illustrate, it was possible to combine opposition to involvement in any 'prospective engagement' with support, at least in principle, for the Concert.

(v)

A 'prospective engagement' need not necessarily be embodied in a treaty, convention or act. It can take the form of a note, a speech, or even of a verbal assurance by a minister or a diplomatic representative. Could it not be said, for example, that Russell's communications in connexion with the Schleswig-Holstein question during Palmerston's second administration placed Britain under an obligation to assist Denmark in their defence, should that prove necessary? His principal critic's views on this subject are well known.[37] However, on 9 March 1864, Russell wrote a dispatch to Paget, the minister in Copenhagen, claiming that he had never gone beyond 'offering advice' to Denmark; he had given no 'promise of material support'.[38] In due course this dispatch was laid before Parliament.[39] Indeed, Russell may well have written it with this object in view. At all events, in the House of Lords censure debate in July 1864 on the government's handling of the Danish question, he cited it as proof that he had given Denmark no pledge of armed support.[40] Even so, Russell would, no doubt, have been wiser not to have gone even to the point of 'offering advice'.

Again, should Palmerston's statement in the House of Commons on 23 July 1863 be regarded as having placed Britain under a moral obligation to assist Denmark in case of attack on the duchies? On that day Palmerston answered a question, put by a Liberal-Conservative member, Seymour Fitzgerald, on the subject of the relations between the 'Germanic Confederation' and Denmark,[41] with a declaration of the government's desire that the independence, integrity and rights of Denmark might be maintained, adding an assurance of his conviction that 'if any violent attempt were made to overthrow those rights and interfere with that independence, those who made the attempt would find in the result, that it would not be Denmark alone with which they would have to contend'.[42]

It would be interesting to know precisely what Palmerston had in mind, when he uttered these words.

Several other powers might reasonably be expected to

consider that the maintenance of the integrity of the possessions of the Crown of Denmark against the claims of the 'Germanic Confederation' was a matter that concerned them. The Czar was head of the elder branch of the House of Holstein-Gottorp, a fact of which the London treaty of 1852 served as a reminder.[43] France had been Denmark's ally in the era of the first Napoleon. Indeed, little more than three years previously Palmerston had warned Russell that 'a military inroad of German Troops into any part of the Danish Territory might lead to bringing France into Play, and might produce serious Consequences'.[44] More recently, on 19 July 1863, Manderström, the Swedish foreign minister, had shown concern at what he termed 'les mesures aggressives de l'Allemagne', pointing out that Sweden's own vital interests could hardly allow her to remain indifferent to the spectacle of her neighbour being crushed.[45] It is also noteworthy that Palmerston went on to express his trust 'that these transactions will continue to be, as they have been, matters for negotiation, and not for an appeal to arms'.[46]

As a matter of fact, Palmerston's statement of 23 July 1863 did not immediately arouse much comment either in the House of Commons or in the London press. In the course of the next few months the situation was transformed by the death of King Frederick VII of Denmark, the accession of Christian IX and his signature of the new constitution, and the intervention of Prussia and Austria, acting in their own interests. A not unfair comment was that of Stanley, who during the censure debate of July 1864 abjured any intention of dwelling on Palmerston's 'famous statement', since, as he explained, he allowed that 'those words were uttered under circumstances somewhat different from those which exist now'.[47] Nevertheless, whatever change of circumstances occurred during the year that followed Palmerston's reply to Seymour Fitzgerald, the words that he employed on that occasion were certainly ill-chosen.

The notes exchanged by Salisbury with Corti, the Italian ambassador, on 12 February 1887, did not, of course, contain the letter of any *casus belli*.[48] Salisbury's own estimates of their significance varied. In a letter to Queen Victoria, written on 5 February, he emphasized that it was only possible to speak with certainty 'for the existing ministry'.[49] When submitting to the Queen the documents approved by the cabinet he pointed out that this country would be bound only by the British note.[50] This did, in fact, differ in important respects from the Italian. In a letter to Paget, now ambassador in Vienna, he described the notes as 'more effusive perhaps than precise'.[51] To Malet, the ambassador in Berlin, he remarked that the professions contained in the British note were 'so guarded', that they did not seem to him 'to amount to more than might have been assumed without any despatches at all'.[52] On the other hand, in a memorandum, dated 23 February 1887, which he sent to the Queen, he expressed the opinion that Britain had given 'the utmost assurance that a Parliamentary State can give, to the effect that "in case of a war between France and Germany she would join herself actively to those Powers who constitute the police of peace in the East" '.[53]

It is significant that neither the British and Italian notes of 12 February 1887, nor the British and Austro-Hungarian of the following 24 March, were laid before Parliament. Nor were those, exchanged by Salisbury with the Austro-Hungarian and Italian ambassadors on 12 December of the same year, under which the three powers declared their wish to preserve the *status quo* in the near east and claimed the right, in the event of a certain course of action on the part of the Porte, to occupy selected points on the territory of the Ottoman Empire. Neither the existence nor the terms of the agreement embodied in these notes was to be communicated to the Ottoman Empire or to any other power that had not already been consulted, without the consent of all the parties.[54] The notes were not even put on record in the appropriate department of the Foreign Office. Instead, they were kept by the permanent under-secretary.[55] In view of their contents and of Salisbury's previous experience of the problems of security, the fact that these precautions were considered necessary is not surprising.

(vi)

What of the world outside Europe? It would be difficult to argue that all British governments systematically avoided 'prospective engagements' in Asia. The best known example of a British pledge relating to any part of Asia given during the nineteenth century is probably that contained in the 'convention of defensive alliance' with the Ottoman Empire, signed in Constantinople by Layard, the British ambassador, on Salisbury's instructions,[56] on 4 June 1878.[57] Under this convention the Sultan undertook to introduce a programme of reforms in Turkey-in-Asia and to permit Britain to occupy Cyprus; Britain, for her part, promised that, should Russia retain Batum, Ardahan or Kars and at any future time attempt to seize any more Turkish territory in Asia, she would assist the Sultan in its defence. W. H. Smith called the arrangement, according to Sandon, a member of the cabinet and an assiduous diarist, 'the most important move since the days of Pitt'.[58] It was aimed at a European power—in fact, the largest. Moreover, once a British government had gone to war against Russia in defence of Turkey-in-Asia, it might well have had difficulty in avoiding involvement in military operations in Turkey-in-Europe as well.

Less than a year after the conclusion of what Gladstone, echoing the fifteenth Earl of Derby, described as 'an insane covenant',[59] Britain entered into another commitment to an Asian ruler.

By the Treaty of Gandamak of 26 May 1879, concluded with the Amir Yakub, after Lytton's war against Afghanistan, Britain imposed terms, the effect of which was to deprive that country of any real independence. Conditionally upon the Amir's conduct of his foreign relations being in accordance with the British government's advice and wishes, he was to receive support against any foreign aggression in the form of money, arms, or troops, to be employed, however, as the British government might judge best.[60]

The provision of troops, as distinct from other kinds of support, was not, of course, obligatory. Further, as Lytton pointed out to Cranbrook, the secretary for India, the engagement involved 'no inconvenient definition of Afghan territory', thereby leaving the British government considerable latitude, should it have to decide whether the *casus foederis* had actually arisen. In short, the Treaty of Gandamak entailed, in Lytton's words, 'limited liabilities . . . on behalf of our ally'.[61] Once again, however, the liabilities incurred related unmistakably to Russia.

In the following year, after the renewal of war, the change of government in London, the resignation of Lytton and the appointment of Ripon as his successor, Lepel Griffin, the political officer on the spot, redefined Britain's relations with Afghanistan in a letter to Abdul Rahman, who was destined to be amir for more than twenty years. The Kabul ruler was to have no political relations with any foreign power, other than Britain. If he were the victim of unprovoked aggression by a foreign power, Britain would, if necessary, aid him to repel it, provided that he followed the British government's advice in regard to his foreign relations.[62] Although Griffin's letter was even less specific than the Treaty of Gandamak as to the nature of the aid to be given, it nevertheless constituted an indubitable, although limited and conditional pledge to assist Afghanistan against an unnamed foreign power, in fact, of course, Russia, not greatly different in essence from that given on behalf of Lytton the previous year.

The period saw other examples of undertakings in connexion with extra-European territories, entailing either an unequivocal *casus belli* or, at least, an obligation difficult to honour without resort to force.

A case in point was the joint note, presented to the Khedive on 6 January 1882, in which the British and French governments expressed their resolve to maintain the established order in Egypt.[63] Another was the secret convention, signed in Bangkok on 6 April 1897, under which Britain promised to assist Siam in resisting any attempt by a third power to acquire dominion or establish influence in any of the territories or islands to the south of Muong Bang Tapan, that is, the region then known as the Siamese Malay States.[64] Yet another was the convention, also secret, of 30 August 1898, under which Britain and Germany agreed to oppose the intervention of any third power in Mozambique, Angola and Portuguese Timor.[65] Balfour, who signed this convention, described the arrangement as 'a complete defensive alliance with Germany against any third Power desiring to intervene in Mozambique or Angola'.[66]

Again, quite apart from entering into such written under-takings, Britain incurred an obligation to defend, if it should be necessary, every one of the numerous territories that successive governments annexed, occupied or placed under a protectorate.

Egypt provides the obvious example. From the time that Wolseley's forces occupied the country in the autumn of 1882 Britain was as fully committed to defending Egypt from attack as she would have been, had the foreign secretary put his signature to a solemn treaty of alliance. Moreover, the collapse of khedivial authority in the Sudan rendered an attack on Egypt itself by the forces of the Mahdi a possibility that had to be considered and that only Britain's own forces were in a state to resist. 'Egypt being army-less', Edward Hamilton asked himself a few weeks after the battle of Tel-el-Kebir, 'who are to act as the defenders of Egypt but our forces?'[67]

The British government, having once assumed responsibility for the defence of Egypt proper, could not easily remain in-different to the fate of Dongola, Kordofan and other regions further south. Henry Labouchere appreciated this situation. 'The result is that we are now told that we have a new frontier somewhere in the direction of the Equator, and that our honour is concerned etc. etc.', he wrote to Joseph Chamberlain little more than a year after the beginning of the British occupation of Egypt.[68]

Other parts of the world witnessed a similar process of what politicians had not yet learned to call escalation. The fact is that no European power that was engaged in acquiring 'a new frontier somewhere in the direction of the Equator' could expect to avoid incurring new responsibilities, however bare its actual treaty-safe. *Imperium et libertas* did not constitute a feasible combination.

(vii)

The governments of the period also inherited some important 'prospective engagements'.

The alliance with Portugal is the most obvious example. It rested on a long series of treaties, the earliest of which dated from the reign of Edward III. On 22 January 1815 Castlereagh, while in Vienna, attending the Congress, comprehensively renewed these 'ancient treaties'.[69] In the years that followed one foreign secretary after another acknowledged the British treaty obligation to Portugal.[70]

Another inherited engagement was that embodied in the three treaties of 'alliance and friendship' with Austria, Prussia and Russia, signed by Castlereagh and Wellington on the same day as the Second Treaty of Paris.[71]

Three years later, at the Congress of Aix-la-Chapelle, the representatives of the four victorious powers declared the alliance of 1815 to be in full force 'pour le casus foederis et belli'.[72] The 'Quadruple Alliance', as the reserved protocol of 15 November 1818 termed it,[73] was the expression of the four powers' determination to maintain the settlement that they had imposed on France. As long as successive British governments took the view that the national interest required the maintenance of that settlement—and Palmerston made it clear to Grey during his first foreign secretaryship that he did so[74]—the alliance remained a commitment.

Another commitment, at least of a kind, and one that was also inherited, arose from the fact that until 1837 the King of Great Britain was also King of Hanover. The personal union did not, of course, constitute a 'prospective engagement' in the strict sense of that term, but, as previous experience had shown, it was liable to prove an involvement. So long as it lasted no British government could remain wholly indifferent to an attack on Hanover, the ruler of which had, nevertheless, his own foreign policy, as William IV reminded Palmerston.[75]

(viii)

There was also frequent talk of an 'understanding' or 'entente' with one power or another, either as a fact or as a desideratum. In the time of Louis-Philippe and Aberdeen there was said to be a 'cordial understanding' or 'cordiale entente' with France.[76] During Derby's second administration Edmund Hammond, the permanent under-secretary at the Foreign Office, wrote of the 'perfect good understanding' that formed the basis of Franco-British relations.[77]

However, 'understanding' and 'entente' are both elastic terms. They could be and were applied to transactions, the existence of which the government of the day preferred not to avow publicly, as the documents relating to the agreements of 1887 with Italy and Austria-Hungary illustrate.[78] Indeed, Granville considered that even an 'understanding' could be 'prospective' and, therefore, open to objection. 'The Policy of successive Governments in this Country', he wrote in 1872 to Buchanan, the ambassador in Vienna, 'has been to avoid prospective understandings to meet contingencies which seldom occur in the way which has been anticipated.'[79]

Again, the fact that in 1814 Britain had been intimately concerned in the establishment of the new kingdom of the United Netherlands could easily be construed as entailing some sort of obligation to maintain the integrity of that brittle amalgam. On 3 September 1830, after the outbreak of the Belgian uprising, Aberdeen wrote to Bagot, the ambassador at The Hague, of Britain's 'engagements' to the Netherlands. He even considered the possibility of the *casus foederis* having arisen. 'We have guaranteed the union of Holland and Belgium', he added, with scant respect for terminological exactitude, 'and if the King has faithfully performed his part, we must perform ours.'[80] He based his attitude on fundamental considerations of policy. 'For if there is a principle of policy in my mind stronger than any other', he wrote to Bagot a few weeks later, 'it is to preserve and improve our union with Holland.'[81]

(ix)

One could, no doubt, go on multiplying examples of temporary, limited, conditional, implied, inherited, obsolete or extra-European commitments almost indefinitely. Nevertheless, the fact remains that during the period of almost eight decades that elapsed between the beginning of Canning's second foreign secretaryship and the end of Salisbury's last administration the sum total of 'prospective engagements' with other European powers, entered into by successive British governments, that placed this country under an explicit, unequivocal and new obligation to go to war on the continent of Europe in a hypothetical contingency and in circumstances that were not merely temporary, was small. They numbered altogether three.

The treaty of 21 November 1855, signed in Stockholm, pledged Britain, together with France, to defend the Kingdom of Sweden and Norway against aggression by Russia.[82] Even this treaty was concluded in time of war. However, it remained in force after the restoration of peace.

Under the Tripartite—or Triple—Treaty of 15 April 1856 Britain, Austria and France declared that they would consider any breach of the terms of the Treaty of Paris, signed sixteen days previously, as a *casus belli*,[83]

On 16 March 1899 Salisbury instructed the British ambassador in Madrid to inform the Spanish government of Britain's readiness, if the occasion should arise, to give military and naval assistance to prevent any hostile landing or attack by sea on the coast of the Bay of Algeciras.[84]

Do these three transactions suffice to dispose of the view that it was a long-established principle of British foreign policy to avoid any 'prospective engagement', at least in regard to Europe and in time of peace? Or should they be regarded as mere aberrations from a general rule? Considered in the context of the events of nearly eighty years, they do not constitute an impressive series of commitments.

On the other hand, even if it had been possible to show that in the entire period from 1822 to 1902 not one British government gave a pledge that entailed the *casus belli* in any part of the world, that would not in itself be conclusive proof that successive governments refrained from doing so in obedience to a principle.

CHAPTER III

'A dangerous game to play'

(i)

More than one historian has expressed the opinion that over a long period successive British governments systematically avoided, not only any alliance, but any guarantee.[1] But what is a guarantee? How does it differ from an alliance? In fact, the dividing line between the two types of pledge was not, and is not, clear cut. Nevertheless, contemporaries held that there was a difference between an alliance and a guarantee, and that the difference was important. This was the view of, amongst others, George Canning.[2]

Moreover, some contemporaries maintained that, although both alliances and guarantees were undesirable, the objections to the latter were even greater than those to the former. Thus, in 1872 the *Times* observed:

A Treaty of Guarantee is of all Treaties the most onerous, the most dangerous, the most prejudicial to the independent action of the State which makes it. All the objections which apply to . . . Treaties of alliance for definite objects as subjecting a State unduly to the caprices of a neighbour, apply with tenfold force to a Treaty which in the nature of things must endure for ever, and which places it in the power of a foreign enemy to present to us at any time the alternative of war or dishonour.[3]

It was frequently said at the time that there was an objection in principle on the part of the British government to giving any guarantee.

Thus, in 1861 Russell was engaged in one of his periodic attempts to solve the problem of Schleswig, Holstein and Lauenburg. On 19 April of that year he circulated a proposal for a programme of reforms, the acceptance of which by the King of Denmark was to be followed by a guarantee to the Crown of Denmark of the possession of the Duchy of Schleswig.[4]

On 4 May 1861 Napier, the ambassador in St Petersburg, sent Russell a dispatch, reporting a conversation with Gorchakov, who, he related, had remarked that the British proposal was 'rather repugnant to at least the modern policy of England which did not willingly admit guarantees', adding that, when, in 1852, the powers had attempted to settle the question of the succession to the territories of the Crown of Denmark, 'the word guarantee had not been inserted . . . from deference to the views of Her Majesty's Government'.[5]

In due course Russell submitted the correspondence in connexion with his proposal to Queen Victoria,[6] who replied on 27 May 1861, observing that Gorchakov was correct in stating that 'the engagements taken in 1852 did not contain a formal guarantee . . . in deference to the opinion of the British Government which, on general principles, has always objected to such engagements'.[7]

The Queen's use of the epithet 'formal' is significant. She was evidently trying, no doubt with the Prince Consort's assistance, to make it clear to Russell that she was employing the word 'guarantee', not in any broad, non-technical sense, such as was and is common, but in the sense of a pledge, embodied in a treaty or comparable contract, and specifically described therein as a 'guarantee'.

The record of European diplomacy affords numerous examples of such guarantees, relating to the execution of the provisions of a treaty, possession of territory, a country's independence, neutrality or institutions, or to some comparable matter. Among the best known guarantees, in this sense of the term, are those given by Louis XVI and Catherine II at Teschen in 1779, in connexion with the peace-treaty that had resulted from their mediation, and those of the integrity of their respective possessions, exchanged by Napoleon I and Alexander I under the terms of the Treaty of Tilsit of 1807.

In endorsing the Russian foreign minister's reported statement concerning both the powers' omission to give any guarantee in 1852 and the fact that this omission had been in deference to the opinion of the British government, Queen Victoria was on firm ground. To be precise, the absence of any guarantee from the London treaty of 8 May 1852, concerning the succession to the Crown of Denmark, had been more particularly in deference to the opinion of Palmerston, who had been, on the British side, the person chiefly responsible for the negotiation of the treaty, although he had no longer been in office at the time of its final signature, and who had strongly opposed Britain's participation in a proposed guarantee relating to Schleswig.[8]

On the other hand, in maintaining that the British government had always objected 'on general principles' to giving any 'formal guarantee', the Queen was on very shaky ground indeed. In the eighteenth century this country had given numerous guarantees of the most formal kind, relating to a variety of matters. That of the Pragmatic Sanction, given under the Treaty of Vienna of 1731 is probably the best known example.[9] Castlereagh had continued the practice. Under article xvii of the Treaty of Vienna of 1815 Britain, together with Austria, France and Russia, had guaranteed to Prussia the possession of the territories that, under article xv of the same treaty, she had acquired from Saxony.[10] Again, by the act of 20 November 1815, signed in Paris, Britain, together with all the other great powers, had guaranteed the integrity and inviolability of the territory of Switzerland and the neutrality of the northern part of Savoy, which at that time formed part of the Kingdom of Sardinia.[11]

The first example during the period under review of an explicit guarantee, relating to the territory of a foreign country and embodied in a treaty, convention or act, to which Britain was a party, was that contained in the twenty-fifth article of the treaty with Belgium, signed in London by Palmerston on 15 November 1831.[12] Under this article Britain and the other great powers guaranteed the execution of the preceding twenty-four articles, the seventh of which provided that Belgium, within certain defined territorial limits, should form an independent and perpetually neutral state.

This treaty had, however, a short life. On 19 April 1839 it was formally abrogated and replaced by new treaties, also signed in London. By separate treaties with the Netherlands and with Belgium the five great powers took under their guarantee twenty-four articles of a Netherlands-Belgian treaty, the seventh of which likewise provided that Belgium should form an independent and perpetually neutral state.[13] It was on the treaties of 19 April 1839 and, more especially, of course, on that with Belgium, that the famous Belgian guarantee thereafter rested.

However, the pledge given to Belgium should not be regarded as a mere exception to a general rule. The convention of 7 May 1832, signed in London by Palmerston, provided that Greece, under the sovereignty of a Bavarian prince and the guarantee of Britain, France and Russia, should form a monarchical and independent state.[14] By the convention of 26 January 1855, signed in Turin, Britain and France guaranteed the integrity of the possessions of the King of Sardinia, although only for the duration of the war with Russia, then in progress.[15] The Treaty of Paris of 30 March 1856, which brought that war to an end, contained no fewer than four guarantee articles. Article vii related to the independence and integrity of the Ottoman Empire; article xv to the navigation of the Danube; article xxii to the privileges and immunities of the Principalities of Wallachia and Moldavia; and article xxviii to the rights and immunities of the principality then known as 'Servia'.[16] Under the Tripartite—also known as the Triple—Treaty of 15 April 1856, signed by Clarendon in Paris, Britain, together with Austria and France, guaranteed 'jointly and severally'— 'solidairement'—the independence and integrity of the Ottoman Empire.[17] The convention of 19 August 1858, also signed in Paris, provided that the now united Principalities should continue to enjoy their privileges and immunities under the guarantee, on this occasion qualified as 'collective', of six contracting powers.[18] The treaty of 13 July 1863, signed in London by Russell, declared that Greece formed, not only, as hitherto, a monarchical and independent, but also a constitutional, state, under the sovereignty of a Danish prince and the guarantee of the same three powers as in 1832.[19] Finally, the treaty of 11 May 1867, signed, albeit unwillingly, by Stanley in London, placed the principle of the neutrality of the Grand Duchy of Luxemburg under the sanction of the 'collective' guarantee of Austria, Britain, France, Italy, Prussia and Russia.[20]

In short, it is apparent that for a considerable period British governments, irrespective of party, gave, when circumstances,

in their judgment, so required, formal and explicit guarantees
relating to a variety of important matters. That this was so wa:
widely recognized. Thus, in 1871 Salisbury told the House o1
Lords:

It has been the practice of many Powers of Europe, on the conclusion
of a treaty, to guarantee the resolutions to which they have come as
to the territory it might assign to any particular Power. That was a
dangerous game to play—a game to which all nations have committed themselves more or less, but none so much, or so frequently,
as England.[21]

The nature of the objects of these guarantees varied, in fact,
more than Salisbury's words would lead one to suppose. Moreover, Britain cannot be said to have played this 'dangerous
game' more frequently than did any of the other great powers.
Nevertheless, Salisbury's statement that Britain—or, as he
preferred to say, England—had given numerous pledges of this
type is incontrovertible. Nine years later Gladstone spoke to
similar effect. 'The United Kingdom', he reminded an Edinburgh audience, '... has been and is involved in many
guarantees for the condition of other countries.'[22]

(ii)

Does the record of the years from 1831 to 1867 dispose of the
theory of the systematic refusal of successive British governments to give any guarantee? As far as those years are concerned, it clearly does. Nevertheless, during more than half the
period under review no British government gave a new and
explicit guarantee, embodied in an article of a treaty, convention or act, and relating to the territory or institutions of a
foreign country. Moreover, more than one foreign secretary
expressed strong objections, on grounds of principle, to giving
any pledge of this type. As far, therefore, as a considerable part
of the period is concerned, the view put forward by the historians cited in the first chapter of this book is certainly
plausible.

CHAPTER IV

'An undertaking to defend'

(i)

It is easy to show that in the early and mid-nineteenth century Britain was a party to numerous guarantees, relating to a variety of matters and stipulated in a long series of treaties, conventions and acts. Nevertheless, an important question remains. Did a guarantee, such as that embodied in, for example, article xvii of the Treaty of Vienna, pledge the powers that gave it to resort, if necessary, to force of arms in defence of the object guaranteed? Was it, to employ a term much favoured at the time, a 'binding engagement'?

This is a difficult question to answer, partly because the term 'guarantee' was not in the nineteenth century and is not today reserved exclusively, even in an international context, for pledges of the type specified in article xvii of the Treaty of Vienna.

Queen Victoria, as has been seen, showed her awareness of the ambiguity of the term, when, in her letter to Russell of 27 May 1861, already quoted, she referred to a 'formal guarantee'.[1] Palmerston, who was a stickler for terminological precision, wrote of a 'specific guarantee',[2] Russell of a 'special guarantee',[3] Napier of a 'real guarantee'.[4] All four appreciated that the question whether the actual word 'guarantee' was to be found in the text of a treaty was important. They also appreciated the necessity of distinguishing between a pledge specifically so named in a treaty and those other arrangements to which the word 'guarantee' was also frequently applied.

(ii)

A guarantee was certainly a pledge that bound the state giving it to go to war, should that be necessary, according to a former historical adviser to the Foreign Office. The obligation involved, wrote the late Sir James Headlam-Morley, 'the final sanction of war'.[5] A more recent authority has written:

To accept the position of guarantor meant for any state that it placed itself under a legal obligation to go to war in circumstances of which the exact nature was not always foreseeable and in which war was not certain to be for the immediate advantage of the state concerned.[6]

A well-known diplomatic historian has also emphasized the obligation to resort to force of arms:

In general, we may say that a guarantee was wedded to the *status quo* and implied a freezing of the boundary or agreement to which it was applied. Enforcement of guarantee lay in the hands of the participants, the implication being that they would support their guarantees by diplomacy and, ultimately, by force of arms.[7]

On the other hand, the late Sir Robert Ensor wrote of the neutrality of Belgium:

Great Britain was one of its guarantors under the Treaty of 1839. She had thus a right to defend it, although not in all circumstances an obligation.[8]

If the guarantee of the neutrality of Belgium entailed so limited an obligation, it cannot be said to have constituted a particularly stringent commitment. What then of Britain's other guarantees, some of which related to matters that concerned her far less closely than did the maintenance of Belgium's neutrality? Did they also confer rights, but not in all circumstances involve obligations?

(iii)

The nature of the obligation entailed by a guarantee is a problem that has engaged the attention of international jurists since the time when it became common for powers to give pledges of this type. More than one writer has stressed the obligation to resort, if necessary, to force of arms, incurred by a guarantor. Thus Vattel wrote:

Quand ceux qui font un Traité de Paix, ou tout autre Traité, ne sont point absolument tranquilles sur son observation; ils recherchent la

Garentie d'un Souverain puissant. Le *Garent* promet de maintenir les conditions du Traité, d'en procurer l'observation. Comme il peut se trouver obligé d'employer la force contre celui des Contractans qui voudroit manquer à ses promesses; c'est un engagement qu'aucun Souverain ne doit prendre légèrement et sans de bonnes raisons. . . . La *Garentie* est une espèce de Traité, par lequel on promet assistance et secours à quelqu'un, au cas qu'il en ait besoin pour contraindre un infidèle à remplir ses engagemens.[9]

Georg Friedrich von Martens made much the same point:

La garantie oblige de prêter secours, même les armes à la main, à celui en faveur duquel on est devenu garant, et qui en fait la réquisition lorsqu'il y a lieu.[10]

Montague Bernard, a leading British authority, also left no doubt that the obligation incurred by a guarantor included the use of force:

. . . a guarantee . . . is an undertaking to defend, in case of need, a right of some kind vested in another Power, with whom the contract is made. A guarantee of a territory is an undertaking to defend the possession of the territory; a guarantee of a dynasty is an undertaking to support the dynasty; a guarantee of a Treaty is an undertaking to prevent by force, if need be, the Treaty from being violated by any of the parties whom it binds.[11]

These are, of course, only academic opinions. However, more than one person who participated in the actual conduct of international relations during the nineteenth century expressed similar views. Thus, in 1823 Canning wrote, in a dispatch to Sir William à Court, the minister accredited to King Ferdinand VII of Spain:

A guaranty is one of the most onerous Obligations which one State can contract towards another. . . .
A guaranty, strictly construed, knows no limits either of time or degree. It would be, unless distinctly restricted in those respects, claimable in a War commenced by the Power to whom the guaranty is given, as well as in a War of unjust Aggression against that Power; and the integrity of the territory of that Power must be maintained at whatever cost the effort to maintain it, is prolonged: Nay, though the guaranteed Power itself should contribute almost nothing to the maintaining it.[12]

Nearly four decades later, in his dispatch of 4 May 1861, describing his interview with Gorchakov, Napier quoted the Russian foreign minister as referring to 'guarantees in the old sense of positive engagements to maintain and defend by force of arms'.[13] No doubt, Queen Victoria had these words in mind, when, in her letter to Russell of 27 May 1861, she defined the import of a guarantee as '*obliging* to take up arms for the defence of the object guaranteed'.[14]

Is this consensus of academic, ministerial and royal opinion conclusive?

The writings of international jurists do not necessarily afford reliable guidance to the intentions of those who are actually responsible for the negotiation and wording of a treaty. As for the definitions given by Canning in 1823 and by Gorchakov, as reported by Napier, and by Queen Victoria in 1861, it is significant that in each case the author concerned was turning down a proposal for a guarantee. Canning was refusing a request from the Spanish foreign minister, made through à Court, for a sole guarantee of a settlement, to be effected through British mediation, of the conflict in Spain between the forces of the Cadiz government and those of France.[15] Gorchakov and Queen Victoria were objecting to a plan, formulated by Russell, that involved a guarantee to the Crown of Denmark by Britain, France, Russia and Sweden of the possession of the Duchy of Schleswig.[16] In the circumstances Canning, Gorchakov and the Queen may all have exaggerated the onerousness of the obligation entailed by a guarantee in order to justify their refusal to give one in the particular case.

(iv)

Indeed, the precise nature of the obligation entailed by a 'formal' guarantee is less easy to define than the theoretical writings of international jurists or the official correspondence of more exalted persons might lead one to suppose.

There was, for example, the difficult question of the duration of a guarantee, which, unless the contrary was specifically provided for, was generally held to have no time-limit, as the *Times* pointed out in 1872[17] and the fifteenth Earl of Derby reminded the House of Lords six years later.[18] A guarantee could, of course, be terminated by means of a formal act of abrogation on the part of all the powers concerned. In practice, however, this procedure was not common. Was Britain during the period under review still bound, then, by the guarantees given by her monarchs in the eighteenth century and never formally abrogated? In 1864, at the time of the Schleswig-Holstein crisis, the cabinet, the Foreign Office and the law officers of the crown did have to consider this question.[19]

There were other difficult questions.

Did a guarantee bind a guarantor actually to go to war, if necessary, in defence of the object guaranteed? The Turin convention of 1855 and the Tripartite Treaty of 1856 did, indeed, each contain an explicit guarantee and did also unequivocally specify the *casus belli*. In this, however, they were exceptional, as far, at least, as Britain's engagements during this period were concerned.

Again, it not infrequently happened that the state, in favour of which a group of powers gave a guarantee, was not itself a party to the relevant treaty, convention or act. Was a state that found itself in this position entitled to invoke the guarantee? To argue that it was not so entitled was to make nonsense of the definitions of a guarantee given by some of the leading international jurists of both the eighteenth and the nineteenth centuries. Nevertheless, in 1877, when war between Russia and the Ottoman Empire was imminent, the then British foreign secretary did employ this argument.[20]

Again, like the guarantees for which Castlereagh had been responsible in 1815, those given by successive British governments in the years from 1831 to 1867 were all multipartite. On no occasion did Britain have fewer than two co-guarantors. On some occasions she had five. Even when a multipartite guarantee was specifically 'several', the obligation incurred by each guarantor was less clear than might at first sight appear. The obligation entailed by a multipartite guarantee that was not specifically 'several' was still less precise. Did it bind an individual guarantor to defend the object guaranteed, even though not one of the other guarantors was willing to do so? Did it bind an individual guarantor to defend the object guaranteed, if that object were to be attacked by some or all of the other guarantors themselves? As for the obligations entailed by a guarantee that was specifically 'collective', 'common' or 'joint', the possibilities for argument were almost limitless. [21]

There remains the further question of whether a guarantee, even if undeniably valid, was likely to be acted upon. A small state, the independence or neutrality of which had been guaranteed, might, if attacked, prefer to offer no resistance to the invader and to make no appeal for armed assistance to the guarantors, rather than allow its territory to become a battle-field for the forces of great powers. In such circumstances a guarantor might well decide to take no action. Again, a guarantor was unlikely to go to war in fulfilment of its obligation, unless to do so was in accordance with its own interests, real or supposed, unless it was confident of being able to act effectively, and unless the state that had appealed for its assistance enjoyed public respect and sympathy.

In fact, the question whether a 'formal' guarantee bound each power that had given it to resort, if necessary, to force of arms in defence of the object guaranteed cannot be answered in a single sentence. The opinions of contemporaries on this point clearly differed widely. As was demonstrated on more than one occasion, there was not a single guarantee, to which Britain was a party, that a prime minister or foreign secretary, who so desired, could not with a little ingenuity explain away. Whether, in the event of a guarantee being invoked, the government of a guarantor-power decided to go to war, to protest, or to abstain from all action, it would not lack arguments to justify whichever course it chose. In short, a guarantee constituted a 'binding engagement', in as far as those responsible for the conduct of the foreign relations of a guarantor-power looked on it as such.

CHAPTER V

'In this instance'

(i)

Did Canning really act, as that professed Canningite of a later generation, Sir William Harcourt, claimed, on the principle of 'a free hand for England'?[1]

Canning was certainly given to expressions of robust insularity, which are often quoted. His dispatch of 18 September 1823 to à Court is well known as an exposition, not only of the nature of the obligations entailed by a guarantee,[2] but of the objections to such pledges.

In August 1823 Ferdinand was at Cadiz with the government, which had come to power as a result of the events of 1820. The French army, which, under the command of the duc d'Angoulême, had invaded Spain the previous April, was a few miles away at Puerto de Santa Maria. À Court was at Gibraltar. On 23 August Yandiola, the foreign minister *ad interim* in the now precariously situated Spanish government, sent a note to à Court, asking him to mediate between Ferdinand and the French authorities in Spain, with a view to bringing about a durable peace under Britain's guarantee—'bajo la garantía de la potencia mediadora'.[3]

À Court replied to Yandiola politely, but without mentioning the proposed guarantee.[4] He also attempted unsuccessfully to comply with the foreign minister's request for mediation.[5] On 31 August he reported to Canning, arguing strongly against giving any guarantee, except—and the qualification is significant—'against foreign aggression'. 'We can hardly guarantee any form of Government', he pointed out, 'against the efforts of the very people for whom such Government is established.'[6]

It so happened that the day on which à Court wrote these words was also the day on which Angoulême's forces captured the fortress of the Trocadero. The Cadiz government was now clearly *in extremis*, a fact which strengthened the case for avoiding any involvement in its affairs. Accordingly, on 18 September Canning wrote to à Court, warmly approving his reticence. He stated in general terms the British government's unwillingness to 'undertake any guaranty whatever, either of territory or of internal Institutions', justifying his refusal on the ground of the onerousness of the obligation entailed. He also argued that, powerful as were the objections to a 'territorial guaranty', those to a 'guaranty of internal institutions' were 'infinitely stronger'. 'It is difficult to say whether these objections apply with greater force to the party giving', Canning added, 'or to that which receives, such a guaranty'.[7] On 3 October Canning wrote again to à Court, expanding his argument. 'The objection to a Guarantee is', he explained, '. . . the extensive latitude of it's [*sic*] obligations both as to time and circumstances.'[8]

These declarations raise an important question. Did Canning's practice conform with his precept? To this question there is one obvious answer, namely, that throughout the five years from 1822 to 1827, when he was successively foreign secretary and prime minister, Canning did not once commit the country to a single, explicit guarantee, specifically described as such in an article of a treaty, convention or act, and relating either to the territory or internal institutions of a foreign country. Such an answer would, however, be far from complete. There still remains the question whether Canning, even if he did not actually commit Britain to a new pledge of this type, was at any time willing to do so. In fact, on at least two occasions he was.

The first occasion was in the spring of 1826 and resulted from a war that had broken out between the newly independent states of Brazil and Buenos Aires over the territory known as the 'Banda Oriental' and had led to interference with shipping on the River Plate. On 18 March 1826 Canning, in a dispatch to Ponsonby, who was on his way to take up his post as minister in Buenos Aires, suggested terms for a settlement. Buenos Aires was to have Monte Video and to pay Brazil pecuniary compensation; uninterrupted enjoyment of the navigation of the River Plate was to be secured to Brazil. If, Canning explained, these terms were embodied in a treaty, Britain would be willing to guarantee its observance:

His Majesty would, if required, not refuse to lend his guarantee for the observance of such stipulations. The British Government would indeed rather, on the general principle of avoiding as much as possible engagements of this character, that the Treaty could be adjusted to the satisfaction of both parties, without the necessity of such guarantee. But if it were required by both parties, His Majesty would consent to give it in this instance, rather than the Treaty should not be concluded.[9]

There appears to be no doubt that what Canning was offering Brazil and Buenos Aires on this occasion was an explicit guarantee, in the strict sense of that term, of the observance of a treaty, to be given in the event of his mediation between the parties to the dispute over the Banda Oriental proving successful. For such a guarantee, intended to ensure the durability of a settlement brought about by mediation, there were plenty of precedents. It is significant, moreover, that what Canning evidently had in mind was a 'sole' or 'individual' guarantee. However, his offer of mediation failed to gain acceptance. The further question of a British guarantee of the settlement did not, therefore, arise.[10]

The story of Canning's handling of the Greek question is also revealing. Early in 1826 Wellington was sent to St Petersburg to congratulate Alexander I's successor on his accession. On 10 February Canning signed the duke's instructions. The British government was willing to consult the new Czar on the subject of the terms of a settlement to be effected between the Turks and the Greeks and to place that settlement, when achieved, 'under the guarantee of Russia, jointly with that of Austria, Prussia, and France'. Canning did not, however, suggest Britain's participation in the projected guarantee.[11]

The outcome of Wellington's visit to the Russian capital was the famous protocol, signed on 4 April 1826. Britain and Russia were to bring this protocol to the knowledge of the other three great powers, who were to be invited to guarantee, in concert with Russia, the final reconciliation between Turkey and Greece, which could not, however, be guaranteed by Britain—'cette transaction ne pouvant être garantie par Sa Majesté Britannique'.[12]

In the months that followed Canning endeavoured to transform the bipartite agreement embodied in the St Petersburg protocol into an arrangement in which all the great powers would participate. Before the end of the year, however, he had reached the conclusion that, as he warned Liverpool, if the British government were to persist in its refusal to join in a guarantee, the project would fall to the ground. 'But', he argued, 'surely a guarantee limited in object, and common to *all* the Powers, cannot be very onerous to us.' He thought that the government might venture 'the Guarantee of our own work in Greece, with five or six auxiliaries'.[13]

Liverpool feared that it would be difficult to guarantee autonomy to the Greeks without also guaranteeing their dependence on the Porte, and that such a pledge might lead to embarrassment in the future.[14] In the event, the condition stipulated by Canning as a *sine qua non* of Britain's participation in a Greek guarantee proved to be impossible to realize.[15] Accordingly, the London treaty of 6 July 1827 merely provided for a guarantee of the settlement by those powers that considered it expedient or possible to contract such an obligation—an obvious escape-clause for Britain.[16]

(ii)

The views of Wellington and Aberdeen are also of interest. Towards the end of 1829 Aberdeen wrote to Bagot, expressing his wish to place the future Greek state 'under the general guarantee of the great Powers of Europe, by an invitation to that effect, when the State is finally constituted'.[17] However, his hope that all five great powers would participate in the eventual Greek settlement was, like Canning's, disappointed. The protocol of 3 February 1830 left it open, accordingly, to each of the three signatories to refrain from giving any guarantee.[18] Wellington, too, took the view that the eventual Greek act of guarantee 'should be so drawn as that all the Powers of Europe might be parties to it'. He did not want Greece to be under the exclusive tutelage of three powers only. 'If we cannot attain this object', he wrote on 17 February 1830, 'we ought not to guarantee.'[19] At all events, when, in November 1830, Wellington and Aberdeen left office, Britain had not yet agreed to participate in a guarantee of the eventual Greek settlement.

(iii)

Canning, as has been seen, expressed an objection, not only to any guarantee of territory or of institutions, but to any pledge whatsoever that would fetter the government's 'decision upon future contingencies'.[20] The transaction of July 1827 envisaged a contingency that might arise in the future, but in the very near future. Within a few weeks of Canning's death Dudley had misgivings concerning the course that the government had adopted. 'To say the truth', he wrote to the British ambassador in Paris on 31 August 1827, 'I am not sure we did right ever to engage in that business.' He thought that 'Russia would evidently get us into a war' and that 'that would never do'. 'We cannot', he added, 'be too cautious in coming under any fresh engagements.'[21] On the following day Stratford Canning, the ambassador in Constantinople, notified Admiral Codrington that the instruction to prevent supplies from reaching the Turkish forces in Greece was to be carried out, if necessary, 'by cannon-shot.'[22] On 20 October 1827, in the Bay of Navarino, Codrington and his colleagues made, in Palmerston's words, 'a Bonfire of the Fleet of our good Ally'.[23] Officially this incident was known as the 'untoward event'.[24]

On at least two occasions Canning showed willingness to give a pledge that would have been even more difficult to reconcile with his own carefully worded declaration of principle. Thus, in his dispatch to à Court of 3 October 1823 he pointed out that the objection to a guarantee did not preclude a less onerous undertaking. 'There are engagements short of guarantee', he explained, 'which might be safely contracted by the British Government without the same inconvenience; and which yet might be in no small degree efficient for the preservation of a peace once made.' 'An engagement tripartite', he added, 'or a defensive Alliance with Spain, would be of this nature.' The ambassador should 'not decline taking *ad referendum* any proposal short of guarantee'.[25]

On 31 March of the following year Canning wrote to à Court,

now, after the restoration to power of King Ferdinand VII
back in Madrid, urging the recognition by Spain of the independence of Mexico and, in due course, of the other former
mainland colonies.[26] Three days later he wrote again, stressing
the desirability of the maintenance of Spain's possession of
Cuba, and offering, as soon as the Madrid government accepted
the suggestions contained in his previous dispatch, to enter into
a 'formal Engagement', binding Britain 'to employ, when
called upon, her maritime power to defend that Colony for
Spain against any external aggression'.[27] On the following day
he elaborated his proposal. The engagement was to be embodied, not in a treaty, but in an 'Exchange of Ministerial
Notes'; it was to be limited to Britain and Spain; the protection
promised by Britain was to be *general*, that is, not pointed at
any particular power.[28]

Owing to the condition attached to it Canning's offer was
declined by Ofalia, the Spanish foreign minister.[29] Canning
referred more than once to the engagement that he had offered
to Spain as a 'guarantee'.[30] However, a guarantee, in the sense
of a pledge of the type given, for example, to Switzerland in
1815, was not usually embodied in an exchange of notes. Nor
were the obligations that it entailed normally explicitly limited
to maritime operations. What Canning had in mind in the
spring of 1824 was not, in all probability, a guarantee, in the
technical sense of that term, such as that embodied in the act of
20 November 1815, but simply a defensive pact. However, he
clearly intended the 'formal Engagement' in regard to Cuba to
be a serious undertaking. It had been, he afterwards told Bagot
'a great offer', which might, had it been accepted, have involved the country in difficulties. 'But', he added, 'it is refused.'[3]

The fact is that Canning believed that Britain, in her own
interests, could not afford to be indifferent to the fate of Cuba
an island of obvious strategic importance. On 21 June 1825 he
wrote to the British ambassador in Paris, instructing him to
warn Villèle amicably against meddling in the internal affairs
of the colony. The British government, he explained, sincerely
wished Cuba 'to remain with the mother'. Next to that
Canning added, he himself wished it to be 'independent either
singly or in connection with Mexico'. 'But what cannot, and

must not be', he insisted, 'is that any great maritime Power should get possession of it.'[32] In the light of this expression of opinion Canning's offer of a pledge to defend, if necessary, Spain's possession of the island is easily intelligible.

(iv)

Canning's elaborately phrased statements of principle need not be taken completely literally. They admitted, in certain circumstances, of exceptions. Canning was willing to enter into an engagement, by whatever name one prefers to call it, that entailed the *casus belli*, when, in his opinion, considerations of Britain's interests rendered such a course necessary. It is significant that the areas, in regard to which he was prepared to undertake commitments, all lent themselves to the use of sea-power.

CHAPTER VI

'The strongest and most refined guarantees'

(i)

There would be little point in discussing the question whether Palmerston shared the objection to guarantees, expressed by the man for whose principles he often affirmed his reverence.[1] His own record speaks for itself.

On 20 January 1831, some two months after becoming foreign secretary in Grey's administration, Palmerston signed a protocol, under which Britain and the other great powers agreed to guarantee the neutrality and the territorial integrity and inviolability of Belgium.[2] It is probably significant that, when Palmerston informed Grey of the signature of this important protocol, he did not mention the guarantee.[3]

The protocol of 20 January 1831 was the germ of the London treaty of 15 November of the same year—the first treaty containing an explicit guarantee in connexion with the territory of a foreign state to which Britain had been a party since 1815.[4] Aberdeen found this reversion to former practice disquieting. 'It has been, for a long time past, the acknowledged policy of the government of this country to be extremely scrupulous of guaranteeing anything', he told the House of Lords on 26 January 1832.[5]

The convention of 7 May 1832 provided that Greece should form a monarchical and independent state under the guarantee of Britain and of two other great powers, namely France and Russia.[6] In other words, it disregarded Canning's stipulation that Britain should participate in a guarantee of the Greek settlement, only if all the other great powers did likewise. Moreover, whatever obligation Britain incurred under the fourth article of this convention related specifically to Greece's internal institutions.

However, to say that Palmerston involved the country in a

umber of guarantees and that he began this process within a
hort time of becoming foreign secretary is not to say that he
ave such pledges indiscriminately. On the contrary, his corres-
ondence abounds with illustrations of the caution that he
xercised in such matters.

Thus, in 1841 he pointed out to Clanricarde, the ambassador
1 St Petersburg, that the convention, then under negotiation,
ntended to settle the question of the Straits, contained 'nothing
ut what we ourselves, the Four Powers chose that it should
ontain'. 'That is to say', he explained, 'it has no Stipulation
bout Guarantees either for the Turkish Empire or for the
yrians or for Commercial Roads through Egypt to Syria,
which were all schemes for intitling France to interfere at a
iture Time in the internal affairs of Turkey.'[7] The Straits
Convention, as finally signed on 13 July 1841, contained, in
ict, no guarantee article.[8]

Again, during his third foreign secretaryship Palmerston
eclined to agree to British participation in a proposed guarantee
elating to Schleswig—or, as he preferred to write, 'Sleswig'.
I own I am strongly against our being Parties to any such
Guarantee as is suggested about Sleswig', he wrote to Russell,
n 26 June 1849, pointing out the disagreeable responsibilities
hat such participation would involve.[9] In fact, the protocol of
he London conference on the integrity of the Danish monarchy,
nitialled by Palmerston on 4 July of the following year, made
o mention of any guarantee.[10] Moreover, Palmerston's corres-
ondence makes it clear that, as far as he was concerned, this
mission was deliberate.[11] Nor did the London treaty, finally
gned by Malmesbury on 8 May 1852, contain any reference
o a guarantee.[12] Nine years later Gorchakov reminded Napier
hat this omission had been made in deference to the views of
he British government.[13]

It would be easy to multiply instances of Palmerston's wari-
ess, when he found himself confronted with a proposal for a
ledge of this type. In July 1855 he insisted that the treaty with
weden, then under negotiation, should be 'without the Form
f a Guarantee'.[14] In December of the same year he demurred to
hat he called 'a *Guarantee* of the Institutions to be given to the
rincipalities'.[15] In 1863 he declined firmly, and, as subsequent

events proved, most wisely, to guarantee the Archduke Maxi-
milian's position in Mexico.[16]

Nevertheless, it is noteworthy that on not one of these variou
occasions does Palmerston, unlike Canning at the time of th
Spanish government's request in 1823, appear, so far as one ca
judge from the available documents, to have maintained tha
for Britain to give a guarantee would have been contrary to th
established principles of the country's foreign policy.

(ii)

The guarantees, for which Palmerston, first as foreign secretar
and then as prime minister, was responsible, raise an importan
question. What obligation did he himself believe them t
entail? Did he uphold the strict doctrine of the extrem
onerousness of a guarantee, held by some of his contemporaries
Or was his view more latitudinarian?

It so happens that some years after Palmerston's death tw
of his former colleagues gave conflicting accounts of his opinio
on this point. Russell, in a small book, published in 1871
recalled that 'Lord Palmerston used to say that in certain case
a State was bound to make war'; one such case was 'where
guarantee has been given'.[17] On the other hand, in the follow
ing year Gladstone told the House of Commons that he ha
often heard Palmerston express the opinion that 'while
guarantee gave a right of interference it did not constitute o
itself an obligation to interfere'.[18] In 1877[19] and again in 187
Gladstone spoke in the House of Commons to similar effect
attributing this opinion, not only to Palmerston, but also to th
Foreign Office.[20] In 1882, in correspondence with Granville
he appealed to what he called 'Palmerston's definition'.[21]

Fortunately, there is no need to rely solely on other people'
recollections of Palmerston's *dicta*. In 1832, for example, whe
defending his first Belgian treaty in the House of Commons, h
gave a definition of 'guaranteeing', explaining that it 'implie
an agreement to use all possible means for effecting a certai
object'.[22] Although Palmerston was, in fact, defining this ter
only in connexion with the financial provisions of the treaty
his words, nevertheless, deserve quotation.

There also exists, preserved in the Netherlands archives at The Hague, a document, which, although not written by Palmerston himself, is, nevertheless, contemporary. On 26 February 1848, two days after the proclamation of the second French republic, Palmerston had a conversation with the Prussian minister in London, Freiherr Christian von Bunsen, to whom he explained his attitude towards the treaties of 1815.[23] Probably in order to remove a misunderstanding as to what Palmerston had said on this occasion,[24] Bunsen subsequently drew up a memorandum, dated 6 March 1848, a copy of which he at some time gave to a Dutch diplomat, van Zuylen van Nijevelt. During the Crimean War, when he was his country's representative in Constantinople, van Zuylen van Nijevelt sent home a dispatch, explaining that he had among his papers 'une communication qui m'a été faite dans le temps, très confidentiellement', a copy of which he enclosed in the belief that, in the circumstances then prevailing, it would be of interest.[25]

The document, which is in French and entitled, 'Opinion exprimée par Lord Palmerston au Chévalier de Bunsen', is expressed in the first person:

Je distingue *un traité* et *une garantie*. Le fait d'avoir été une des puissances signataires d'un tel traité, donne le droit d'intervenir, mais ne lui en impose pas l'*obligation*, dans le cas où l'état de possession fut changé.

Il en est autrement d'une *garantie* qui involve l'obligation de *maintenir* l'état de possession.

Une pareille garantie a été donnée par l'Angleterre *au Roi de Prusse* pour la Province de Saxe; à la *Suisse* et à la *Belgique* pour leur neutralité et intégrité.

L'Angleterre n'a garanti ni la Lombardie à l'Autriche, ni les Provinces Rhénanes a la Prusse.

Elle a le *droit* de les aider en cas d'attaque mais elle n'en a pas l'*obligation*.[26]

Palmerston's correspondence in connexion with some of the other international transactions of the period is also instructive.

In his letter to Russell of 26 June 1849 he gave his view of the implications of the guarantee that had been suggested in connexion with 'Sleswig'. 'The real and only Meaning of such a

Guarantee', he wrote, 'is that the Parties to it should put down by Force of Arms the Resistance of the Sleswickers to the King Duke.' This, he pointed out, would constitute 'an armed Interference in the internal Affairs of Sleswig'. He was sure that Russell would not like to employ British troops for this purpose. Nor did he think that the prime minister would like to make himself 'by a joint Guarantee responsible for the Manner in which the Troops of any other Government might conduct such an Operation'.[27]

Again, on 24 July 1855 Palmerston approved Clarendon's proposal for what he termed, not strictly accurately, a 'Convention' with Sweden. 'It does not mention the word Guarantee', he wrote, 'though it contains an Engagement virtually equivalent to it.'[28] The Stockholm treaty unquestionably bound Britain and France to defend Sweden and Norway by force of arms against Russia.[29]

(iii)

It would be interesting to know also Palmerston's view of the obligations entailed by the guarantees, for which he himself, either as foreign secretary or as prime minister, was directly responsible.

What obligation did he believe that Britain incurred under, for example, the guarantee in article xxv of the Belgian treaty of 15 November 1831?[30] The treaty specified no *casus belli*.

In November 1830, just before the fall of Wellington's administration, Matuszewic, one of the Russian plenipotentiaries to the London conference, which had been meeting under Aberdeen's chairmanship, wrote to Nesselrode, outlining a plan, under which the five powers were to guarantee the existence of the projected Belgian kingdom 'en commun'.[31] However, neither this nor any comparable formula was included in the actual text of the treaty, as finally signed. On the other hand, the preamble to the convention with France of the following year declared that under article xxv of the treaty of 15 November 1831 the execution of the preceding twenty-four articles had been 'conjointement garantie' by the five powers.[32] These words, although not contemporary with the event to which they refer, may be regarded as affording an indication of Palmerston's—and Talleyrand's—opinion of the nature of the guarantee.

What is indubitable is that article xxv of the London treaty of 15 November 1831 stated that the five great powers guaranteed to Belgium the execution of the preceding twenty-four articles. This reference to execution is significant. The King of the Netherlands was not a party to the treaty. He had not withdrawn his forces from the territory that it assigned to the new kingdom. Execution of the twenty-four articles necessarily meant in the first place, therefore, execution directed against the King of the Netherlands. On the day following the signature of the treaty Palmerston wrote to Bagot at the Hague, enquiring whether the king expected 'to subdue by his arms a Country whose Independence and Integrity is [sic] guaranteed by the Five Great Powers of Europe'. 'Not even if the Tromps and Ruyters could revive', he declared, 'would that be possible.'[33]

However, although Britain and France promptly ratified the treaty, the three autocratic powers took their time. Meanwhile, vital points on Belgian territory remained under the occupation of the forces of the King of the Netherlands. On 11 March 1832 King Leopold of the Belgians wrote to Palmerston, pointing out that it was time that the treaty was executed.[34] Palmerston acknowledged the obligation, as far as Britain and France were concerned. Two days later he instructed Bagot to make the Dutch foreign minister understand that the treaty was 'a formal and serious engagement, at least for England and France; and one which they are determined to make good'.[35] 'Belgium has a Right', he told Heytesbury, the former Sir William à Court, now ambassador in St Petersburg, on 15 March, 'to exact from the Parties who have ratified the Treaty, the full Enjoyment of all the Provisions of which the Ratifiers have guaranteed the Execution.'[36]

On 1 June 1832 Palmerston was able to inform Heytesbury that the treaty had at last been ratified by all five great powers.[37] The question of its execution still remained, however. Palmerston took the view that not to get the treaty carried into execution would be to 'violate our Guarantee to Belgium'.[38]

On 5 June he held a conference with the plenipotentiaries of the other guarantor-powers. 'I said', he reported to Grey, '. . . that if other Powers refused to fulfil the Engagements they have contracted, we would fulfil ours in concert with such as might be equally prepared to act up to their guarantee.'[39] 'Our Interests require that this Belgian Squabble should at last be put an end to', he wrote to Matuszewic the following day, 'and our Honor demands that we should see that a Treaty which we have guaranteed, be faithfully executed.'[40]

On 17 July 1832 King Leopold claimed the execution of the treaty.[41] Since the three autocratic powers declined to take part in exerting pressure on the King of the Netherlands, Palmerston collaborated with Talleyrand, with whom he worked out a plan for what, in a memorandum submitted to King William IV, he called 'decisive measures'.[42] Even so, the scope of these measures was limited. On 2 October Palmerston informed Grey that he had seen the King, who had insisted 'with great vehemence' that the one thing to which he would never agree was 'Co-operation with France by Land'. 'I said', Palmerston added, 'that I was sure there was not a Member of the Cabinet who would think of advising such a Measure.'[43] Nor was there to be any formal declaration of war on the Netherlands, despite the juridical difficulties to which this omission might give rise at sea, 'while we are not at war', as Palmerston reminded Grey.[44] In short, although Palmerston acknowledged that Britain, as one of the powers that had 'guaranteed the execution' of the twenty-four articles, had an obligation to Belgium,[45] in practice he carefully limited its application.

The outcome of the efforts of Palmerston and Talleyrand was the convention of 22 October 1832, under which Britain and France declared that, having been requested by Belgium to execute the terms of the treaty of the preceding year, they would require the King of the Netherlands to promise to withdraw his forces from that country. In the event of his refusal they would place an embargo on all Dutch ships in their ports, would give orders for the detention of all Dutch ships encountered at sea, and for this purpose would station a combined squadron off the coast of the Netherlands. If, by 15 November

1832, the King of the Netherlands had not withdrawn his forces, France would send troops into Belgium. [46]

There ensued what Aberdeen called 'our quasi war with Holland',[47] which quickly achieved its immediate object, although the King of the Netherlands continued to decline to recognize the independence of Belgium. Thus it was not until 19 April 1839 that a final settlement of the Belgian question was achieved and placed under the guarantee of the five great powers. [48]

Even after the signature of the treaties of 19 April 1839 there was still room for disagreement as to the precise nature of the obligation that they—more especially the five power treaty with Belgium—entailed. In this respect the new treaties were no more explicit than the one that they replaced. They contained no reference to any *casus belli*. They did not specify whether each guarantor was individually responsible, or, if not, in what manner the five guarantors were to share their responsibility.

Nor do the reports of debates in Parliament at the time supply clear answers to these and similar questions. Indeed, it is impossible not to be struck by the lack of interest paid by the House of Commons in, for example, its debates on the service estimates, to the implications of the obligations incurred by this country under both the treaty of 1831[49] and those of 1839.[50]

On the other hand, quite apart from any question of treaty obligation, Palmerston upheld what he called, in a letter to Melbourne, written in 1838, 'the antient and hereditary Policy of England with respect to the Low Countries'.[51] That policy had lain behind the establishment in 1814–15 of the united Kingdom of the Netherlands. However, the union created by Castlereagh had collapsed and clearly could not be restored, as Palmerston himself regretfully acknowledged. 'We should have preferred a Reestablishment of the Union'; he told Matuszewic in 1832, 'but Events had made that impossible, even before the Conference began.'[52] Palmerston, accordingly, strove for what he regarded as, from the British point of view, the next best solution, namely, an independent Belgium. 'As to England', he impressed on the Russian plenipotentiary, 'our Object is, to make Belgium Independent.'[53]

The 'antient and hereditary Policy' had long been aimed at

France, whereas in 1832 Britain collaborated with France against the King of the Netherlands. Nevertheless, both Grey and Palmerston considered that there was still a danger of French designs on Belgium. In 1830 Grey wrote of the threat of 'the annexation of Belgium to France'.[54] After the signature of the protocol of 20 January 1831 he observed with satisfaction to Princess Lieven that the neutrality of Belgium was 'the best barrier that existing circumstances afford against France'.[55] Some six weeks after the conclusion of the treaty Palmerston expressed to the British ambassador in Paris his conviction that 'the Conquest of Belgium is an object which the French Nation still keep in view'.[56] In other words, neither the prime minister nor the foreign secretary considered that all Frenchmen were as moderate in their approach to the Belgian question as was Talleyrand.

Many years later Palmerston gave Clarendon a frank explanation of the considerations that had lain behind his handling of the Belgian problem during his first foreign secretaryship, and the letter in which he did so deserves quotation, despite having been written more than two decades after the conclusion of the treaties of 1839:

There were thousands of Frenchmen ready to rush over the Border to assist the Belgians and if England had not interfered diplomatically the matter would have ended not by the Belgians being eat up by the Dutch, but by Belgium being swallowed up by France.[57]

(iv)

Palmerston's correspondence does not tell us a great deal concerning his view of the obligation entailed by the convention of 7 May 1832 between Britain, France and Russia, on the one hand, and Bavaria, on the other, by which the three powers regularized the position of the new Greek state. 'La Grèce', read article iv, 'sous la Souveraineté du Prince Othon de Bavière, et la garantie des trois Cours formera un Etat Monarchique Indépendant.'[58]

The late Sir James Headlam-Morley took the view that these words did not constitute a guarantee at all.[59] Indeed, they were certainly ambiguous, like those employed in many other treaties and conventions, before and since. Nevertheless, there is no doubt that Palmerston considered that the three powers gave a genuine guarantee. 'France Great Britain and Russia guaranteed the integrity and Independence of the Kingdom of Greece', he wrote in 1841 to the ambassador in Vienna.[60] Greece, herself, however, was not a party to the convention.[61]

(v)

The multiplicity of the guarantees contained in the Treaty of Paris, signed by Clarendon on 30 March 1856, was certainly striking. However, during the negotiations in Vienna in the spring of the previous year Gorchakov had made it clear that Russia would not give an undertaking to make any infringement of the territorial integrity of the Ottoman Empire 'un cas de guerre'.[62] She would not give 'une garantie territoriale active'.[63] Thus it was that, although under article vii of the Treaty of Paris the powers, including Sardinia, entered into an engagement to respect the independence and territorial integrity of the Ottoman Empire and guaranteed the observance of this engagement 'en commun', they merely declared that they would consider any act tending to its violation as 'une question d'intérêt général'. Moreover, articles xv, xxii and xxviii of the treaty, under which the powers guaranteed the arrangements for the navigation of the Danube, the privileges of Wallachia and Moldavia, and, collectively, the rights and immunities of 'Servia', certainly do not read as though they were intended unequivocally to entail the *casus belli*.[64]

The precise origin of the Tripartite Treaty of 15 April 1856 is not easy to pin-point.[65] In 1835 Palmerston worked out a scheme for a treaty with France and Austria for the defence of the Ottoman Empire. This project, however, proved abortive.[66] During the Vienna conference in the spring of 1855 Russell wrote to Clarendon, telling him that he had been anxious to get Austria to agree to a treaty with Britain and France, separate from Russia. He had had a conversation with Drouyn de Lhuys, who had drawn up a 'project of treaty', of which Franz Joseph approved.[67] Owing to the failure of the Vienna negotiations nothing immediate came of this scheme.

However, the Buol-Bourqueney memorandum of 14 Nove
ber 1855, which laid down the lines for a general settleme
provided that the eventual peace-treaty should be supp
mented by 'un traité d'alliance entre l'Autriche, la France et
Grande Bretagne, garantissant l'integrité et l'indépendance
l'Empire Ottoman, et rétabissant comme *casus belli* toute
fraction portée par la Russie aux stipulations de la dite paix

On 19 November 1855 Persigny, the French ambassador
London, communicated this memorandum to Clarendon
During the Congress of Paris, of the following year, when t
signature of the final peace-treaty was in sight, Clarend
reported to Palmerston that Buol had told Napoleon III tl
he was ready to sign 'the tripartite Alliance guaranteeing t
Treaty', but that 'the Emperor was disposed to back out'.
added that he had encouraged Buol, telling him that the Brit
government attached great importance to the proposed ad
tional treaty and would be glad if Prussia, too, would join.[7]

On the day after the signature of the Treaty of Pa
Clarendon informed Palmerston that the Emperor still wish
'to avoid the tripartite Treaty with Austria for the maintenar
of the General Treaty' on the ground that the latter contair
'sufficient guarantee against Russia'—a view from which he c
not himself dissent. 'Shall we have this Treaty or not?'
asked. 'If we do', he warned the prime minister, 'I must p
some pressure upon the Emperor.'[71]

As was to be expected, Palmerston was strongly in favour
an arrangement that would pledge both France and Austr
and perhaps another great power as well, to maintain by fo
of arms the provisions of the treaty that embodied what h
long been the object of his own eastern policy. In any case, th
were abundant precedents for an additional treaty, such as tl
on which Buol and Bourqueney had agreed in Vienna t
previous November.

On 1 April 1856, accordingly, Palmerston wrote to Clar
don, urging him to persist in his efforts to obtain what
termed 'the Triple Treaty between England, Austria a
France for maintaining the Integrity and Independence of t
Turkish Empire', and impressing on him his conviction that
would be very unadvisable to give that up and no good Reas

could be assigned for doing so'. 'Such a Treaty', he added, 'would be a good additional Security and Bond of Union.' He hoped that not only Prussia, but also Sardinia, would be included among the signatories.[72] 'We ought not', he wrote the following day, 'to give up the Triple Treaty for the Defence of the Turkish Empire.'[73]

Clarendon carried out Palmerston's instructions. On 12 April he reported French reluctance to meet Britain's wishes, and outlined the argument that he had employed:

I of course insisted upon the utility of recording the dangers that were likely to occur and that it was in the interest of peace for the 3 Powers to concert together as to the means of preventing what would lead to war rather than to wait until the casus belli had actually arisen. This was all the more important we said as the Tripartite Treaty was not likely to be acted upon soon . . . .[74]

Clarendon's letter is significant in that the argument that he employed was exactly the opposite of that so often favoured by British foreign secretaries, when declining to give a pledge that would restrict the country's freedom of action.

Three days later Clarendon signed the Tripartite—or Triple —Treaty, which was unique among Britain's diplomatic transactions of the period in that the guarantee contained in its first article was explicitly 'several'. Its second article stated, also explicitly, that any breach of the terms of the Treaty of Paris would be considered as a *casus belli*.[75] The treaty constituted, according to Palmerston, a 'prospective Engagement'.[76] It was designed to ensure the maintenance of the settlement achieved by the victorious war just concluded. 'The objects for which the war was undertaken have been achieved', wrote Clarendon to Delane of the *Times*, 'and as far as Treaty Obligations are binding we have got guarantees for the future.'[77]

Stratford de Redcliffe told Clarendon that the treaty was 'a good leaf taken out of the book of the Congress of Vienna' and might 'be presumed to offer the best security that diplomatic engagements can yield'. However, he was sceptical as to the value of guarantees. 'The strongest and most refined guarantees of that kind', he observed, 'are but cobwebs when passions run high and ambition is on the wing.'[78]

In fact, the Tripartite Treaty was a less onerous commitment than it at first sight appeared. The Ottoman Empire, for the protection of which it was designed, was not a party. The treaty did not, therefore, bind Britain to the Ottoman Empire, but only to Austria and France. In any case, even before the signature of the treaty France, as Clarendon pointed out to Palmerston at the time, was moving towards Russia.[79]

CHAPTER VII

'Inkshed'

(i)

In January 1834 Palmerston wrote to the ambassador in Paris, apropos of what he called a 'Plan for an alliance between England and France', put forward by Talleyrand:

As long as the Interests and Sympathies of the Two Nations are united, as they now are, an alliance does exist, cemented by Motives as strong, as the articles of a Treaty; and if by any unforeseen Circumstances our mutual Relations were to alter, one or other of the Two would find the Treaty inconvenient, and would endeavour to disentangle itself from its obligations.

But such a Treaty with any Power would not be well received in this Country.[1]

Fourteen years later Palmerston explained his attitude more simply and more forcefully to the House of Commons:

I hold with respect to alliances, that England is a Power sufficiently strong, sufficiently powerful, to steer her own course, and not to tie herself as an unnecessary appendage to the policy of any other Government.[2]

These pronouncements prove, of course, little or nothing concerning Palmerston's actual conduct of foreign affairs. They merely raise the same question as do Canning's statements of his objections to guarantees. In fact, during his first two periods as foreign secretary Palmerston certainly envisaged more than one engagement not easy to reconcile with his declarations of principle.

Thus, in the autumn of 1833, shortly after the conclusion of the Treaty of Unkiar-Skelessi and of the Münchengrätz agreement, when Palmerston, not for the last time, was entertaining suspicions of Russia, he sounded Grey about a scheme for a treaty with Sweden. Britain, in return for an assurance that, in the event of being at war, she would enjoy certain facilities in Swedish waters, was to promise Sweden, should the latter be attacked as a result of honouring this engagement, to afford her naval assistance.[3] Grey did not immediately object to what he called '*a strictly defensive engagement*' with Sweden, promising support 'against any attempt to alter the distribution of Power in the Baltick'.[4] Nevertheless, he came to the conclusion that to make an overture to Sweden along the lines suggested would be imprudent. The Swedes, he thought, might leak the proposal to Russia, 'making a merit with that government of their refusal'.[5] Palmerston acknowledged the force of this argument. The idea, he told Grey, a trifle lamely, was not his own. It had been suggested to him by the British minister in Stockholm.[6]

The treaty of 22 April 1834 with France, Portugal and Spain had, as its preamble explained, a limited purpose, arising out of the situation in the Iberian Peninsula.[7] But Palmerston hoped that it would have a wider and more lasting significance. He impressed on the ambassador in Paris his conviction that the treaty 'would have a most powerful Effect in Europe'; that 'it would not only settle at once the affairs of the Peninsula, but create a moral and Political Force in the West which would effectually counterbalance the Eastern League'; that 'it would tell as far as Constantinople, and the Shores of the Euxine'.[8] He told his brother, William Temple, that the treaty established 'a Quadruple Alliance among the Constitutional States of the West'.[9] He even contemplated extending its membership and purpose. Three days after signing it he wrote to Grey, suggesting the inclusion in the treaty of the Two Sicilies. He thought that the accession of the southern Italian kingdom would tend to separate it from Austria and thus 'to defeat Metternich's favourite Scheme of an Italian Confederation of which Austria should be the Chief and Directress'.[10]

Towards the end of 1835 Palmerston wrote to the ambassador in Paris, informing him that the government had come to the conclusion that 'something must be done to protect Turkey from Russia'. He accused Russia of aiming at the dismemberment of Turkey and complained that the Treaty of Unkiar-Skelessi was a step towards that end, since it made Turkey dependent on Russia for support. The remedy was to 'let another Treaty give to Turkey a broader Basis of Support from other Powers, and enable her thus to shake off the yoke of Russia by being secure of aid without Russian assistance, and by being secure of Protection against Russian Menace'. Britain and France were to be parties and Austria, too, if she were willing. The point of the treaty was to be 'Defence against External attack'. Its stipulations were to be 'few and simple':

The Sultan engages to make no Cession of Territory to any foreign Power. The other Contracting Parties engage that if the Sultan is threatened by any Foreign Power, they will endeavour by good offices to persuade that Power not to attack the Sultan, and failing in that will give the Sultan effectual aid for his Defence.[11]

The French government agreed to this scheme, but with a modification to the effect that, in Palmerston's words, 'we should begin by a Treaty between England and France'.[12] Early in 1836 Palmerston submitted drafts for a treaty to Melbourne.[13] 'I am convinced', he wrote on 14 January, 'that the announcement of such a Treaty with France would be received with general applause by the Whole Country.'[14] However, according to Palmerston, several members of the cabinet, including, more especially, the prime minister himself, strongly objected to the scheme in its modified form, preferring 'a preliminary overture to be made to Austria by England and France jointly'.[15] Eventually, therefore, Palmerston abandoned the project. 'We will let the Question about the Turkish Treaty rest for the present', he wrote to the ambassador in Paris on 8 March 1836.[16]

One project that did materialize was that, devised during the Crimean War, for a pact with France and Sweden—to be strictly accurate, Sweden and Norway—for the defence of the latter's territory against Russia.

Soon after the British and French declarations of war on Russia the King of Sweden, Oscar I, made approaches to Britain, which, however, produced no immediate result.[17] In June 1855 Palmerston himself proposed the conclusion of a pact that would bind Sweden not to cede any fishing or pasturage rights or any territory to Russia without Britain's consent.[18] Clarendon took the view that the King would be unlikely to promise to make no territorial concession to Russia, unless Britain undertook to aid him with a naval force in resisting any attempt by Russia to obtain such a concession. He also thought that France should be invited to participate in the proposed arrangement.[19] On 19 July he informed Palmerston that the King wished to 'have all his possessions guaranteed'.[20] Although Palmerston was not in favour of giving such a pledge in so many words, he thought that Britain and France might undertake to support Sweden in resisting any Russian demand for the cession of any of her territory. Indeed, he even contemplated the formation of what he called 'a League virtually though not offensively against Russia', that would include not only Britain, France and Sweden, but Denmark as well.[21]

Not surprisingly, this more ambitious and somewhat fanciful suggestion came to nothing. Clarendon went ahead, however, with the scheme for a three-power pact. On 24 July 1855 Palmerston approved his proposals.[22]

Although these negotiations were conducted in time of war, Palmerston did not look on them as a mere war-time expedient. On the contrary, he hoped for important long-term advantages. On 26 July 1855 he pointed out to Clarendon that 'with regard to the proposed Treaty with Sweden the Benefit which we should derive from it would be the preventing Russia from establishing a great naval Station in never freezing waters'. He thought that that was 'a great object for us looking well to the Future' and that Britain would also 'gain incidentally the advantage of securing Sweden on our Side in Peace or in War, if we chose to avail ourselves of her Resources'. At all events, Britain would have Sweden 'as a friendly Neutral in War, and as a Commercial Friend in Peace', instead of 'a Member even reluctantly of a Northern League against us'.[23]

The wisdom of the proposed treaty did not go unquestioned. In August the Duke of Argyll, a junior member of the cabinet, wrote Clarendon a long letter, the argument of which precluded almost any pledge that entailed the *casus belli*.[24] It was probably as a rejoinder to this criticism that, on 25 September, Palmerston sent Clarendon a detailed justification, not only of the particular transaction under consideration, but of what he called 'prospective Precaution' in general. The treaty, he claimed, would be 'the attainment by anticipation of Part of the Objects of the War', the main object of which was 'to curb the aggressive ambition of Russia':

We went to war not so much to keep the Sultan and his Mussulmen in Turkey, as to keep the Russians out of Turkey; but we have a strong interest also in keeping the Russians out of Norway and Sweden, and if we can do so by Inkshed instead of by Bloodshed surely it is wise to take the opportunity to do so.[25]

Palmerston contested the view that the government could safely leave Sweden to take care of her own territory and to call upon Britain and France when it was in danger:

First of all the Knowledge of such a Treaty would be a powerful check upon Russia and would prevent her from pressing Sweden à la Menchikoff which she might otherwise endeavour to do and to carry her Point by a Coup de Main before application for Support and Assistance could be made, considered, agreed to and complied with. In the next Place Sweden if left free to act as she liked might have Inducements held out to her which might make her willing to consent to what Russia wants. Suppose for instance that Russia were to propose an Exchange of Aland and Bomarsund for the Fiord at the Top of Norway; the Swedish Government if unshackled might think the Bargain a good one for Sweden, but it would be a very bad one for us; and yet if there was no Treaty we should have no Right to object.[26]

He saw the treaty as part of a great security-system, designed to prevent Russian aggression in the future:

The treaty we propose would be a *Part of a long Line of Circumvallation* to confine the future Extension of Russia even if the Events of the War should not enable us to drive her outposts in, at any Part of her present Circumference. . . . We must never forget, that whatever the Conditions of Peace may be the Russian Government will set to work the moment Peace is concluded to strengthen all that has been found weak, to prepare for aggression everything that has hitherto been ineffective, to redeem by Encroachments on the weak the Position and Power which she will have lost by the assaults of the Strong, and that by endeavouring to Bar her up on all sides as well and as much as we can, we are taking the best means of avoiding future Collisions.[27]

Such were the arguments adduced by Palmerston in justification of the treaty, eventually signed in Stockholm on 21

November 1855, under which Sweden undertook not to cede
territory to Russia, and Britain and France promised Sweden,
in the event of Russia demanding the cession of any of her
territory, to provide military and naval assistance.[28]

Palmerston entertained high hopes of this arrangement. 'I
cannot but think', he wrote to Clarendon on 17 December,
'that the Treaty will be well received here when People understand the Evil which it is intended to guard us against.'[29] After
the conclusion of peace in the following year he even suggested
to Clarendon the inclusion in the Stockholm treaty of Austria.
'The accession of Austria', he wrote on 29 May 1856, 'to our
Treaty about Sweden would no Doubt add a good Deal to the
political Strength of the Security which that Treaty is intended
to afford Sweden against Russian aggression, and in a Military
Point of view it would also strengthen our Hands, and therefore
the accession of Austria would I think be desirable.'[30]

The Treaty of Stockholm was supplemented by the Tripartite Treaty of the following year, which, with its specification
of the *casus belli*, illustrates the difficulty of drawing a clear
distinction between a 'treaty of alliance' and a 'treaty of
guarantee'. Palmerston himself described the arrangement
embodied in the Tripartite Treaty as 'an important alliance'.[31]
In the House of Commons he dwelt on the long-term planning
that lay behind the two-fold system of security, established by,
on the one hand, the Stockholm treaty, and, on the other, what
he called, 'the triple alliance of England, France, and Austria'.[32]
'These alliances are not the offspring of a day, or the chance
products of accident', he told the House, 'but the results of full
deliberation, and the tendency of great material and political
interests.'[33]

However, although the Treaty of Stockholm and the Tripartite Treaty both embodied engagements that were unquestionably 'prospective', neither treaty specified the number
of troops that each signatory was to contribute to the joint war
effort, or what subsidy, if any Britain was to pay her allies,
should the *casus foederis* arise. Thus, the actual military or
financial contribution that Britain would be required to make,
in the event of either treaty being invoked, was a matter that
would have to be decided when the occasion arose. In this

respect, therefore, the obligations undertaken by Palmerston and Clarendon in 1855–6 were less well defined than those incurred by Castlereagh in comparable circumstances in 1814–15.

(ii)

Palmerston's denials of Britain's need for any alliance should not be regarded as expressions of a rule that admitted of no exception. Indeed, Palmerston does not appear to have been regarded by his contemporaries as a minister for whom the avoidance of any such involvement was a matter of high principle. Nassau Senior, the economist, even suspected that he and the other politicians of the period were not above giving secret pledges to other powers behind the back of Parliament and the public. 'But in England, alliances, guarantees, and all the other mischiefs of diplomacy, may be concocting in Downing Street, while the Bank Parlour and the Royal Exchange enjoy a fancied security'; he wrote, 'and the nation may be awakened from its dream of safety only by the presentation of Papers and the demand for a Vote of Credit.'[34]

Senior was unfair, at least to Palmerston, who was less addicted to secret transactions than were certain other prime ministers and foreign secretaries. Whatever its framers' original intentions, the Tripartite Treaty, as finally concluded, had no secret article. Palmerston did not, indeed, encourage discussion in Parliament of a treaty before it had been ratified. 'With us', he wrote to the ambassador in Paris in 1834, 'it is a sufficient answer in Parliament to say that one cannot discuss a Treaty till it has been ratified and laid before Parliament.'[35] However, once a treaty had been ratified, he insisted on it being promptly laid. Thus, on 2 May 1855 he wrote to Clarendon, pointing out that the Tripartite Treaty, signed little more than two weeks previously, had 'not been laid before Parliament.' He enquired whether the treaty had been signed, and, if so, whether the delay was due to the fact that the ratifications had not yet been exchanged.[36] In short, the man, who, according to Russell, had 'everything at his fingers' ends', kept Parliament informed of the country's commitments, at all events after they had been contracted.[37]

CHAPTER VIII

'Still obligatory'

Early in 1859, when relations between France and Austria were deteriorating, Derby was at pains to impress on the House of Lords the fact that Britain was not bound by any 'secret engagement' that would fetter her freedom of action in any contingency that might arise.[1]

It may, perhaps, have been in consequence of Derby's desire to establish this point that in August 1859, that is, some two months after the resignation of the Conservative government, there was laid before Parliament an interesting compilation, entitled 'Treaties of Guarantee'. This consisted of a return of the texts, or extracts therefrom, of a number of treaties, conventions and acts, under which Britain had given explicit guarantees, in connexion with the territory or institutions of various countries, or with comparable matters, as well as those of several others that contained no specific reference to such a pledge. It thus served as a reminder that these so-called 'treaties of guarantee' were officially considered to be 'still obligatory'.[2]

The 'ancient treaties' with Portugal constituted the largest single group included in the return. They numbered altogether eight, ranging from the original treaty of 1373 to that of 22 January 1815, signed in Vienna by Castlereagh. Even without the Foreign Office's assurance that these treaties were 'still obligatory', there would have been no doubt that Britain was bound by them. Both Castlereagh and Canning had acknowledged Britain's treaty obligation towards Portugal. In 1826 a royal proclamation had formally declared that, as a result of recent events in the peninsula, the *casus foederis* had arisen, whereupon troops had been dispatched to the mouth of the Tagus.[3] The British treaty obligation to Portugal had subsequently been acknowledged by both Palmerston[4] and Granville.[5]

The alliance was, in fact, the expression of what successive governments regarded as Britain's own interest in the maintenance of the independence of Portugal. 'We are still bound to protect the independence and security of Portugal against foreign aggression', wrote Wellington in 1831, 'not only by the terms of our treaties, but by that policy which ought to direct every state to provide for its own security.'[6] In the following year Palmerston expressed the opinion that 'Great Britain especially has a paramount Interest in the Independence of Portugal'.[7] Moreover, Portugal's geographical position lent itself to warfare of the type in which Britain, as a great naval power, would be at an advantage. The British war-ships, which for many years were stationed in the estuary of the Tagus, served as visible tokens of the binding force of the 'ancient treaties', of Britain's interest in the maintenance of the independence of Portugal, and of her ability both to honour her obligation and to defend her interest.[8]

There was a close dynastic link between the British and Portuguese royal families. Moreover, Britain's treaty obligation to Portugal, unlike her other continental responsibilities, was one that she shared with no other power. It could not, therefore, be explained away, should Portugal ever invoke the 'ancient treaties', as being dependent on the willingness of some other signatory or signatories to act. On the other hand, the alliance clearly did not rest on a basis of co-equality.

The remainder of the contents of the return varied considerably in importance, in stringency and in relevance to the conditions actually prevailing in Europe in the second half of the nineteenth century.

It would be interesting to know what precisely the Foreign Office conceived the British obligation to Prussia under article xvii of the Treaty of Vienna to be. It clearly did not consider that Britain was under no obligation at all. What the attitude of the British government would have been, if Prussia had ever had occasion to invoke the guarantee, is a matter concerning which one can only speculate.

The obligation entailed by the act of 20 November 1815, under which Britain and the other four great powers had guaranteed the integrity and inviolability of the territory of

Switzerland and the neutrality of the northern part of Savoy, is also difficult to state precisely. However, the act had not lost all relevance to the contemporary situation. As recently as 1845 Aberdeen had considered himself entitled to offer the Swiss government advice on the strength of 'the relation in which Great Britain stands towards the Confederation as one of the Parties to the Act guaranteeing the Swiss national independence'.[9]

The guarantee of the independence of Greece, provided for by Britain, France and Russia in the convention of 7 May 1832, had not sufficed twenty-two years later to deter the first two of these powers, who were then at war with the third, from occupying Athens.[10] This, however, had not, in the eyes of the Foreign Office, caused the convention to cease to be 'obligatory'.

The treaties of 19 April 1839 with Belgium and with the Netherlands related to matters in which Britain's vital interests were more obviously involved. Nevertheless, it was clear that the pledge given to Belgium was one that Britain could not honour unaided—at least, not against a great power. Clarendon appreciated this point. In 1852, when there was concern at the possibility of French designs on Belgium, he had written to Henry Reeve, of the *Times*, impressing on him that, whatever the extent of the British obligation, he would 'fulfill it at all hazards and consider that our honor and our interest were alike concerned in doing so'. To this affirmation he added, however, a significant qualification. He considered that 'it would be of the utmost importance to us not to undertake this work singlehanded'.[11]

The return also gave the texts, or extracts therefrom, of the various treaties and of the convention that together formed the contractual basis of what is sometimes called the 'Crimean System'. Of these the most stringent was the Tripartite Treaty of 15 April 1856 with Austria and France. This treaty was unquestionably valid. However, since Britain's two co-signatories had been at war with each other in the spring and early summer of 1859, it could be presumed to have lost much of its probable effectiveness. On the other hand, the return did not give the text of any treaty, convention or act, signed before 1815, other than those with Portugal. In the opinion of the

Foreign Office the numerous guarantees given by Britain in the eighteenth century were evidently no longer in force. Nor did the return give the texts of Castlereagh's treaties of 'alliance and friendship' of 20 November 1815. Another significant absentee was Palmerston's treaty of 22 April 1834 with France, Portugal and Spain. Yet in 1847 Portugal had invoked the assistance of her allies under that treaty, and, at a conference held in London, they had agreed to comply with her request.[12] The sequel had been a brief but effective intervention in the internal affairs of Portugal.[13]

CHAPTER IX

'Non-intervention'

(i)

'I think I know what a Radical is', John Bright remarked in 1853, according to Greville, 'but I have never seen such a one as young Stanley.' Eleven years later Stanley presented the unusual spectacle of a former secretary of state for India, who was also the son and heir of the leader of the Conservative Party, addressing the House of Commons in the language of the Manchester School. 'I believe', he declared during the great debate of July 1864 on the Palmerston government's handling of the Danish question, 'that a policy of neutrality and non-intervention may be not only a safe but a respected and an honourable position.'[2] Richard Cobden's comment on Stanley's speech, expressed in a letter to Henry Richard of the Peace Society, was: 'You and I could indorse every word.'[3]

Since the 1830s Cobden had championed the principle of 'non-intervention' in the politics of the continent. There was no means, he wrote in 1835, by which a body of members of the reformed House of Commons could so fairly achieve for itself the patriotic title of a national party as by associating for the common object of 'deprecating all intervention on our part in continental politics'.[4] 'We avow the principle of non-intervention', he declared at Manchester in 1862, 'which means neutrality.'[5] The corollary of this principle was clearly the avoidance of any pledge that would place Britain under an obligation to take part in any continental war.

It was natural to interpret the debate of July 1864 as a victory, not merely for the decision to refrain from intervening in the conflict over Schleswig and Holstein, but for the principle of 'non-intervention' in general. On 19 October Stanley developed this theme in a speech to his constituents:

We had a discussion last July on the conduct of foreign affairs . . . and the object with which many members—I among the rest—went into it was to obtain from Parliament a distinct and decided expression of opinion in favour of a policy of non-intervention in Continental disputes. In that we perfectly succeeded. The feeling upon that point came nearer to unanimity than I ever recollect to have been the case in Parliament upon any occasion equally important. I believe the feeling of the country went the same way, and, unless I greatly mistake it, the debate of 1864 will mark the beginning of a new era in the history of British diplomacy.[6]

For a time Cobden, perhaps influenced by Stanley's prophecy, was of the same opinion. 'Non-intervention', he wrote to Michel Chevalier, the French economist, on 5 November, 'is the policy of all future governments in this country.'[7] On reflection, however, he was less sanguine. 'There is much to be done', he confessed to Henry Richard five days later, 'before we bring the great political parties to an honest recognition of the *principle* of non-intervention.'[8]

(ii)

In the summer of 1866, only a few days after the outbreak of what was destined to be remembered as the Seven Weeks War, Russell's second government resigned and Queen Victoria sent for Derby.

In the situation then prevailing on the continent there was clearly a strong case for a policy of the kind about which so much had been said and written two years previously. The *Spectator* declared that the general wish was 'to hold absolutely aloof from the complications of European politics, to abstain from all counsel even which savours of obligation, and resolutely to avoid every shadow of international engagement that might limit our freedom for the future'. Of the men available to carry out this wish the *Spectator* considered Stanley to be 'the very best'.[9]

In fact, Derby's choice for the Foreign Office did eventually fall on his son. When Queen Victoria expressed her alarm[10] he acknowledged that both he and the future foreign secretary would desire 'to keep this country as far as possible from any entanglement in Continental politics'.[11] Stanley, for his part, on seeking re-election, impressed on his constituents his conviction that politicians of all parties were agreed on 'the duty of keeping out of these Continental quarrels'. He also attempted to clear up any misunderstanding as to the real meaning of a 'policy of non-intervention', which he defined as a 'policy of abstinence from war-like interference in Continental disputes'.[12]

(iii)

Less than a year later Stanley signed a treaty that exposed him to the charge of inconsistency with his own pronouncements.

The Grand Duke of Luxemburg, who was also King of the Netherlands, had been a member, in the former of these two capacities, of the 'Germanic Confederation', set up in 1815. The city of Luxemburg had been a fortress of the Confederation, with a garrison supplied by Prussia. Despite the dissolution, as a result of the war of 1866, of the Confederation and the fact that the Grand Duke was not a member of the new North German Confederation, the Prussian garrison remained in the fortress. Early in 1867 Napoleon III and his foreign minister, Moustier, attempted to acquire the Grand Duchy by purchase from the King of the Netherlands. This attempt was thwarted by Bismarck. They then, in April 1867, demanded the withdrawal of the Prussian garrison from the fortress of Luxemburg.[13]

Prussia, the head of the newly formed North German Confederation and the ally of the south German states, could not be expected to comply with this demand forthwith. Bernstorff, the Prussian ambassador in London, saw Stanley on 15 April and read him a communication from Bismarck, explaining the Prussian point of view. 'If I am to believe what Bismarck says in his despatch read to me yesterday', wrote Stanley to Cowley, the ambassador in Paris, 'Prussia will not give way on any terms.'[14] 'He [Bismarck] says that on no conditions whatever will Prussian consent to evacuate the fortress', the foreign secretary informed his father on 17 April.[15] For several days there was an impasse. Loftus, the British ambassador in Berlin, took a gloomy view of the situation. 'War is inevitable I think, and within the shortest period', he wrote on 19 April to Buchanan, his colleague in St Petersburg. 'Prussia cannot and will not evacuate the Fortress of Luxemburg', he added, 'and the French Government apparently consider their occupation as illegal under Treaties and therefore a menace to Herself.'[16]

Bismarck did not expedite a solution of the crisis by leaving Berlin to spend a few days at Varzin. Stanley could only await the news of his return. 'I do not absolutely despair of peace', he wrote to Clarendon, with whom he maintained a polite correspondence, on 23 April.[17] On the same day he warned Bloomfield, the ambassador in Vienna, that, if Bismarck took the line that German national feeling did not allow him to give way, there could be 'no possible result except war'.[18] It was also on 23 April that Buchanan telegraphed from St Petersburg the news that Gorchakov had instructed Brunnow, the Russian ambassador in London, to propose a conference in the British capital, with a view to preserving peace by means of a settlement on the basis of the neutralization of the Grand Duchy and the extension to it of the guarantee already enjoyed by Belgium.[19]

Gorchakov's proposal, which Bismarck supported, placed the British foreign secretary in a difficult position. Although Stanley wished peace to be preserved, he was most reluctant to involve Britain in a new commitment to defend Luxemburg. However, after some two weeks of negotiations, the conference met in London—to be precise, at 10 Downing Street—on 7 May 1867. Four days later Stanley signed a treaty, the second article of which provided that the Grand Duchy of Luxemburg should form a perpetually neutral state, and placed this principle under the sanction of the collective guarantee of Austria, Britain, France, Italy, Prussia and Russia. Under subsequent articles the city of Luxemburg was to cease to be a fortress; Prussia was to withdraw her garrison; and the King-Grand Duke was to carry out the demolitions necessary for the conversion of the fortress into an open city.[20]

It was the guarantee contained in the second article of the London treaty of 11 May 1867 that exposed Stanley to the charge of inconsistency.

How was it that the champion of a 'policy of non-intervention in Continental disputes' brought himself to put his signature to a treaty that contained even a 'collective' guarantee?

Stanley appears to have been sincerely anxious to avoid giving a pledge of the kind proposed. On 27 April he warned Grey, the Queen's private secretary, that the public was determined not to incur any 'fresh responsibilities for Continental objects'.[21] In his circular dispatch of the following day, while agreeing to a conference on the basis of the neutralization of the fortress and the withdrawal of the Prussian garrison, he made no reference to any guarantee.[22] This omission, as we know from Hammond's correspondence, was deliberate.[23]

On 3 May Stanley circulated proposals for a treaty, which served as a reminder that possession of the Grand Duchy was already guaranteed to the King-Grand Duke under the treaty of 1839 and made no provision for any additional guarantee.[24] In his dispatch to Cowley of the same day he reported having impressed on Bernstorff and on Bentinck, the Dutch minister, his 'sense of the great difficulty which would attend the giving of any fresh guarantee'.[25] On the following day, in a dispatch to Loftus, he emphasized the adequacy of the existing guarantee and the impossibility of giving a new one.[26]

However, both the King of Prussia and Bismarck insisted on the neutralization of the Grand Duchy under a European guarantee as an indispensable pre-condition of the withdrawal of the Prussian garrison.[27] On 4 May the Chancellor, according to Loftus, commented unfavourably on the omissions that characterized Stanley's draft treaty.[28] 'I fear', cabled the ambassador the following day, 'that Prussia will not withdraw from fortress unless the Grand Duchy is neutralized and placed under an European guarantee.'[29] Gorchakov also insisted on these conditions.[30] On 5 May Brunnow, the Russian ambassador in London, produced a counter draft treaty: the Grand Duchy was to form a perpetually neutral state; this principle was to be placed under the sanction of a collective guarantee; further—and the order was significant—the city of Luxemburg was to cease to be a fortress and the Prussian garrison was to be withdrawn.[31] According to La Tour d'Auvergne, the French ambassador, Brunnow saw Stanley and tried to persuade him that Britain could give a collective guarantee without thereby greatly increasing her obligations; to this Stanley replied that he would promise nothing—even collectively.[32]

On 6 May the Foreign Office accordingly drew up another draft treaty, based on Brunnow's, but omitting any reference to a new guarantee. This draft it circulated to the various plenipotentiaries.[33] Hammond also sent a copy to Cowley, pointing out that the text was really Brunnow's, but with this important omission, and explaining that it was this draft that Stanley intended to present to the conference. He did not think that there was any chance of the British government going any further, so far as the guarantee was concerned. 'It would be repugnant to the principles and feelings of Parliament and the Public to do more', he declared, 'and surely, though we are very ready to do our best for the peace of Europe, we cannot reasonably be expected to forgo all our own principles and views to accommodate the fancies of Prussia.'[34] Hammond's attitude towards the guarantee required by Bismarck was clearly in line with that of the foreign secretary.

However, to the pressure already being exerted on Stanley by Bismarck in Berlin and Gorchakov in St Petersburg was added that of certain people in his own country, whose views he could scarcely afford to ignore. On 5 May Queen Victoria wrote to the foreign secretary, urging him to agree to the extension to Luxemburg of the existing guarantee of neutrality, already enjoyed by Belgium.[35] Grey reinforced the Queen's argument,[36] and wrote to Disraeli to the same effect.[37] On the same day—it was a Sunday—Bernstorff called on Derby, who, according to the former's account of the conversation, eventually undertook to speak to his son.[38] At all events, the prime minister wrote that night to Stanley, impressing on him his view that the settlement of the question at issue depended on the course taken by the British government. 'If the "European Guarantee" can be accepted in the sense in which Prussia is willing to accept it', he observed, 'I do not see that it need interpose an insuperable obstacle to a settlement.' He expressed a wish to see Stanley 'if not at breakfast to-morrow, as early as you can after'.[39]

Disraeli took the same line. On the evening of 6 May he had a conversation with Stanley at the House of Commons, after which he wrote to the Queen, expressing his confidence that the foreign secretary would 'accept the proposition of general guarantee'. He had, he related, emphasized the strength of feeling in the House of Commons, the City of London and society generally 'in favour of Peace, at the price of general guarantee'.[40]

This pressure on the young and still comparatively inexperienced foreign secretary by the Queen, by the prime minister, who was also his father, and by the chancellor of the exchequer and leader of the House of Commons, was clearly too powerful to resist. Later the same evening Hammond, after receiving a message from Stanley, while on his way home, sent the foreign secretary a long, avuncular letter, acknowledging the impossibility of continued refusal. 'If Lord Derby and Mr Disraeli, backed by the Queen, press you to give way on the guarantee point', he wrote, 'there can be no question, I think, but that you should give in.' This, however, was not to be 'till after a decent fight recorded on the Protocol'.[41]

The permanent under-secretary then proceeded to brief his official chief as to the right course to adopt. Stanley was not to 'breathe a syllable to any foreign diplomatist' about the possibility of his giving way. When, on the following day, the conference met, he was to submit his draft for consideration, without alluding to the question of a guarantee. If, as was probable, Bernstorff insisted on a guarantee, Stanley was to remind the conference that the guarantee of 1839 applied to Luxemburg, no less than to Belgium, to declare that he considered an additional pledge of this kind unnecessary, but to offer to join in an engagement to neutralize the Grand Duchy and to respect its neutrality. If Bernstorff were still to hold out for a guarantee, Stanley was to say that, in view of the importance of the question at issue, 'involving an engagement which might at some day or other prove the cause of England being engaged in war', and 'the strong objection to guarantees on the part of Parliament and the Country', he must, before giving a definitive answer, consult the cabinet and take the Queen' pleasure. He was then to propose the adjournment of the conference for two days.[42] 'You would thus get on record your objections', Hammond concluded, 'and show to Parliament and the Country that you consented to guarantee only under the sanction of your colleagues and of the Queen.'[43]

Stanley did not, in fact, follow Hammond's advice to maintain complete reticence as to his intentions. On 7 May, the day
of the conference, but before it actually met, he saw Bernstorff,
who cabled to Bismarck that the foreign secretary had made it
clear that, if the other powers were unanimous, he would not
stand out against the guarantee.[44]

On the same day and also before the meeting of the conference, Stanley wrote to Cowley, acknowledging that he had
made up his mind to give the guarantee of neutrality, if it was
'absolutely pressed'. It would, he explained, not do to break up
the conference on what was 'really so small a point'.[45] To
Grey, too, he expressed his readiness 'to give way on the point
in dispute rather than break up the conference'.[46] Thus, even
before the conference met Stanley had made up his mind to
agree to guarantee the neutrality of Luxemburg, if Bernstorff,
supported by the other plenipotentiaries, insisted, as in all
probability, he would.

On the afternoon of Tuesday 7 May the conference duly met
at 10 Downing Street. The protocol records that the ambassador
of Italy was admitted and the representatives of Luxemburg
were present. Bernstorff complained that the draft treaty
circulated by the Foreign Office was a departure from the
programme, on the basis of which his government had agreed
to take part in the conference, namely a European guarantee
of the neutrality of the Grand Duchy. Brunnow, La Tour
d'Auvergne, Apponyi, the Austrian ambassador, and Bentinck
all supported this contention. Stanley reminded the conference
of the guarantee given to the King of the Netherlands in 1839.
Bernstorff pointed out, correctly, that this guarantee did not
relate to Luxemburg's neutrality. When the plenipotentiaries
came to discuss the second article of the draft treaty, Bernstorff
proposed the addition of a sentence, placing the principle of the
neutrality of Luxemburg under the collective, or common,
guarantee of the signatory powers, with the exception of
Belgium. Stanley thereupon undertook to consult the cabinet
and to inform the conference of its decision at its next meeting.[47]

It so happened that, after returning from the conference to
the Foreign Office, Stanley had to go immediately to the House
of Commons.[48] However, Hammond kept Cowley abreast of

the situation. The foreign secretary, he wrote, had not disguise
from the plenipotentiaries the fact that in all probability h
cabinet colleagues would assent to the guarantee of the ne
trality of Luxemburg, on which Prussia insisted.[49] Bernstorf
for his part, informed Bismarck that Stanley had told him aft
the meeting that he would answer for the guarantee.[50]

Meanwhile, in Berlin, Bismarck was resorting to more con
pelling arguments. At 4 o'clock on the afternoon of 7 Ma
Loftus cabled that the Chancellor had that day informed hi
that, in view of France's military preparations, Prussia could r
longer remain passive. If the conference did not within the ne
three days achieve a peaceful settlement, the mobilization of tl
Prussian army would be ordered. Prussia would accept r
arrangement that did not include a 'European guarantee'
the neutrality of the Grand Duchy.[51]

On 8 May the cabinet met.[52] On the same day Stanle
notified both Cowley and Loftus of his decision to agree to tl
guarantee. 'I have accepted the inevitable guarantee, as prefe
able to setting all Europe by the ears', he told Cowley.[53] 'I ha
agreed—not very willingly, but seeing it as a matter of necessi
—to join in the general guarantee', he wrote to Loftus, addir
that he had told Bernstorff that he would do so formally at tl
next meeting of the conference on the following day.[54]

When, on 9 May the conference reassembled, Stanle
announced his government's decision to defer to the wishes
the other powers, and to accept Prussia's proposed amendme
to the draft treaty. A passage was, accordingly, added to tl
second article, placing the principle of the neutrality of tl
Grand Duchy under the sanction of the collective guarantee
the signatory powers, apart from Belgium.[55] Even Hammor
saw 'nothing to object to' in this arrangement. 'If you were
refuse to give this guarantee', he wrote to Stanley, 'it is qui
clear you would be impeached!'[56]

On the same day Stanley informed the Commons that tl
conference had reached agreement, declaring that he shared tl
strong feeling of susceptibility that existed in the House on tl
subject of guarantees, and minimizing the responsibility th
the government had incurred.[57] 'The House of Common
Hammond reported to Cowley, 'cheered loudly the announc

ment that all was settled, and received with complacency Lord Stanley's explanation about Guarantee.'[58] 'Not a word of objection has reached me', wrote Stanley to Grey the following day.[59] From Berlin Loftus cabled that the Prussian government had abandoned its intended mobilization.[60] On Saturday 11 May the treaty was signed.

What Stanley had, in fact, done was to sign a treaty based, in all essentials, on the Russian draft of 5 May 1867. On 13 May the prime minister and the foreign secretary announced in their respective Houses of Parliament the signature of the treaty.[61] On the following day Stanley wrote to Bloomfield. 'We have averted war for the moment—for the year I think certainly', he claimed. 'The relief of the mercantile classes here is great', he added, 'and the public has swallowed the guarantee more easily than I thought possible.'[62]

Bernstorff shared in the general euphoria. On 15 May he informed the King of Prussia that numerous politicians had assured him that he had rendered the British government an immense service, 'en lui forçant la main par rapport a la garantie et en lui procurant ainsi contre sa propre volonté un succès diplomatique que depuis longtemps aucun Cabinet anglais n'avait obtenu'.[63]

On 14 June the treaty, having been ratified and laid before Parliament, was debated in the House of Commons. Labouchere observed that some of its provisions 'appeared to be directly at variance with the principles of non-intervention supposed of late years to regulate our foreign policy'.[64] Another Opposition back-bencher, Robert Aytoun, protested against 'conduct involving us in a guarantee of foreign territory'.[65] Stanley, for his part, declared that the idea of a new guarantee had been so distasteful to him and so contrary both to his own principles and to those of his colleagues, that he had hesitated for 'two or three days' before agreeing to give one. On the other hand, he told the House, if the project of a 'collective European guarantee' had fallen through, the conference would have been broken off and 'a rupture would have ensued'.[66]

Six days later the treaty was debated in the House of Lords. Derby admitted that guarantees were unpopular. The 'collective guarantee' had, however, he pointed out, been made a '*sine qua non*'. To have refused to participate in it would have been to incur 'the heavy responsibility of a European war'.[67]

(iv)

Stanley was also accused of having first agreed to give the pledge required of Britain by Gorchakov and Bismarck, and of having then gone back on his word, before finally yielding. Thus, a week after the signature of the treaty, Clarendon wrote to Cowley, relating that Bernstorff had told him in confidence that 'when the demand for a European guarantee first came S. made no objection or rather he so completely assented that B. wrote to Bismarck that as far as England was concerned it was a fait accompli'.[68] When, on 20 June 1867, the House of Lords debated the treaty, Granville, in his turn, referred to a report, which, he said, 'was generally credited upon the continent', to the effect that the government had 'at the beginning of the negotiation . . . agreed to the guarantee' and that 'they afterwards withdrew from that position'.[69]

There is, of course, no doubt that at the end of April and the beginning of May 1867 some of those who were closely concerned in the negotiations believed that the British government had consented to give the pledge required of it. On 26 April Bismarck informed Bernstorff that Loftus had that day enquired whether Prussia would participate in a conference in London for the purpose of maintaining the independence of Luxemburg under a European guarantee.[70] On the following day the King of Prussia, in a letter to Queen Victoria, referred to the fact that, according to Loftus, the British government appeared to be willing to agree to the neutralization of the Grand Duchy under a European guarantee.[71] On 4 May Van de Weyer wrote to Grey that Stanley himself had proposed to Prussia, as a basis for negotiation, 'the *neutralisation* of Luxemburg with a *European guarantee*'. 'It now seems', he complained, 'that Lord Stanley shrinks before the clause of *guarantee*.'[72]

It would be interesting to know what substance, if any, there was in these statements. It may well be that one or more of those who took part, on the British side, in the negotiations concerning the future of Luxemburg employed in the course of conversation the ambiguous term 'guarantee' with a looseness that was and is common. It may also well be that a misunderstanding arose from the fact that on more than one occasion in the past the great powers, including Britain, had secured—or had attempted to secure—the neutralization of a territory by a guarantee. It may have been assumed in some quarters in 1867 that one arrangement implied the other.

At all events, an examination of many of Stanley's letters and dispatches has not yielded any evidence that he personally consented to give an explicit guarantee of the neutrality of Luxemburg at any time before the late afternoon or evening of 6 May 1867. Indeed, Hammond, in a memorandum, which he drew up for Stanley's use on 21 June 1867, that is, the day following the Lords' debate on the treaty, specifically denied the truth of what he described as 'a cock and bull story', told by Granville.[73] 'Lord Stanley', he wrote to Cowley the following day, 'never until the last moment gave way about the guarantee or entertained the notion of giving it.'[74]

CHAPTER X

'Moonshine'

(i)

During the crisis of April-May 1867 Prussia had insisted on a European guarantee of the neutrality of Luxemburg. The guarantee stipulated in the second article of the treaty of 11 May 1867 was, indeed, European, in the sense that all the great powers of Europe were parties to it. It was also explicitly 'collective'. But what precisely is a 'collective'—or, for that matter, a 'common' or a 'joint' guarantee? What obligations do the parties to such a guarantee incur?

There are no simple answers to these questions. For one thing, in 1867 the number of precedents for a specifically 'collective', 'common' or 'joint' guarantee, given in connexion with the territory or institutions of a foreign country, was small. The guarantees given to Prussia and Switzerland in 1815 had not been explicitly qualified in any such way. The statement in the preamble of the convention with France of 22 October 1832, concerning the guarantee contained in article xxv of the Belgian treaty of the previous year, had been significant as an interpretation, but not as a literally accurate description, of the pledge given to Belgium by the five powers.

In December 1854 Britain, Austria and France had presented a memorandum to Russia, proposing a 'collective' five-power guarantee of the privileges of the Principalities and of 'Servia'.[2] In fact, perhaps owing to an oversight, the guarantee of the privileges and immunities of the Principalities, contained in article xxii of the Treaty of Paris, had not been qualified in this way. On the other hand, the guarantee of the rights and immunities of 'Servia', contained in article xxviii, was explicitly 'collective'. This was, accordingly, the first unquestionably 'collective' guarantee, relating to the institutions of a foreign country, ever given by Britain. The guarantee of the observance of the engagement to respect the independence and integrity of the Ottoman Empire, contained in article vii of the Treaty of Paris, had been given 'en commun'.[3] According to the English text of the Tripartite Treaty, Britain, Austria and France guaranteed the independence and integrity of the Ottoman Empire, not only 'severally', but also 'jointly'.[4] The convention of 19 August 1858 had provided that the now united Principalities should continue to enjoy their privileges under a guarantee specifically qualified as 'collective'.[5]

The first proposal for a specifically 'collective' guarantee of the neutrality of Luxemburg, put forward at the time of the crisis, was, as far as can be judged from the available documents, that contained in the Russian draft treaty of 5 May 1867. Brunnow, a diplomat of great experience, trained in a service that appears to have attached much importance to terminological precision, evidently considered the epithet significant. According to La Tour d'Auvergne, Brunnow told Stanley that 'une garantie collective n'engageait pas au même point qu'une garantie *spéciale*'.[6] Bernstorff seems to have regarded the terms 'collective' and 'common'[7] as interchangeable, at least in the context of a guarantee.[7] However, this does not materially simplify the task of finding a definition of these terms, as understood by contemporaries.

If we may believe Hammond's account, admittedly written some weeks after the conference, the significance of the epithet was appreciated by Julian Fane, the protocolist. In his memorandum of 21 June 1867 Hammond wrote:

Fane told me that the word 'collective' was first put forward by Brunnow in the Conference. Some time later in the discussion when Bernstorff was writing down the terms of his amendment and had come to the word 'garantie', he hesitated for a moment as to the Epithet, apparently doubting whether it should be 'Européenne', on which Fane put into his mouth the word 'collective' which he at once adopted, adding in parenthesis 'en commune [*sic*]'.[8]

Hammond's recollection, recorded in the same document, of his own remarks to Stanley on the latter's return to the Foreign Office from the conference also deserves quotation:

It was only on your return from the Conference that I heard from you that the Guarantee was '*Collective*', and my remark to you was that you might very safely undertake for that, as it amounted to nothing.[9]

On the following day Hammond sent Cowley a more lively account of this conversation on the subject of the 'collective guarantee', concluding with the words: 'I wished him joy as it was no guarantee at all.'[10]

In short, there was a considerable measure of agreement, at least in diplomatic circles, that the epithet 'collective', when employed in connexion with a guarantee, was a significant term, the effect of the use of which was to reduce the onerousness of the pledge to which it was applied. On the other hand, to state positively what obligation a 'collective' guarantee did entail, as distinct from what it did not, is not easy. Mountague Bernard was one contemporary who attempted to define a 'collective' guarantee positively. On 11 June 1867, after the treaty had been laid before Parliament, he wrote, in a letter to the *Times*:

Unquestionably the guarantee is collective, in the sense that each of the six Powers (excluding Belgium) has a right to insist that the aid of the other five be invoked at the same time as its own, and that the liability be borne in common.[11]

Even so, helpful as this passage is, it is a statement, not so much of the obligations of 'collective' guarantors, as of their rights.

(ii)

What caused a stir in 1867 was, of course, the official British explanation, or rather explanations, given in Parliament, of the 'collective' guarantee, contained in article ii of the treaty.

On 9 May, that is, before the actual signature of the treaty, Stanley told the House of Commons that all that the government had done had been to adapt the existing engagement, contracted in 1839, to the changed circumstances of the time. It had not incurred any fresh responsibility. On the contrary, the responsibility that formerly existed had actually been narrowed.[12] On 14 June he maintained that the guarantee was a case of 'limited liability'. It had the character of a 'moral sanction', rather than of a 'contingent liability to make war'.

'It would, no doubt, give a right to make war', he declared, 'but it would not necessarily impose the obligation.'[13]

Derby went even further. On 20 June, speaking in the House of Lords, he emphasized the 'collective' character of the guarantee, as distinct from the individual and separate character of that given in 1839:

That is a most important difference, because the only two Powers by which the neutrality of Luxemburg is likely to be infringed are two of the parties to the collective guarantee; and therefore, if either of them violate the neutrality, the obligation on all the others would not accrue.[14]

As to the power whose designs on Luxemburg, Prussia had most reason to fear, Derby declared:

It is quite true that, if France were to invade the territory of Luxemburg, the other Powers, though they might be called upon to resist the invasion, would not be bound to do so.[15]

This idiosyncratic interpretation did not, however, pass unchallenged. Russell, who had initially expressed his approbation of the government's handling of the crisis, declined, after hearing Derby's statement, to accept the prime minister's interpretation of the treaty. He declared his belief that, if France were to invade Luxemburg, the other parties to the treaty would be bound to call upon her to retire.[16] Granville called attention to the contradiction between Stanley's reluctance to give the pledge required by Prussia and the infinitesimal significance that the prime minister attached to it. He considered that, in fact, an 'undesirable increase' in Britain's foreign liabilities had taken place.[17] Argyll thought that Derby's argument reduced the guarantee to 'a sham, and a farce'.[18]

The explanations given by both Stanley and Derby aroused indignation in Berlin. Bismarck complained, according to Loftus, that the effect of Stanley's speech in the House of Commons was to render the guarantee 'entirely illusory'. He could not understand how Britain, after giving an undertaking in so formal a manner, could thus repudiate the duties that it entailed.[19] The Berlin press was eloquent in its wrath. 'Bindet Euch Besen vom Ginsterbusch der Plantagenets und verkauft Euren Shakespeare an den cheesemonger', the *Neue preussische*

Zeitung, popularly known as the *Kreuzzeitung*, advised the people of Britain.[20] The semi-official *Norddeutsche allgemeine Zeitung* was severely critical of Stanley's explanation of the guarantee. It found that given by Derby 'noch exorbitanter'.[21]

On 25 June Bernstorff called on Stanley. According to the latter's official report, conveyed to Loftus in the form of a dispatch, Bernstorff complained of the explanation given by Derby in the House of Lords, quoting a newspaper, which represented the prime minister as having said, in substance, that, if Luxemburg were to be attacked by France, Britain 'would not be bound to defend it'. Stanley related that in reply he had commented on the poor acoustics of the Lords' chamber and the consequent unreliability of the reports of debates held in it. He could not undertake to defend words attributed to the prime minister, without knowing whether he had really used them. However, he offered to explain his own idea of the obligations involved in a 'collective' guarantee, pointing out the absurdity of supposing that each of the powers that had given such a pledge could be held 'singly and separately responsible for its being enforced'.[22]

In a private letter to Loftus, written the same day, Stanley expressed himself more frankly:

Lord Derby's language about the guarantee was, I suspect, not quite accurately reported: but I have admitted to Bernstorff that if he said what appears in the newspapers, he went rather further than I should have done in denying the existence of any obligation. I think I satisfied him.[23]

Stanley's explanation of the 'collective' guarantee in his dispatch of 25 June 1867 was a good deal less latitudinarian than those that he had previously given in the House of Commons. His letter of the same day was a guarded repudiation of the more extreme argument employed in the House of Lords by his father. A few days later Stanley informed Loftus that Bernstorff had once again called at the Foreign Office to discuss the guarantee, but had 'seemed easier in his mind'; he would not 'press the subject'.[24]

Hammond, for his part, fully endorsed the doctrine enunciated by Derby. In his memorandum of 21 June he compared the Luxemburg guarantee with those embodied in the two treaties concluded in Paris after the Crimean War. 'Reading the Treaty of 1867 by the light of those of 1856', he wrote, 'it is clear that the construction put by Lord Derby on the Treaty of 1867 is correct.'[25] In his letter to Cowley of the following day he argued that Stanley's reluctance to agree to the Prussian demand was in no way inconsistent with Derby's statement that the obligation entailed by the guarantee was 'infinitely small'.[26] In another letter to Cowley, written on 25 June, he made light of the complaint lodged that day by Bernstorff:

Bismarck as you will see professes to be shocked at the small account we take of collective guarantee . . .

The truth is, as Latour [sic] d'Auvergne told me, that Bernstorff and Bismarck were fully aware that the collective guarantee was moonshine if it was supposed to mean more than the previous words as to respect of neutrality; but they held that the term 'guarantee' must appear to satisfy the susceptibilities of the Fatherland.[27]

Derby, at all events, held to his doctrine. On 4 July, after the Opposition peer, Houghton, had raised the matter of the Luxemburg treaty in the House of Lords,[28] he asked:

Suppose that Prussia with a view of making war on France, or France with a view of making war upon Prussia, were to enter the territory of Luxemburg . . . does the noble Lord [Houghton] mean to say that all the guaranteeing Powers in this Treaty of 1867, or each singly, would be bound by the obligations thrown on them by this treaty to go to war against the Power—whichever it might be— which entered Luxemburg with an army? Would Prussia desire this interpretation of the treaty?[29]

A few days later Bernstorff, after further complaints from Berlin,[30] paid another fruitless call on Stanley, and there the matter rested.[31]

The fact was that the Luxemburg treaty represented a substantial concession by Prussia to France. All that Bismarck had obtained, in exchange for the surrender of Prussia's right to garrison a strategically vital fortress, was the 'collective' guarantee, the significance of which was then explained away, first by Stanley and then by Derby. However, if we may believe Loftus, Bismarck had already at an early stage in the crisis placed himself in a weak position by some remarks that showed scant respect for any guarantee whatever.[32] Loftus's report of the Chancellor's observations on this delicate subject had not escaped the notice of either the foreign secretary[33] or the permanent under-secretary.[34] Moreover, Derby's letter of 5 May to his son leaves the impression that Bernstorff had, in the intimacy of a private conversation, minimized the onerousness of the pledge exacted by Bismarck.[35]

Whether Bismarck and Bernstorff really went as far in discounting the onerousness of the 'collective' guarantee as Hammond claimed is, of course, another matter. On the other hand, if they believed that the British government would regard an undertaking extracted from it by forcing its hand—'en lui forçant la main'—as entailing a stringent obligation, they showed remarkably little discernment.

At all events, Bismarck made the best of a bad bargain. In the autumn of 1867 he defended the treaty in the North German Reichstag. The neutralization of the Grand Duchy under a European guarantee, in the reliability of which, despite all strained interpretations—'trotz aller Deuteleien'—he expressed his confidence, was, he declared, a complete substitute, from the military point of view, for Prussia's right to garrison the fortress.[36] Nevertheless, the behaviour of Derby and Stanley remained a grievance. Bismarck was still nursing it eighteen years later.[37]

Long after the settlement of the Luxemburg question the views expressed in Parliament by Derby and Stanley continued to be belaboured by international jurists, especially in Germany.[38] On the other hand, it was reasonable to hold that the fact that a guarantee was specifically 'collective' did make the responsibility of each individual guarantor dependent on the willingness of at least some of the others to act. In a letter written by her secretary to the Queen of Prussia in July 1867 Queen Victoria placed her own gloss on the explanations given by her ministers. 'With regard to the guarantee', wrote Grey, 'the Queen does not imagine that either Lord Derby or Lord Stanley meant to say more . . . than that if the other Powers, Parties with England to the Luxemburg arrangement—and more especially, if France and Prussia were to decline to be bound by it, and England should thus be left alone, she would be free to consider what course it would be proper for her to adopt.'[39]

(iii)

The controversy over the Luxemburg treaty also served to illustrate the multiplicity of interpretations that could be placed, not only upon a 'collective', but upon any multipartite guarantee that was not explicitly 'several'. The guarantee of the integrity and inviolability of the territory of Switzerland, contained in the act of 20 November 1815, for example, was not qualified by any of the epithets that were so much bandied about in 1867. Did it then bind the five guarantors individually or only collectively? Stanley spoke of it as though it amounted to no more than the pledge given to Luxemburg. On 14 June 1867 he told the House of Commons:

Take an instance from what we have done already. We have guaranteed Switzerland; but if all Europe combined against Switzerland, although we might regret it, we should hardly feel bound to go to war with all the world for the protection of Switzerland.[40]

What then of Belgium? The guarantee given in 1839 was not explicitly qualified in any way. On 20 June 1867 Derby told the House of Lords that it was 'binding individually and separately upon each of the Powers'.[41] Clarendon agreed, at least in the House of Lords. 'I look upon our guarantee in the case of Belgium as an individual guarantee', he declared in the same debate, 'and have always so regarded it.'[42] However, in a letter to Hammond, written three days previously, Clarendon had expressed a different opinion. He agreed that 'the so called guarantee given in the Luxemburg Treaty is . . . no guarantee at all because it is collective and no Power engages to enforce it individually'. As for the guarantee given to Belgium; he wrote:

I cannot say that the guarantee of 39 has much more validity or binding force. The words 'se trouvent ainsi placés sous la garantie de leurs dites Majestés' would not make it obligatory upon any single Power to interfere, and the same obstacles to collective action would probably arise as those which are now thought to render the Luxemburg guarantee a nullity.[43]

(iv)

From the point of view of what Stanley called 'theories of foreign policy',[44] the Luxemburg crisis was significant in a number of ways. It is probably best remembered for the controversial doctrine, propounded by Derby in the House of Lords. It deserves to be remembered also for the uncertainty that it revealed as to the obligations entailed, not only by a 'collective', but by almost any other type of guarantee. It elicited numerous expressions of opposition to guarantees in general and claims that they were unpopular with the public at large. It probably had the effect of increasing the suspicion with which pledges of this kind were already regarded.[45] On the other hand, it served to demonstrate that highly placed persons were still willing to involve the country in the responsibilities of yet another guarantee, even, as far as one can judge, one that was not specifically 'collective'.

(v)

Nearly four decades later the man who at the time of the Luxemburg crisis had served as Stanley's private secretary gave his explanation of a 'collective' guarantee. In August 1905 Sanderson, now the experienced permanent under-secretary at the Foreign Office, to whom Sir George Clarke, the secretary of the Committee of Imperial Defence, had sent a memorandum on 'Treaty Guarantees and the Obligations of Guaranteeing Powers',[46] replied at some length from Scotland, where he was on holiday, 'far away from all documents':

I take it that a collective guarantee of the integrity or neutrality of a State by the Great Powers of Europe is a declaration that they hold the principle so guaranteed to be one of general interest which they desire to maintain, that if it be threatened they will give their support towards maintaining it, and that they will not allow it to be abandoned or modified without general agreement. To construe it as a positive policy on the part of each of them to use material force for the maintenance of the guarantee, in any circumstances, and at whatever risk or inconvenience would be to read into it what no Government can reasonably be expected to promise.[47]

Sanderson's considered verdict on the 'collective' guarantee, incorporated in the Luxemburg treaty, is also of interest:

The collective guarantee of Luxemburg was made a *sine qua non* condition for the acceptance by France and Prussia of an arrangement to avert a great war. The British Government entered into the guarantee with much reluctance rather than wreck the settlement, and Lord Derby's speech in the House of Lords was intended to defend them from the charge of having placed the Country under an obligation to go to war for a matter which did not directly concern it. But it was generally agreed that he had gone too far in his disclaimer, and I think that if within a short period either France or Prussia had violated the agreement all the other co-signatories would have felt themselves bound to give something more than mere moral support to the other Party, supposing that a conflict had ensued. They could scarcely have formally declared themselves neutral.[48]

(vi)

Quite apart from the collectivity of the guarantee, the obligation incurred by Britain under the treaty of 11 May 1867 was less onerous than it at first sight appeared. Luxemburg was a member of the Zollverein. Its inhabitants had much in common with their eastern neighbours. Was it certain that, in the event of a violation of Luxemburg's neutrality by Prussia, now at the head of the North German Confederation, its Grand Duke would order his minuscule forces to resist the invader? Would he invoke the treaty of 11 May 1867, thereby inviting France to send an army into his Grand Duchy? Or would he adopt a passive attitude, justifying it on the ground that, under the terms of the treaty, his capital had been converted into an open city? In the light of subsequent events it is easy to see that this might well be the reaction of the Grand Duke to a violation by Prussia—or Germany—of the Grand Duchy's neutrality.

CHAPTER XI

'Engagements to go to war'

(i)

Unlike many of his contemporaries, Gladstone did not uphold the principle of 'non-intervention' in disputes between continental powers. On the contrary, he went out of his way more than once to dissociate himself from the doctrine that the Manchester School had made fashionable. Thus, in the autumn of 1864, little more than three months after Cobden had asked the House of Commons why Britain interfered 'in these affairs abroad',[1] and the *Times* had declared that the wish of the country was not to be involved in war 'in order to adjust to our satisfaction the relations of foreign States',[2] he told an audience at Liverpool:

It is impossible that to a country like England the affairs of foreign nations can ever be indifferent. It is impossible that England, in my opinion at least, ever should forswear the interest she must naturally feel in the cause of truth, of justice, of order and of good government.[3]

Nearly five years later Gladstone expressed himself to General Grey, that is, in effect, to Queen Victoria herself, in strikingly similar terms. 'I do not believe that England ever will or can be unfaithful to her great traditions', he wrote on 17 April 1869, 'or can forswear her interest in the common transactions and the general interests of Europe.'[4] He was certainly prepared, should the situation, in his opinion, so require, to commit the country to what he called 'engagements to go to war', the obvious examples of which were the treaties concluded in August 1870 with Prussia and France.[6]

These treaties invite a question. Why, in view of the fact that in 1839 the great powers had guaranteed the independence and neutrality of Belgium, did Gladstone and Granville consider in 1870 that new treaties were necessary?

The answer to this question is to be found, in part at least, in the dispatch written by Loftus on 13 April 1867, at the time of the dispute over Luxemburg, reporting a conversation that he had had that day with Bismarck. According to the ambassador, Bismarck had hinted that Prussia might 'come to an under-standing with France and enter into an alliance with her'; the French Emperor 'would require no more than Belgium'. On being reminded of the guarantee given to Belgium by the powers, he had replied that 'a guarantee was in these days of little value'. Later in the conversation Bismarck had, according to Loftus, 'in referring again to a war with France observed that the Emperor after a battle or two might propose to Prussia an alliance at the cost of Belgium'.[7]

Bismarck's observations clearly left a deep impression on Loftus, who during the next three years sent repeated warnings to London of the danger of a Franco-Prussian deal at Belgium's expense.[8] In 1869 he advised Clarendon, in the event of a war between France and Prussia, to make Britain's neutrality conditional on a formal pledge by each belligerent to respect the independence and neutrality of Belgium both during the war and after it.[9] On 16 July 1870, that is, three days before France's declaration of war on Prussia, he urged the same suggestion on Granville. Britain's neutrality should be 'condi-tional on the Belligerents giving an assurance that they will respect the neutrality of Belgium during the War, in accordance with their Treaty Engagement, and the Independence of Belgium *after* the War, or they might shake hands at the end of the Campaign at the expense of Belgium'.[10]

Loftus's warning gained added force, when, on the day of the outbreak of war, Bernstorff saw Gladstone and Granville and read to them the so-called Benedetti draft treaty.[11] On 25 July, a Prussian embassy official having supplied Delane with a copy,[12] the *Times* published the draft treaty in full.[13]

Gladstone and Granville could hardly ignore this well publicized evidence that at some time not precisely specified, but presumably in the summer of 1866, Napoleon III had been plotting the annexation of Belgium in the expectation of Prussia's connivance and promise of assistance against a third power. On 26 July Edward Hertslet, the Foreign Office

librarian, drew up a memorandum on the 'supposed Negotiations' between France and Prussia, in which he quoted
Loftus's dispatch of 13 April 1867 at length.[14] The government
had accordingly to decide whether it could regard the existing guarantee and the promises to respect the neutrality of
Belgium, already given by both belligerents, as sufficient safe-
guards.

Some rough jottings, evidently made by Gladstone at the
time, serve to illuminate the considerations that lay behind his
course of action. 'We cannot', he noted, 'pass by the publication
of the Treaty in silence.' A 'new act', entered into with both
belligerents or with one only, would be an impediment to a
'dangerous combination'. It would also tend to increase
Britain's 'liberty on the question of defending her [Belgium]
single-handed'.[15]

On 30 July the cabinet met and decided, as Gladstone
reported to Queen Victoria, that the best course would be 'to
find a new point of departure, from which new securities if
possible may be taken for the safety of Belgium, and against the
possibility of any combination of the two belligerents for the
purpose of its destruction as a neutral and independent State'.
It therefore authorized Granville to ask each belligerent
separately whether it was willing, not only to respect the
neutrality of Belgium, but also to join in upholding it, if
Belgium should be invaded by another power. He was to invite
Russia and Austria to adhere to each of the two arrangements,
if completed. In addition Parliament was to be asked for a vote
of credit of two million pounds and for authority to increase the
size of the army by twenty thousand men.[16]

Not everyone agreed that to negotiate new pacts with
France and Prussia was the wisest course in the circumstances.
Hammond warned Granville of the imprudence of raising a
question that might cast doubt on the sincerity of the pledges
to respect Belgium's neutrality, which both belligerents had
already given. These pledges, he added, although satisfactory,
had not been needed 'to impose upon them the obligations long
since contracted towards us and other Powers to respect it'.[17]
Lyons, the ambassador in Paris, feared that the proposed pacts
might involve the country in war, without leaving the govern-

ment any choice, either as to the right moment to intervene, or even as to which side to support.[18]

John Bright, on the other hand, differed from Gladstone and Granville on grounds of fundamental principle. He had not, owing to poor health, been attending meetings of the cabinet in recent months.[19] On learning from Gladstone of the decisions taken on 30 July,[20] he replied, explaining his inability to 'sanction our entering into any new engagement for the military defence of Belgium' or to 'consent to ask Parliament to raise men and money for supporting the independence of any foreign state'. 'To adopt the policy of the Cabinet', he added, 'would be for me to abandon principles which I have held and advocated during all my public life.' With this affirmation of Manchester School principle Bright tendered his resignation.[21]

Gladstone replied to Bright at some length in a letter, which, likewise, is of interest as a statement of principle. For Britain to undertake single-handed the defence of Belgium against a combination of France and Prussia would, he pointed out, be 'Quixotic'. But it was precisely that combination that constituted the 'only serious danger'. He hoped that the proposed engagements would render it 'improbable to the very last degree'. To this defence of his policy Gladstone added a 'Confession of Faith':

If the Belgian people desire, on their own account, to join France or any other country, I for one will be no party to taking up arms to prevent it. But that the Belgians whether they would or not, should go plump down the maw of another country to satisfy dynastic greed, is another matter. The accomplishment of such a crime as this implies would come near to an extinction of Public Right in Europe. And I do not think we could contentedly look on while the sacrifice of freedom and independence was in course of consummation.[22]

On the day after the signature of the treaty with Prussia Gladstone defended the government's course of action in the House of Commons, explaining that 'it was the combination, and not the opposition, of the two Powers which we had to fear'.[23] There was some criticism of the treaties, notably by John Bright's brother, Jacob, who declared that 'there was no wise policy for this House and for the Government of this country to pursue but that of keeping entirely free from

Continental entanglements'.[24] Nevertheless, there was no nation-wide outcry. Parliament was about to rise for the summer recess. Indeed, the treaty with France was not signed until after Parliament had risen.

Although the plan to include Austria and Russia in the transaction came to nothing, Granville was able to claim on 20 August, in a letter to Buchanan, that the government had attained its object.[25] By the time that Parliament had re-assembled in February 1871 the international situation had been transformed. There was no longer any danger that France and the new German Empire would combine to settle their differences at the expense of Belgium.

(ii)

Nearly a decade later Gladstone again had occasion to differentiate his own principles from those of Cobden and his followers.

At the outset of the general election campaign of 1880 Beaconsfield's open letter to the Duke of Marlborough contained a disparaging reference to 'the passive principle of non-interference'.[26] To this Gladstone replied in a speech at Edinburgh, dissociating himself from that principle, and declaring that the 'Manchester School' had 'never ruled the foreign policy of this country—never during a Conservative Government, and never especially during a Liberal Government'.[27] The disproof of the implication that he and those who thought like him belonged to the 'Manchester School' or to a 'Peace Party' lay, he declared, in 'the engagements to go to war . . . if necessary, for the sake of the independence of Belgium', which his own government had concluded in the summer of 1870.[28]

CHAPTER XII

'Diplomatic liabilities'

(i)

In the years when there was so much talk of a policy of 'non-intervention' it was, nevertheless, recognized that Britain did not actually possess complete freedom of action in any possible eventuality. Stanley himself, for example, acknowledged the existence of what he called 'diplomatic liabilities',[1] although he minimized both their number and the likelihood of their having to be acted upon. 'I do not deny that there are within the range of possibility exceptional cases where the solemn faith of the country has been pledged to a particular course of action', he told his constituents in 1866, explaining, however, that these cases were 'few' and that 'the improbability of their arising' was 'extreme'.[2]

(ii)

On several occasions it became necessary to consider the implications of one or another of these 'diplomatic liabilities'.

Early in 1860 Palmerston and Russell became aware that the ministers of Napoleon III and Victor Emmanuel II were preparing a deal, under which France would obtain, in compensation for Sardinia's—or, if one prefers, Piedmont's—acquisitions in central Italy, the whole of Nice and Savoy, including the neutralized zone of the latter (Chablais, Faucigny and the Genevese).[3] France and Sardinia were, in fact, planning to violate both the Treaty of Paris of 20 November 1815 and the act of the same day, which contained the arrangement for the neutralization of northern Savoy, under the guarantee of all five great powers.

This prospect did not worry Palmerston. 'I should think a large addition of Territory to Piémont well purchased by the

Sacrifice of Savoy', he wrote to Russell on 5 February 1860, 'if that was an inevitable Condition for the Italian arrangement.'[4]

On 2 March 1860 the House of Commons debated the situation. 'I say, perish Savoy', declared John Bright, ' . . . rather than we, the representatives of the people of England, should involve the Government of this country with the people and the Government of France on a matter in which we have really no interest whatever.'[5] A few days later Russell reported to Palmerston that, in reply to an enquiry by the Prussian minister as to whether Britain intended 'to make *serious* remonstrances on the subject of Savoy—meaning such remonstrances as might lead to war', he had stated that he could not answer such a question without consulting the Cabinet, but that he 'did not think this country was prepared for a war for Savoy'.[6] Nor were the other great powers eager to take action. 'With Russia bribed or cajoled', Russell warned Palmerston, 'and Austria silent and sulking the annexation of Savoy will be effected, very probably, by a coup de main.'[7]

The Swiss Federal Council having made representations to the King of Sardinia, on 15 March 1860 Kern, the Swiss minister in Paris, pointed out to Cowley, the British ambassador, that any annexation of the neutralized area of Savoy by another power would be contrary to the arrangement made and guaranteed in 1815, protesting formally against any measure aimed at the annexation of the territory to France before the other great powers had given their opinion.[8]

Russell was pessimistic. On 17 March he admitted to Cowley that what he called 'the Savoy business' would 'look very ugly for the present and the future'. The Cabinet, he explained, wished him to protest strongly against it, but he himself looked on the matter as a *'fait accompli'*.[9] Nevertheless, it was undeniable that Britain was under some sort of obligation, arising out of the act of 20 November 1815. Russell acknowledged to Cowley the fact of 'the neutral territory being guaranteed by Europe, in the same way as Switzerland herself'. He thought that Britain could not 'refrain from consulting with the other powers about it'.[10]

On 24 March 1860 France and Sardinia concluded the Treaty of Turin, providing for the transfer to the former of Nice and Savoy.[11] On the following day Queen Victoria wrote to Russell, reminding him of the British obligation. 'We are parties to a Treaty of Guarantee, together with other Powers', she pointed out, 'and have as such a clear and solemn *duty* to perform.' She thought that the proper course would be to summon the representatives of the contracting powers, including the French ambassador, to the Foreign Office and 'to go with them into the matter'.[12]

Russell saw no practical advantage in this proposal. His own view was that the neutralized part of Savoy ought to be given to Switzerland. However, he questioned whether any power was willing to enforce such an arrangement. Not one of them, he noted, had said that it was. Without some previous agreement he saw 'no use, and much danger of discredit in a meeting of the nature proposed'.[13] In fact, no meeting of the representatives of the contracting powers took place. The 'Savoy business' remained a *'fait accompli'*.

In October 1862 the deposition of King Otho presented the 'three protecting Powers', as Palmerston called them,[14] with the problem of what action they should take in the light both of the arrangements that they had made for Greece at the time of her liberation and of the events of the intervening years. Palmerston took the line that it was 'not good that we should volunteer to start Doubts as to the Validity of subsisting diplomatic Engagements, the Maintenance of which is for our Advantage'. He also considered that 'the Greeks having been declared and guaranteed to be an independent Nation have a right to exercise that Privilege of Independence which consists in changing the reigning Dynasty upon good and sufficient Cause'.[15] Russell reported to the prime minister that Brunnow wished to 'renew the guarantee'. He himself opposed this course. Greece, he reminded Palmerston, was 'thirty years old'. His advice was: 'Let her defend herself and take care of her own concerns.'[16]

Eventually, after agreement had been reached on the choice of a Danish prince to occupy the vacant Greek throne, Russell, on 13 July 1863, signed a new treaty between Britain, France and Russia, on the one hand, and Denmark, on the other. Article iii declared Greece, under the sovereignty of Prince

William of Denmark and the guarantee of the three courts, to
be a monarchical, independent and constitutional state. Article
v stipulated that the Ionian Islands, when their union with the
kingdom of Greece should have been effected, should be comprised in the guarantee.[17] Greece was not a signatory to this
treaty, but she was to that of the following year, under which
Britain ceded to her the Ionian Islands, and, together with
France and Russia, reiterated the guarantee.[18]

In the following year there occurred an incident that served
to illustrate the dialectical refinements to which the existence
of pledges of this kind could give rise.

By an act, signed by a plenipotentiary at Frederiksborg on
23 July 1720 and countersigned by himself at Herrnhausen
three days later, King George I had promised the King of
Denmark 'de lui garantir et conserver dans une possession
continuelle et paisible la partie du Duché de Sleswick, laquelle
Sa Majesté Danoise a entre les mains, et de la défendre le
mieux possible contre tous et chacun qui tâcheroit de la
troubler, soit directement ou indirectement, le tout en vertu du
Traité conclu en 1715 avec Sa Majesté Britannique, comme
Electeur de Brunswick et Lunebourg'.[19] Could it possibly be
maintained in the seventh decade of the nineteenth century
that this act was still in force? Britain had, after all, been at
war with Denmark from 1807 to 1814. The act had not been
included in the Foreign Office's return of 1859.

On 11 February 1864 Hammond wrote to ask the law
officers of the crown whether, in their opinion, the act of 1720
was still in force. Had it been abrogated by the state of war that
had prevailed between Britain and Denmark in the years
1807–14? If so, had it been revived by the Treaty of Kiel,
which had brought that war to an end?[20] Three days later he
wrote again to report that the Danish minister in London had
invoked the act of 1720.[21] On the same day Russell informed
Queen Victoria of the Danish minister's *démarche*, adding that
many members of the cabinet were of the opinion that Britain
was bound by the act, and also by the earlier treaty, 'to oppose
the separation from Denmark of the Duchy of Sleswig'.[22]

On 17 February Phillimore, the queen's advocate, gave his
opinion that the guarantee of 1720 was still in force, since the

Treaty of Kiel had revived all previous 'Treaties of Peace' between Britain and Denmark.[23] However, Roundell Palmer, the attorney-general, and Collier, the solicitor-general, did not share this opinion. The act of guarantee, they considered, having been abrogated by the subsequent state of war, the obligation entailed by it had not been revived by the Treaty of Kiel.[24]

A more significant commitment was that embodied in the treaty of 19 April 1839 between the five great powers and Belgium.

In April 1867, at the time of the Luxemburg crisis, Loftus's report of Bismarck's hint at a possible Franco-Prussian deal at the expense of Belgium raised the difficult question of what Britain's attitude should be, if the country whose independence and neutrality she had guaranteed were to fall victim to the designs, not merely of one, but of both its powerful neighbours.[25] On 23 April Stanley wrote to Disraeli, expressing his readiness to go as far as might be necessary in support of Belgium—'short of giving an absolute pledge to fight for its independence'. 'Suppose we gave such a pledge', he asked, 'that France and Prussia came to an understanding, Russia and Austria standing aloof, where should we be?'[26]

A few weeks later the official explanations of the Luxemburg guarantee had the effect of casting doubt on the stringency of that given twenty-eight years previously to Belgium. Could the guarantee of 1839 also be explained away? Clarendon thought, although he did not say publicly, that it probably could.[27]

In 1869 the dispute over the Belgian railways raised once again the question of Britain's obligation.[28] On 6 March 1869 Clarendon, whose correspondence at this period reveals his sensitiveness to the opinions on Britain's role in Europe that were then fashionable, wrote privately to Lumley, in Brussels:

England is no doubt a guarantor of Belgian independence and neutrality, but it is only in conjunction with other Powers—and in the present state of public opinion here I apprehend that the Government would not be allowed to go singlehanded into a defence of Treaty obligations while other Guarantors stood aloof. Nor have we the means even if we had the will to go to war with France and as that must be as well known to the Belgian Government as to ourselves it should make them chary of relying upon our aid.[29]

A few weeks later he wrote to Gladstone, insisting on his intention of 'maintaining perfect freedom of action for the Government upon a question that might be of such vital importance to England as taking part with Belgium against France'.[30]

On 13 April 1869, while the Belgian question was still in the air, Clarendon had a conversation with the veteran Portuguese politician, Saldanha, who, he reported to Gladstone, had come 'to enquire whether Portugal might depend on the assistance of England, in the event of her being attacked by Spain'—a revolution having occurred in the latter country a few months previously. 'I said', Clarendon related, 'I couldn't entertain the question as to how England would fulfil any obligation imposed on her by Treaties and that sufficient to the day was the evil thereof.'[31] To Queen Victoria he sent an account of the interview,[32] which, the Queen thought, gave the impression that his reply to Saldanha had been 'peremptory'. She would, she wrote, deeply regret either Portugal or Belgium being led to imagine that they must not look to Britain for support in case of need.[33]

This episode served Clarendon as the occasion for a disquisition on the motives of the Belgian and Portuguese governments and on Britain's treaty obligations in general. He assured the Queen that the Belgian and Portuguese governments' real object was to hold out to their enemies, real or supposed, that Britain's whole material force was at their disposal. His object, he explained, was to preserve complete freedom of action, to be used as circumstances might arise and as treaty obligations might impose duties. The British government's duty, he added, was to consider Britain's own interests and 'not to disguise from themselves the many difficulties of our position and the exceeding delicacy of calling upon Parliament to give effect to Treaties which, if public opinion years ago had been what it now is, would not have been sanctioned'.[34]

In the following year, after the outbreak of war between France and Prussia and the publication by the *Times* of the Benedetti draft treaty had raised once again the question of Britain's obligation under the treaty of 1839, Gladstone, in correspondence with Bright, adopted the common-sense attitude that to undertake single-handed the defence of Belgium against both its great power neighbours, acting in combination, would be foolhardy.[35] In the House of Commons he dissociated himself from the doctrine that the mere fact of the existence of a guarantee was binding on every party to it, irrespectively altogether of the particular position in whch it might happen to find itself at the time when the occasion for acting on the guarantee arose.[36]

There was the further and by no means simple question of the nature of the Belgian guarantee. Was it 'collective', 'common', 'joint', 'separate' or 'several'? The text of Palmerston's treaty provided no answer to this question.

In August 1870 the law officers of the crown, having been consulted by the Foreign Office, reported that, in their opinion, if the treaty were to be construed according to the contract law of this country, the guarantee was a 'joint' one. Nevertheless, they considered that the refusal or inability of one or more of the guarantors to act would not liberate the others from their obligation to do so. Whether, in the event of none of the other guarantors being willing to co-operate, Belgium could reasonably expect Britain to undertake single-handed a war against great continental powers was a question to which the law officers prudently refrained from offering an answer.[37] A few days later Sir Wilfrid Lawson told the House of Commons that there was a variety of opinions as to the extent to which Britain was bound by the Belgian treaty, and that 'many good authorities held that we were only bound collectively, and not separately'.[38]

The question of Britain's treaty obligations was, of course, inextricably bound up with that of her own vital interests. For a period, the length of which it would be rash to specify, successive British governments had taken the view that it was essential to this country's security to ensure that no potentially hostile great power—which for many years meant, in practice, France —should acquire dominion, not merely over Belgium, but over the entire region known as the 'Low Countries'. The 'antient and hereditary policy of England', to which Palmerston had appealed in 1838,[39] applied to the Low Countries as a whole, even though Britain was not pledged by the letter of any actual treaty to defend the more northerly of the two kingdoms comprised in that area. Indeed, it could be argued that, from the strategic point of view, this policy applied even more to the kingdom of the Netherlands than to Belgium, since the former controlled the estuaries of the various rivers, into which the Rhine divided, and of the Scheldt.

When, on 1 August 1870, the House of Commons debated the issues raised by the threat to Belgium's independence, revealed by the *Times*, Disraeli enunciated this policy at some length. He had no doubt, he declared, that the 'representatives of the great Liberal party', who had negotiated the Belgian treaty, had been influenced in the course that they had taken by what he called 'the traditions of English policy'. Those traditions he proceeded to expound:

It had always been held by the Government of this country that it was for the interest of England that the countries on the European Coast extending from Dunkirk and Ostend to the islands of the North Sea should be possessed by free and flourishing communities, practising the arts of peace . . . and should not be in the possession of a great military Power. [40]

Gathorne Hardy noted in his diary that the debate 'certainly showed a strong feeling of our obligations to Belgium and the duty of fulfilling them for our own sakes'. [41]

There was also the guarantee given to Prussia in respect of her Saxon territories, under article xvii of the Treaty of Vienna, which the Foreign Office had acknowledged in 1859 to be 'still obligatory'.

In the debate of 1 August 1870 Disraeli reminded the House of Commons of this pledge, declaring that it was 'probably the most solemn guarantee which England ever made in modern times'. [42] However, this claim did not command universal support, even in Disraeli's own party. Gathorne Hardy recorded his complete disagreement with his leader concerning what he called 'the guarantee of the Treaty of Vienna'. 'Surely Prussia herself has abrogated that', he noted. [43] In the following year Gladstone assured the House of Commons that the undertaking, of which the leader of the Opposition had made so much, was, after all, only a 'joint guarantee'. [44]

In the autumn of 1870 Russia's unilateral abrogation of the

Black Sea articles of the Treaty of Paris raised the question whether another of Britain's 'diplomatic liabilities' should still be regarded as being in force. Russia's action was not only a repudiation of provisions contained in a peace-treaty to which she herself was a party. It was also a challenge to the Tripartite Treaty of 15 April 1856, which had been framed for the express purpose of ensuring her observance of the terms of the Treaty of Paris, and the obligations entailed by which were, Granville acknowledged, 'as binding as were ever contracted'.[45] Gladstone observed that the treaty did not appear 'to have much force as a covenant at present'.[46] At all events, as was only to be expected in the circumstances prevailing in the closing months of 1870, not one of the three signatories invoked it.

The following year saw an interesting reappraisal of Britain's treaty obligations.

In March 1871 Salisbury gave notice in the House of Lords of a motion on the subject, thereby occasioning Granville some concern.[47] On 6 March Salisbury introduced his motion, calling attention to the numerous 'guarantees'—a term that he, like many of his contemporaries, employed to include pledges that were not strictly 'guarantees' in the literal sense of that term— which Britain had at various times given, and also to the inadequacy of the military resources available to her for honouring them, should the need arise. He stressed the solemnity of these pledges, advising the government to 'adapt their promises to their powers, or their powers to their promises'. He also asked for a new edition of the return of 1859, with such additions as the passage of time had rendered necessary.[48] Granville's reply was guarded, but he complied with Salisbury's request.[49] On 7 June 1871 a new and enlarged edition of 'Treaties of Guarantee' was laid before Parliament.[50]

To Sir Wilfrid Lawson the lesson to be drawn from this publication was that the government should forthwith extricate the country from its commitments.[51] On 12 April 1872, in the House of Commons, he accordingly moved the presentation of a humble address, praying the Queen to take the necessary steps for this purpose.[52] Another Radical, Peter Rylands, spoke in his support. 'We must free ourselves from entangling alliances', he declared.[53]

Gladstone opposed the motion. He was not in favour of abrogation, but he systematically minimized the significance of most of the contents of the new return. There was, he pointed out, a 'stringent guarantee' in the Tripartite Treaty, which contained 'a distinct reference to the obligation to take arms'. This, he explained, however, was an exception. The other treaties included by the Foreign Office were 'rather in the nature of . . . strong declarations of policy and of general intention'. The truth was, he added, that guarantees depended for fulfilment 'very much on the national opinion of the time'.[54]

Lawson's motion was easily defeated.[55] It had, however, served to air an important subject. 'The Premier softened down the obligation of a guarantee until he must have persuaded his hearers that it was altogether the most harmless thing in the world', observed the *Times*, 'pledging the country which gives it neither legally nor morally to anything at all which it may find inconvenient.'[56] 'In other words', commented the *Spectator*, 'if we want to defend Belgium when attacked, we shall defend her, and if not, not.'[57]

CHAPTER XIII

'The national honour'

(i)

he outlook on foreign affairs of the fifteenth Earl of Derby, as
:anley had become in 1869 on the death of his father, during
s second tenure of the Foreign Office, did not greatly differ
om that which he had adopted in the 1860s. Thus, in March
374, soon after returning to office, he wrote to Buchanan:

ur national position seems to me stronger than ever it was, if we
oose to make it so, for in the existing uncertainty as to peace and
ar, and the mutual dislike of France and Germany, we can hold
e balance as we never held it before. But to keep this position we
ust be friendly with all, exclusively allied with none, and show
rselves simply bent on the maintenance of treaties, and the
eservation of peace.[1]

In the following year, after the 'war in sight' crisis, he im-
essed on the House of Lords the fact that his actions had
volved no sacrifice of the country's 'freedom of action', and
pealed, as he had so often done before, to what he claimed
be the opinion of the nation at large:

elieve that the policy of non-intervention in general in Continen-
l disputes is the one which finds most favour with the people of this
untry.[2]

ain, in February 1876, after Odo Russell had reported from
rlin a friendly suggestion by Bismarck for 'a timely under-
nding between our two governments' on the Eastern
uestion,[3] Derby sent a frigid reply:

is unnecessary to point out to Your Excellency that England
sires no exclusive alliances, nor do the principles of English policy
mit of such being contracted.[4]

To the question how far Derby's practice as foreign secretary
the second Disraeli administration conformed with his

precept the simple answer would be that during the four yea
from 1874 to 1878 he involved the country in no 'exclusiv
alliance' with any power. Nevertheless, mention should I
made in this connexion of the approaches made to Austri
Hungary in the early stages of the Russo-Turkish War of 187
On 10 June Beaconsfield reported to Queen Victoria that tl
cabinet had unanimously resolved 'to make a distinct offer of a
alliance' to Austria-Hungary, to the effect that, if and whe
Russian forces crossed the Danube, the two powers 'would l
prepared with their fleets and armies to assume positions, wit.
out declaring war against Russia, which would ensure h
withdrawal from the contest'. If Austria-Hungary, he explaine
were to occupy 'the Principalities' and Britain to 'send up h
fleet to Constantinople and occupy Gallipoli', there was r
doubt that 'the war might terminate'.[5] Four days later l
telegraphed the Queen that Derby had made the Austria
ambassador a 'distinct proposal for an alliance as sanctioned l
the last Cabinet'.[6] In the event Andrássy rejected the proposa
which, accordingly, came to nothing.[7] 'I cannot say', wro
Derby to Buchanan, 'that at present I should be inclined
build much on the hope of an Austrian alliance.' 'We shou.
hardly', he added, 'be prepared to move without an ally.'[8]

(ii)

Within a few days of taking Derby's place at the Foreig
Office in March 1878 Salisbury began to prepare the way f
the 'defensive alliance'[9] with the Ottoman Empire, under tl
terms of which Britain was to acquire the right to occupy ar
administer Cyprus and to undertake to assist the Sultan, und
certain conditions, in the defence of Turkey-in-Asia again
Russia.[10] The convention embodying this alliance was not,
course, a contract between co-equal powers, nor did Salisbu
intend it to be one, as his numerous letters to Layard ma)
clear. 'The Porte', he wrote, 'must recognize that it nee
protection.'[11] He insisted on the Porte giving 'specific assu
ances of good government to Asiatic Christians' and investir
Britain with a 'special privilege of advice and remonstrance i
case of any gross abuse'.[12] The language, in which he couche

the telegram to Layard, instructing him officially to offer the Sultan the 'defensive alliance to secure his territory for the future in Asia',[13] caused Cairns, the Lord Chancellor, to object, according to Sandon, to the 'peremptory tone' employed.[14] In fact, the arrangement provided for in the convention of 4 June 1878 was widely regarded as tantamount to a British protectorate over Turkey-in-Asia.[15]

Indian troops would be available to assist in honouring the obligation to the Porte, should the need arise. Indeed, the transaction had more than a little in common with the numerous 'treaties, engagements and sanads', under which the British government in India had for many years undertaken to give the rulers of neighbouring territories armed assistance in case of necessity, while at the same time acquiring a say in their affairs.[16] In fact, Salisbury's attitude to the problems of Turkey-in-Asia was clearly influenced by his years of experience as secretary for India. From Berlin he wrote to Cross, his *locum tenens*, impressing on him the desirability of placing Cyprus under the India Office.[17] In the cabinet, according to Sandon, he pressed the same point. He did not want the island to be assigned to the Colonial Office, which, he argued, 'would infallibly under the Liberals give it a Constitution, which would be fatal to the whole scheme', but to the India Office, which 'under every Government, hated Constitutions'. He also urged that the officials, whom he described as 'the class of men who would be required to act, in fact as "Residents" in Asiatic Turkey under our protection scheme', should be supplied by India. Britain, he reminded the cabinet, was 'a great Asiatic power'.[18]

At all events, the analogy between Britain's existing tutelary relationship with the princely states of India and the new one into which she had entered with the Ottoman Empire in respect of the latter's territory in Asia, did not escape the notice of the former ambassador in Constantinople, Sir Henry Elliot, now in Vienna. In July, after the announcement of the conclusion of the convention, he wrote to his successor in the Turkish capital, observing:

I think few people realize the enormous responsibility of the task we have undertaken. I only hope that there may not be at home a disposition to go too far in trying to treat the Sultan like one of the

Protected Princes in India, by which in a short time Russia would be able to come forward as the advocate of his independence.[19]

The undertaking given to the Sultan on 4 June 1878, even though it applied only to the Asian portion of his empire and was both conditional and, as far as the *casus belli* was concerned, unilateral, was undoubtedly a 'prospective engagement', at least of a kind. How then did Salisbury reconcile it with his view that no British government could enter into any engagement that entailed an obligation to go to war in a contingency that lay in the future? The most probable explanation of this apparent contradiction is that at the time of the conclusion of the Constantinople convention Salisbury did not subscribe to the theory of which he was later so indefatigable an exponent. No trace of it appears in the numerous and lengthy letters that he wrote to Layard in the spring of 1878. 'I think', he wrote on 2 May 1878, 'that we might very properly enter into a defensive alliance with the Porte, undertaking to join in defending her Asiatic Empire from any attacks of Russia.'[20] A week later he expressed his conviction that the Ottoman Empire's only chance of survival lay in obtaining the alliance of a great power. 'Is it possible for England to give that alliance?' he asked. 'I cannot speak yet with confidence': he answered, 'but I think so.'[21]

What Salisbury was attempting to do, in fact, was to bind the country by a pledge that he could be sure would be honoured, if the *casus foederis* ever arose, irrespective of the circumstances prevailing at the time. This he explained to Layard at some length:

For the purpose of acting as a support to the Turks in a period of crisis it [the proposed convention] will have the enormous advantage that it will pledge the national honour of England. A reliance upon the promptings of English interest, however obvious, will be insecure: for when the moment for decision comes, some other motive may intervene—or some party arrangement adverse to intervention may be in force—or the current of attention in England may be turned by other things: and it may always be possible for the partisans of peace *quand même*, to persuade the Government of the day that no urgent interest requires its intervention. But a direct national promise will be regarded by both Government and people, until we have sunk much lower, than we have done as yet.[22]

(iii)

Nor is it easy to see much inhibition, constitutional or otherwise, in the attitude of those responsible for the Treaty of
Gandamak. The treaty gave Britain, according to Lytton, 'that
permanent political position and influence in Afghanistan
which has, at all times, and under successive Administrations,
. . . been the avowed object of British Policy'. The 'Treaty engagement' to support the Amir, 'against foreign aggression with
arms, money, or troops', was the 'necessary consequence' of
Britain's 'demand to control the foreign relations of a neighbouring State'.[23] The treaty was, in fact, less stringent than at
first sight appeared, as the viceroy himself explained to Cranbrook.[24] What view the Beaconsfield administration would have
taken of the obligation that it entailed, had the Amir invoked
it, is a matter concerning which one can only speculate. Not
surprisingly, the Treaty of Gandamak became a dead letter
within a matter of months.

(iv)

As for Disraeli—or Beaconsfield—himself, although at the time
when intervention in the Russo-Turkish War appeared to be a
possibility, he insisted that Britain needed no ally, apart from
the Turks,[25] and in the period of crisis that followed the conclusion of the Treaty of San Stefano he anticipated the com-
placent view of the country's 'isolation' that was later to become
so fashionable,[26] his pronouncements on foreign affairs were
not characterized by any aversion from 'prospective engagements' in general. Indeed, in one of his most celebrated—or
notorious—orations, delivered at the Knightsbridge Riding
School in the summer of 1878, shortly after his return from the
Congress of Berlin, he expressly repudiated the doctrine that
Britain should never, in any circumstances, add to her foreign
commitments:

I, for one, would never shrink from increasing the responsibilities of
this country if they are responsibilities which ought to be undertaken.[27]

In this connexion, an incident, which occurred during th
last year of the Conservative administration, is revealing. O
26 September 1879 Münster, the German ambassador, paid
visit to Hughenden. According to Beaconsfield's account of h
conversation with the ambassador, written for the informatio
of Queen Victoria, Münster proposed the formation of a trip
alliance of Britain, Germany and Austria-Hungary. To this th
prime minister replied that he had himself regretted Derby
abrupt rejection of Bismarck's overture in connexion with th
Eastern Question three and a half years previously, and that h
had always favoured the principle of 'an alliance or goo
understanding with Germany'.[28] To Salisbury he expressed hi
conviction that an alliance with Germany and Austria
Hungary 'might probably be hailed with something lik
enthusiasm by the country'.[29]

Salisbury, after a conversation with Münster, came to th
conclusion that Bismarck perhaps needed Britain no longer. 'I
so', he wrote to Beaconsfield, 'we are well out of it.'[30] The Queer
for her part, strongly objected to any 'alliance' that might seer
to be directed against France.[31] At the end of October North
cote, who shared her views, wrote to Beaconsfield, both on he
own behalf and on his own. Anything that produced coldnes
and distrust between this country and France, he argued
would expose Britain to serious annoyances. 'France alone, an
still more France with Russia', he wrote, 'can do us a thousan
ill turns by intrigue, against which Germany and Austri
would be as powerless to protect us as a Policeman is against
flight of midges.'[32] In fact, whatever the real purpose of Münster'
visit to Hughenden in the autumn of 1879, nothing positiv
came of it. 'At present Your Majesty's is [sic] free as air', wrot
the prime minister to the Queen on 5 November 1879.[33]

(v)

In 1880 Gladstone accused the Conservative government c
having burdened the country with 'needless, mischievous
unauthorized and unprofitable engagements'.[34] It is easy t
guess what he had in mind. However, there was one charge tha
Gladstone could not bring against his opponents. Whateve

its other errors, the Beaconsfield government had not given a 'formal' guarantee, relating either to the territory or to the institutions of any foreign country. No mention of any such pledge by Britain is to be found in any article of the Constantinople convention, the Treaty of Berlin or the Treaty of Gandamak. Moreover, we know that in at least two of these cases the omission was deliberate. When, on 29 July 1878, the Constantinople convention was debated in the House of Lords, Salisbury contrasted the pledge that it contained with the ineffective guarantee embodied twenty-two years previously in the Tripartite Treaty.[35] In September of the same year he objected to what he took to be a proposal 'to offer a guarantee of Afghanistan against Russia', warning Cranbrook of the 'constant charges of bad faith' to which such a course would expose him.[36]

Salisbury's negative attitude on these two occasions in 1878 is certainly significant. Whether it should be regarded as an indication of a general unwillingness to commit the country to any new 'formal' guarantee is, of course, another matter.

CHAPTER XIV

'Misty and shadowy guarantees'

(i)

The record of the Conservative administration of 1874–80, so far as the giving of what the fifteenth Earl of Derby called 'dangerous instruments'[1] was concerned, was not unique. In fact, the London conference of May 1867 proved to be the last occasion in the nineteenth century on which a British government gave a new guarantee, explicitly stipulated in an article of a treaty, convention or act, in connexion with the territory of a foreign country.

The generation that followed the conference witnessed, admittedly, more than one transaction, with which this statement is not, at first sight, easy to reconcile.

The treaties of August 1870 with Prussia and France each acknowledged the validity of that of 1839 and each embodied a pledge that entailed the *casus belli* and was sometimes described by contemporaries as a 'guarantee'.[2] Nevertheless, neither of Granville's treaties contained any mention of any new guarantee.

The Constantinople convention, likewise, embodied a pledge that was sometimes described as a 'guarantee'.[3] Once again, however, this term is not to be found in the text of the convention.

Under article lxi of the Treaty of Berlin the Porte undertook to guarantee the security of the provinces that were inhabited by Armenians against the Circassians and Kurds.[4] Britain, however, did not participate in this pledge.

By the Pretoria convention of 3 August 1881 the British commissioners did, indeed, explicitly 'guarantee' that 'complete self-government' would be accorded to the Transvaal Territory within the space of five days. This formula seems to have been employed, however, principally as a means of emphasizing the solemnity of the undertaking given by the commissioners. In any case, 'complete self-government' was to be subject to the 'suzerainty' of the Queen.[5]

By the London convention of 18 March 1885 Britain and the other great powers undertook either to guarantee or to ask their parliaments for authority to guarantee the regular service of the annual payments of a loan to the Egyptian government.[6] This undertaking, however, related only to the discharge of a financial obligation.

The preamble of the Suez Canal Convention of 29 October 1888 declared that the arrangement agreed upon was 'destiné a garantir, en tout temps et à toutes les Puissances, le libre usage du Canal Maritime de Suez'.[7] But there was no reference to any 'guarantee' in its articles.

The Salisbury-Soveral declaration of 14 October 1899 reaffirmed the 'ancient treaties' between this country and Portugal,[8] including that of 22 January 1815, by which Castlereagh had renewed the previous treaties of 'Alliance, Friendship and Guarantee'.[9] However, as it happened, not one of the pre-1815 treaties with Portugal had contained the actual letter of a 'guarantee'. In any case, whether or not Britain can be said ever to have given a 'formal guarantee' to Portugal, the declaration of 14 October 1899 merely affirmed existing treaties.

(ii)

Is it possible to see in the fact that governments, drawn from both the major political parties, refrained over so long a period from giving any new 'formal' guarantee, relating to the territory or to the internal institutions of a foreign country, the result of steadfast adherence to a principle?

It is, of course, easy to cite objections, raised by a prime minister or foreign secretary, to giving a pledge of this type in a particular case. The fact of such an objection having been raised constitutes, however, no proof that the minister concerned, let alone all the prime ministers and foreign secretaries of the period, acted upon a general principle.

It is also easy to show that numerous members of Parliament,

journalists and others were opposed to giving 'formal' guarantees. This opposition had been voiced in the House of Lords in
the mid-eighteenth century.[10] Bentham had expressed it
vigorously in the 1780s.[11]

In the 1860s and 1870s there were numerous expressions of
this opposition. In 1864 the *Spectator* referred to 'the national
dislike to guarantees'.[12] In 1867, after the conclusion of the
Luxemburg guarantee, Labouchere told the House of Commons
that guarantees did more harm than good; instead of preventing
wars, they tended to turn local into European questions.[13] The
Saturday Review remarked, apropos of this speech, that 'guarantees are generally contrivances for escaping from present
embarrassment at the cost of greater evil in the future'. It
considered that both Castlereagh and Palmerston had given
such pledges too readily.[14] Stratford de Redcliffe impressed on
the House of Lords that what he had heard during the debate
on the treaty had amply confirmed 'the unfavourable opinion
which he had always entertained respecting guarantees'.[15] In
1872 the *Times* declared, with reference to what it called
'Treaty guarantees', that 'as a matter of principle, every man of
reflection must be opposed to them, and must wish that no such
obligations existed'.[16] In the following year a Liberal back-
bencher, Lord Edmond Fitzmaurice, described the feeling of
the nation in regard to 'Treaties of Guarantee' as one of
'horror'. He was confident that 'no Minister would venture to
bind this country to a new guarantee'.[17]

Of greater significance than these expressions of opinion by
organs of the press or by individuals are the pronouncements of
those actually, or potentially, responsible for the conduct of the
country's foreign relations.

Even Clarendon, who only eleven years previously had put
his signature to both the Treaty of Paris, with its four guarantee
articles, and the Tripartite Treaty, with its 'several' guarantee,
acknowledged during the first debate in the House of Lords on
the Luxemburg settlement that 'guarantees . . are naturally
viewed with fear and mistrust by the people of this country'.
He considered that the apprehension with which pledges of this
type were regarded was 'perfectly just'.[18]

In 1874 the fifteenth Earl of Derby explained his objection

at length in a letter to Lytton, at that time the *chargé d'affaires* in Paris, apropos of a suggestion for the neutralization of Denmark, which he took to imply also a guarantee:

Nothing is so unpopular in England: and reasonably so. A guarantee either does not mean a promise to defend by force of arms the settlement which you have guaranteed, in which case it is little better than a delusion: or it does imply such a promise, in which case we are at any moment liable to be called upon to take part in a Continental war, which may not in the slightest degree concern our interests. Nay, if a war breaks out, it becomes the interest of each belligerent to endeavour to induce its enemy to violate the engagement in order to bring about an intervention on the part of England and the other guaranteeing Powers.[19]

Gladstone was also critical of this type of engagement. On 13 June 1878 he told the House of Commons that guarantees were 'somewhat damaged in public estimation'. As far as the eastern question was concerned, they had proved 'an embarrassment and an impediment in the way of right action'.[20]

Perhaps the most significant condemnation of guarantees in general was that uttered by Salisbury in the House of Lords on 29 July 1878 during the debate on the eastern settlement:

Those misty and shadowy guarantees which bound you to everything in theory, and which turned out, in practice, to bind you to nothing, were anything but honourable to the character of European diplomacy. . . . I think it is time that the practice of making pledges of this kind was abandoned in the diplomacy of Europe.[21]

As these words make clear, Salisbury, unlike Canning over half a century earlier, was objecting to guarantees on the ground, not that they entailed uniquely onerous obligations, but that they lent themselves to evasion. He claimed that the pledge contained in the Constantinople convention was, in contrast, unambiguous, and that the government, by placing its intentions on public record in a solemn and unmistakeable manner, had given Britain's diplomacy 'character and plainness and frankness', all of which it had, perhaps, been in danger of losing. The transaction that Salisbury singled out as having been more especially characterized by a lack of these admirable qualities was, of course, the Tripartite Treaty, which had pledged Britain, Austria and France 'in the strongest language possible' to make any breach of the provisions of the Treaty of Paris a *casus belli*.[22]

In fact, in the previous year, when war between Russia and the Ottoman Empire had been imminent, Derby had explained away the obligation entailed by the Tripartite Treaty. The Porte, he reminded the House of Lords on 8 February 1877, was not a party to the treaty, which, therefore, did not bind Britain in any way, except to her co-signatories, Austria-Hungary and France. Accordingly, unless Austria-Hungary and France called upon her to act—a step that in the circumstances then existing they were not in the least likely to take—the Tripartite Treaty bound Britain to 'nothing at all'.[23] Thus, as Salisbury explained to the House of Lords on 29 July 1878, 'when the hour of trial came, and the provisions of the Treaty of Paris were broken', the guarantee contained in the Tripartite Treaty was found to be 'not binding on those who made it'.[24]

This episode made a deep impression on Derby's successor. 'Remember', he wrote a quarter of a century later, 'the fate in 1877 of the tripartite guarantee of Turkey signed in 1856 by Austria, France and England.'[25]

(iii)

Nevertheless, it would be rash to regard these pronouncements— even Salisbury's—as proof that in the later nineteenth century it was an established principle of Britain's foreign policy never again to give a pledge of the type that had once been so common. Even Derby did not in 1874 altogether exclude the possibility of 'pledging England to a new guarantee', although he impressed on Lytton that, before doing so, he would 'hesitate long, and require very clear evidence of public necessity or advantage'.[26] In fact, although for so long a period no British government committed the country to a 'new guarantee', that was not because no prime minister or foreign secretary was ever willing to do so.

Thus, towards the end of 1881 Edward Hamilton recorded a remark by Gladstone to the effect that a major water-way, such as the Suez Canal or the projected Panama Canal, 'should be guaranteed neutral by all the powers'.[27] Nearly a year later a committee, of which both Granville and Dilke were members, appointed to consider the future administration of Egypt, now under British occupation, recommended the conclusion of an agreement between the great maritime powers, under which the Suez Canal 'should be free for the passage of all ships in any circumstances'. 'This arrangement', the committee added, 'should be guaranteed by the Contracting Powers.'[28] On 17 March 1885 Granville signed a declaration, under which Britain and six other powers agreed that negotiations should take place with a view to the establishment by means of a convention of a regime that would guarantee at all times and to all powers the free use of the canal.[29] This principle was incorporated in the preamble of the Suez Canal Convention of 29 October 1888, but not, as has been seen, in any of its actual articles.

Again, on 8 October 1882, that is, less than a month after Tel-el-Kebir, Malet, at that time consul-general in Cairo, wrote privately to Granville, advising him that the Khedive and his ministers wished the tie between their country and the Porte to be rendered even more nominal than it was already and accordingly hoped 'that Egypt would be placed under a guarantee of the Powers'.[30] Ten days later Granville, presumably acting on this hint, drafted a dispatch, in which he stated that the British government would 'be ready to guarantee Egypt from attack'. To this offer he added the expression of his hope that other powers would 'join Britain in such a guarantee'. As a corollary of the proposed arrangement, the fortifications on Egypt's Mediterranean coast would be destroyed.[31] Malet, in fact, was to be instructed to offer the Khedive a sole guarantee by Britain of Egypt's immunity from attack, which was to take effect, even though no other great power was willing to participate.

There was no recent precedent for a sole guarantee by Britain of the immunity from attack of any country. Although British forces were in occupation of Egypt, the length of their stay was not at this time foreseen. Granville's proposal, therefore, struck his cabinet colleagues as more temerarious than, in the light of subsequent events, it now appears. Chamberlain strongly objected to 'the proposal that England should give a sole and individual guarantee to Egypt against attack by any other Power'. He thought that a 'sole guarantee' was too heavy a responsibility for any power that had no system of conscription. He acknowledged that 'a joint guarantee would be a very different matter', but pointed out that it was not certain that the other powers would agree to give such a pledge.[32] Gladstone, too, had misgivings. 'I became', he wrote to Granville, 'a good deal alarmed at the notion of a *sole* guarantee by England.'[33] The cabinet, understandably, did not proceed with the proposed guarantee.[34]

On more than one occasion, too, during Salisbury's last foreign secretaryship, ministers considered the possibility of giving a new guarantee in connexion with territory in one part of the world or another.

On 2 March 1896 Salisbury himself wrote to Devonshire, the chairman of the defence committee of the cabinet, suggesting that consideration be given to 'the arguments for and against guaranteeing the principal Italian ports'.[35] In due course the Directors of both Military and Naval Intelligence gave their views on this subject. The Director of Military Intelligence thought that to give Italy such a guarantee would mean virtually joining the Triple Alliance, a course that would have distinct advantages; on the other hand, a guarantee that merely ensured Britain the support of Italy, without that of Germany and Austria-Hungary, presented only 'trivial attractions'.[36] The Director of Naval Intelligence did not think that there could be any arguments at all for guaranteeing the Italian ports.[37]

In 1897 and 1898 there were negotiations with Portugal, in which Chamberlain, briefed by Bertie, the head of the African and Asiatic Departments at the Foreign Office, played a leading part.[38] At one point Chamberlain proposed to Soveral what he called 'guarantee of territory' in exchange for control of the port at Lourenço Marques and of the railway linking it with the South African Republic.[39] Later Chamberlain discussed with the governor of Mozambique a plan, under which, in Sanderson's words, 'Great Britain should guarantee to Portugal her possessions in Africa, and should enable her to obtain a loan on the security of the revenues of those Possessions'.[40] According to

Bertie, one possibility was for Britain 'to guarantee the Kingdom of Portugal against foreign attack on its Colonial Possessions and spheres of influence', with a reservation of the right
of pre-emption, in the event of Portugal desiring at any time to
part with any of them.[41] There seems to be no doubt that what
Chamberlain and Bertie had in mind in these negotiations was
a sole guarantee to Portugal, in return for a *quid pro quo*, of
possession of territory.

In 1898 there was discussion of the possibility of offering
Spain a guarantee of her sovereignty over the territory in the
vicinity of Gibraltar.

This was the outcome of reports, received during the war
between Spain and the United States, of the construction o
military works on the coast of the Bay of Algeciras. These
included concrete emplacements, presumably intended for
mounting guns for the defence of the coast against a possible
attack from the sea by United States forces. However, it was
evident that up-to-date, heavy guns, mounted on these emplacements, would also be able to shell Gibraltar and ships lying in
the anchorage there. Moreover, the possibility of the Algeciras
district passing under the control of a great power that possessed
such guns could not be disregarded. There was much disquiet
both at Gibraltar and at the Admiralty.[42] Balfour, too, showed
concern.[43]

Salisbury, who spent the latter part of the summer of 1898 in
Alsace, was inclined to discount the danger of Gibraltar being
bombarded from the coast of the Bay of Algeciras, but he
recognized the impossibility of ignoring the views of the
Admiralty. On the other hand, he was pessimistic as to the
feasibility of obtaining from any Spanish government what
would amount to the surrender, in compliance with a demand
from Britain, of the right to defend Algeciras from Spain's own
soil.[44]

Balfour hoped to solve the problem by giving Spain a
guarantee of her sovereignty over what he called, not very
precisely, the 'region immediately surrounding Gibraltar',
together with a promise 'to resist invasion of it by any foreign
Power'. In return Spain was to pledge herself not to erect or
maintain within the region military works or fortifications of

any kind.[45] On 6 September 1898 the Foreign Office cabled a
suggestion along these lines to Drummond Wolff, the ambassador in Madrid.[46] Two days later Wolff warned Salisbury that
the Spaniards would look on the proposal as 'the offer of a
protectorate and consequently a humiliation without any great
advantage'.[47] On 27 October the cabinet agreed to offer Spain,
in return for the required assurance, a guarantee of the Balearic
and Canary Islands.[48] Later in the year Salisbury had a conversation with the Spanish ambassador in London, after which
he notified Wolff that Spain would not promise to refrain from
setting up heavy guns within range of Gibraltar.[49] There was
no mention of any actual guarantee in the undertaking given to
Spain by Salisbury in March of the following year.[50]

In the light of the history of these projects, abortive though
all of them were, it would be rash to maintain that every
British government of the later nineteenth century acted on the
principle that 'formal' guarantees, in connexion with the
territory or institutions of a foreign country, or some comparable
matter, were undesirable. Nevertheless, the fact remains that
many contemporaries strongly objected to pledges of this type;
that powerful arguments were sometimes advanced at a high
level against proposals for a new one; and that the practice of
giving them did for a considerable period fall into disuse.

Moreover, this desuetude was not peculiar to Britain. Whereas it had formerly been a common practice to include a mutual
guarantee in a treaty of alliance—the Austro-Prussian treaty of
1854 and Bismarck's treaties of 1866 with the south German
states are obvious examples—the Austro-German treaty of 1879
and the Triple Alliance treaty of 1882 both lacked the letter of
any such pledge.

CHAPTER XV

'The Liberal view'

(i)

On 27 November 1879, in what was probably the most celebrated speech of his first Midlothian campaign, Gladstone laid down what he called 'the right principles of foreign policy'. He named six such principles, the fourth of which was that 'you should avoid needless and entangling engagements'.[1] This carefully formulated principle was not, of course, categorical. It left a door open for any engagement that, in the opinion of the government of the day, was needed and was not entangling.

(ii)

In fact, within a few months of taking office in the spring of 1880 Gladstone's government entered into an undeniable, although conditional and extra-European, engagement.

Before leaving for India, Ripon, the new viceroy, placed on record his opinion that the future ruler of Afghanistan should be aided by grants of money and arms, but not by troops.[2] Lepel Griffin's letter to Abdul Rahman did not specify the nature of the aid to be given, but it did state that, if the Kabul ruler were the victim of unprovoked aggression by a foreign power, the British government would be prepared to aid him, if necessary, to repel it, provided that he accepted its advice in regard to his external relations.

In the following year Hartington, the secretary for India, enunciated the principle of which this pledge was the expression. 'The present Government have admitted as plainly as any other that the integrity and independence of Afghanistan is a matter to them of vital importance', he told the House of Commons, 'and that they do not intend to permit interference by any foreign Power with the internal or external affairs of Afghanistan.'[3]

Early in 1885 it became apparent that a clash between Afghan and Russian forces was likely to occur in the region between Merv and Herat, where there was no clearly defined boundary—where, indeed, a boundary commission was expected shortly to start work. The probability of such a clash raised the question both of Britain's obligation to Afghanistan and of the applicability of that obligation to the situation that was now in prospect.

Joseph Chamberlain took the view that, whatever the wisdom or otherwise of the course adopted five years previously, Britain was committed. 'Rightly or wrongly (and I think the policy is open to some doubt) we are pledged to assist the Ameer in resisting aggression', he wrote on 17 March. On the other hand, the question whether Russia's advance constituted an aggression of the kind that Britain had promised to resist was more difficult. Chamberlain thought that, if the matter could be regarded as a law-suit, the Afghans would have a very good case, but that the Russians would also have a 'plausible answer'. He also thought that 'under these circumstances the Liberal party would not support the Government in extreme measures'. [4]

Kimberley, who was now secretary for India, agreed that Britain was committed. 'The basis on which the present policy of the British Government in Afghanistan rests', he wrote on 18 March 1885, 'is the engagement entered into with the Amir in a letter given to Abdul Rahman by Mr Lepel Griffin under authority from the Government of India, prior to the evacuation of Cabul in August 1880.' Unlike Chamberlain, however, he considered that this engagement was 'applicable to the present case'. [5]

Nevertheless, it was one thing to argue that the British obligation applied even to the 'No Man's land'[6] to the north of Herat. It was quite another to explain how Britain was to conduct a war against Russia. On 24 March the Cabinet met and, according to Carlingford, considered the problem. Among the difficulties discussed was 'the powerlessness of our navy against Russia'.[7] Less than a week later the anticipated clash between Afghan and Russian forces took place at Penjdeh, a small place on the Kushka river.

It so happened that at the time of the Afghan-Russian collision that made Penjdeh famous Abdul Rahman was on his way to a meeting with Ripon's successor, Dufferin. On 31 March 1885 he reached Rawal Pindi, where the viceroy was awaiting him.[8] During the next few days the two men discussed the situation created by Russia's advance. According to Dufferin's report to Kimberley, the Amir, in reply to an offer to send engineers to fortify Herat, 'deprecated any British troops appearing in his country', pointing out that 'the Afghans would at once imagine that they had come to subjugate it'. On being asked to agree in advance to subscribe to whatever settlement Britain might come to with Russia, he showed himself 'obviously indifferent' to the prospect of the surrender of Penjdeh. In short, if we may believe Dufferin—and there appears to be little reason, if any, for not doing so—Abdul Rahman made it clear that he did not wish his country to become a battle-field for the armies of two great European powers.[9]

It was evident that for the British government in India to send an expeditionary force across Afghanistan to fight a war against the Russians in the little known country to the north of Herat would be a hazardous enterprise. To do so without the cooperation of the Afghans themselves would be to invite disaster.

Dufferin saw this clearly. 'But many and cogent as are the reasons against sending a British army to Herat under the most favourable circumstances', he warned Kimberley, 'the idea of such a thing becomes far more questionable, the moment that the ruler of Afghanistan, no matter from what motive, shows a disinclination to encourage it.'[10] However, the viceroy's talents proved equal to the situation. On 11 April 1885 he reported having induced Abdul Rahman to give the British government 'a free hand in relation to the boundary, and to promise, in the face of Heaven and of the East, to be our faithful friend and ally, and to place himself, his country, and his army at our disposal'.[11]

It was undeniable that Britain was under some sort of obligation to Afghanistan. On 5 May Dufferin reminded Kimberley that the Indian, which in practice meant also the

British, government was bound by the promise given by Griffin 'to protect the territories of Afghanistan from aggression on the part of a foreign foe'. 'Though the compact is very cautiously worded', he added, 'and is strictly conditional on the Amir acting in accordance with our counsels, . . . the promise of effectual assistance is absolute and precise.' However, he explained, this assistance was, by agreement with the Amir, not to be in the form of troops. 'In what other way then', asked the viceroy, 'could our promises be fulfilled and our aid bestowed than by the gift of money, cannon, arms and ammunition?'[12]

A few months later Dufferin briefed the new Conservative secretary for India, Randolph Churchill. He thought that Ripon had 'committed us perhaps to a greater extent than was necessary'. 'Still', he observed, 'there the obligation is, and, as I have already strenuously urged, I think we are bound to respect it so long as our ally fulfils upon his side the conditions attached to it.'[13]

(iii)

To say that Gladstone's second government entered into a commitment, albeit a limited and conditional one, to India's north-western neighbour, is not, however, to say that any prominent Liberal of the later nineteenth century favoured involving the country in an alliance with any great European power. In fact, one leading Liberal after another expressed, publicly or privately and with varying degrees of qualification, his opposition to any such engagement. During the general election campaign of 1880 Hartington told a meeting at Rawtenstall that Britain could best serve the cause of peace 'by having her hands free, and by not being entangled . . . by any separate or special alliance with any Powers'.[14] Shortly after taking office Granville reported having told the French *chargé d'affaires* that the new government 'did not as a general rule feel a preference for special alliances between individual States'.[15] The fifteenth Earl of Derby, who served in Gladstone's cabinet from 1882 to 1885, was, perhaps, the most outspoken of all. In 1885 he declared at Blackburn:

I am quite sure that the less we are mixed up in the sanguinary muddle of Continental diplomacy the better for England. We need no special alliances. We have nothing to gain by being mixed up with the intrigues of despotic or semi-despotic Powers.[16]

(iv)

During Salisbury's second administration the Liberals had to consider their attitude towards a transaction, of which Parliament had not been informed.

At some time, not easy to determine precisely, but probably either at the end of December 1887 or at the beginning of January 1888, Henry Labouchere, who had a keen nose for improprieties of all kinds, got wind of the secret exchange of notes, carried out by Salisbury and the Italian ambassador the previous February. On 3 January 1888 he accordingly wrote to Harcourt, informing him, with understandable exaggeration, that in the spring of 1887 Salisbury had 'entered into a sort of alliance with Italy', under which 'he engaged to protect her coasts should there be war'.[17]

The source of his information, Labouchere explained, was a certain George Sheffield, formerly of the British Embassy in Paris:

I got this from Sheffield who was for years the Private Secretary and tom cat of Lord Lyons, and he would know it, as the dispatches would have been sent to the Paris Embassy for the guidance of Lord L. Pray do not mention to a soul Sheffield's name. I cannot suppose that he is mistaken.[18]

Labouchere displayed suitable indignation at Salisbury's secret diplomacy. 'Is it not impudence', he asked Harcourt, 'to have given this compromising pledge whilst Parliament is sitting and not to have said a word about it?'[19] When, in February 1888, Parliament reassembled, he put a number of searching questions to Fergusson, the parliamentary under-secretary for foreign affairs, but failed to elicit any significant admission.[20] Eventually, on 22 February, he obtained a debate,[21] to which Gladstone made a strikingly non-partisan contribution,[22] and which yielded nothing conclusive.

In 1891 the renewal of the Triple Alliance and a visit by the

British fleet to Italian waters served to revive rumours of a secret commitment. Labouchere again questioned the parliamentary under-secretary in the House of Commons[23] and finally succeeded in obtaining some satisfaction.[24] 'You will observe that now, for the first time', he wrote jubilantly to Harcourt on 7 July, 'Fergusson has admitted that there is an understanding.' He thought that there was strong feeling in the country against 'any understandings that might drag us into war' and that 'to make it clear what Lord S. has done would help us at the Elections'—a general election being then not far distant. However, he explained, Gladstone had intimated to him through Arnold Morley, the chief Liberal whip, that 'it would be undesirable to make too much of the "understanding" between Lord Salisbury and Italy'. To do so 'might render it difficult for a Liberal Government to get out of it'.[25]

Two days later a Liberal back-bencher, Sir George Campbell, proposed a motion in the House of Commons for a reduction in the foreign secretary's salary.[26] Labouchere spoke in support, accusing Salisbury of loving 'secret alliances' and of going to another power 'in a surreptitious manner' and begging it 'to enter into some secret understanding with himself'. 'These understandings with one country', he added, 'lead to misunderstandings with other countries.'[27] James Bryce also spoke, but not in a partisan spirit. The country, he declared, had 'responsibilities enough'. If a conflict were to arise, it would be in a better position to exert its forces on the side of peace, if it were 'free from all engagements beforehand'. 'These are commonplaces of foreign policy', Bryce explained.[28]

It so happened that on the following day Harcourt was a guest at a garden-party at Marlborough House, where he saw Baron d'Estournelles de Constant, of the French embassy. The baron, Harcourt subsequently reported to Gladstone, 'entered into conversation on the subject of the Triple Alliance and the feeling in France as to the suspected complicity of England in the transaction'.[29]

Harcourt's account of his reply deserves quotation. 'I assured him', he wrote, 'that I felt convinced that Salisbury had not in fact entered into any binding engagements.' As for the Liberals, Harcourt took the line:

That in any event we did not and should not recognize any right of the present Government to engage the responsibility of England in the future. That our policy was one of absolute disengagement from Continental combinations of any kind, and that we maintained the right of England to act as her interests demanded when the occasion arose unfettered by any alliances conventions or understandings of any description.

Harcourt added that he had told the French diplomat that these were also Gladstone's views, authorizing him to pass the information on to Waddington, the ambassador, who was in France.[30]

On the morning of 11 July, Harcourt continued, Estournelles de Constant paid him a call, presumably at his house in Brook Street. On this occasion Harcourt referred the baron to Bryce's speech in the House of Commons two days previously, as expressing his own views, only to be met with the comment that 'Bryce's name was not known in France' and a request for 'some more authoritative declaration'. It was obvious whose declaration of the Liberal Party's attitude towards Britain's relations with the Triple Alliance the French embassy would consider most authoritative. 'The matter is so grave', Harcourt told Gladstone, 'that I think it is well deserving of consideration whether in some form or other you should not yourself express your views upon it.'[31]

It so happened that Gladstone at this time was under doctor's orders not to make speeches. He accordingly wrote to Rosebery, reminding him that, although much had been said in recent weeks concerning the Triple Alliance and Britain's relation to it, the expression of 'the Liberal view' in the House of Commons had been left to Bryce and Labouchere. 'But these', he observed, 'are not quite European names.' He had, Gladstone continued, consulted Harcourt and John Morley:

We all three hold in the strongest form the doctrine that it is the business of England to stand absolutely aloof from these prospective engagements. And such we believe to be the general or universal view of the Liberal party . . .

I think there never was a case in which *aloofness* was so imperatively our duty. . . .

We have done Salisbury all along all the justice we could. But with the general Election now coming near I think we ought to state the true principle and reserve our own liberty of action.

'Salisbury I have no doubt', Gladstone concluded, 'has *committed* himself and his Government.'[32]

When Rosebery received this letter he was on holiday at Bad Gastein, whence he replied politely in terms of general concurrence. He was, he assured Gladstone, in agreement with him 'as to the paramount necessity of holding aloof from the Triple Alliance, or any other such engagement'. His reason, he explained, was the same as that which made him 'hostile to the Channel Tunnel'. He was 'anxious to obtain the full advantage of the insular position with which Providence has endowed us'.[33] This profession Harcourt pronounced 'satisfactory'.[34] The leaders of the Liberal Party were agreed as to the undesirability of involvement in an alliance with any of the other great powers.

Meanwhile, Waddington had returned to London. On 14 July he forwarded Estournelles's impressions of the situation to the Quai d'Orsay. Both parties would, Estournelles thought, be in agreement not to enter into any commitment, for that was the indisputable will of the country—'car c'est là le voeu, la volonté indiscutable de l'Angleterre'.[35]

As for the alleged lover of 'secret alliances', he had not found it necessary to reply publicly to the accusation brought by the energetic and public-spirited editor of *Truth*. However, Salisbury evidently appreciated the fact that numerous hazards lay in the path of whoever was the Foreign Office's spokesman in the House of Commons. A few months after these events he recommended Fergusson for appointment as postmaster-general, and, accordingly, had to find a new parliamentary under-secretary for foreign affairs. According to his own account, given in a letter to Hicks Beach, he passed over with much regret George Curzon, who 'had pledged himself awkwardly in regard to one or two foreign questions'. He would, he wrote, like Curzon 'in any other place better than as the champion of F.O'. 'A certain amount of impenetrable apathy', Salisbury added, 'is necessary in the man who is to answer Labouchère [*sic*].'[36]

(v)

When, after the Conservative defeat in the general election of
the following year, Salisbury resigned, instead of seeing his
successor at the Foreign Office in person, he addressed a letter
to Currie, now the permanent under-secretary, emphasizing
the importance of Britain's relations with Italy and, through
Italy, with the Triple Alliance, but denying having given any
assurance of 'material assistance'.[37] Rosebery's report to
Gladstone of this incident served as an indication of the attitude
that he intended to adopt towards the exchanges entered into
by his predecessor five years previously:

Salisbury has written a letter to Currie (to be shown to me) instead
of the usual interview, in which he says that he promised the
Italians no material assistance. I have not investigated this point;
partly because it does not press, as Salisbury's promises, whatever
they were could only be personal to himself.[38]

Rosebery's attitude was, in short, that the Liberal government was not bound by the transactions carried out by Salisbury
in 1887 and that the less that he knew about them the better.
'Lord Rosebery refused to look at any of the Agreements of
1887', wrote Sanderson some years later.[39]

Moreover, the Liberal foreign secretary discouraged attempts
to revive the agreements, showing, in doing so, his awareness
of the distrust of continental entanglements felt by his colleagues.[40] Early in 1894 he pointed out to Malet that, although
Britain could theoretically join the Triple Alliance or enter into
a secret treaty with Italy, neither of these steps was 'in the range
of practical politics'. 'In fact our only sure policy is to strengthen
our fleet', Rosebery added, 'and that will be done.'[41]

CHAPTER XVI

Our popular constitution'

(i)

During his second and third administrations Salisbury more than once enunciated principles that precluded him from involving this country in what so many of his contemporaries termed 'entangling alliances'.[1]

Even 'isolation', he wrote to Queen Victoria in January 1896, was preferable to 'the danger of being dragged into wars which do not concern us'.[2] A few weeks later he reminded Lascelles that Britain's 'insular position' made 'the burdensome conditions of an alliance unnecessary for our safety'.[3]

However, Salisbury's favourite argument, which, with minor variations, appears over and over again in his correspondence and memoranda, was the constitutional one. No British government, he maintained, could give a pledge that entailed an obligation to go to war in a contingency that might arise in the future, because it could not be sure that, should the *casus foederis* arise, Parliament—in other words, the House of Commons—would allow the pledge to be honoured. That was something that would depend on the state of public feeling prevailing at the time, and there was no means of foreseeing what that feeling would be. Thus it was, Salisbury explained to Lascelles, that his administrations had 'kept free from any engagement to go to war in any contingency whatever'. That was 'the attitude prescribed to us . . . by our popular constitution'.[4]

It would be interesting to know when Salisbury first adopted this theory and from what source he derived it. He had not, so far as one can judge from his letters to Layard, held it at the time of the negotiations that preceded the conclusion of the Constantinople convention. Had he then held it during his first administration? In August 1885 Philip Currie, who was on holiday in Germany, informed Herbert Bismarck that, if his father would help bring about a settlement of the Russo-Afghan frontier dispute, he would 'be laying the foundations of a closer and more intimate alliance between the two Countries'—that is, between Britain and Germany. 'The present Prime Minister of England', Currie added, 'is known to be favorable to such an alliance in the fullest sense of the terms.'[5] Was this statement by the assistant under-secretary at the Foreign Office really an accurate description of Salisbury's views at the time? It would not, in fact, be easy to point to any occasion before the period of his third foreign secretaryship on which Salisbury resorted to the constitutional argument, of which he became so fond.

However, the view had long prevailed on the continent, especially in the German-speaking countries, that the sudden changes of government, to which Britain was subject, rendered her an unreliable ally. This belief went back to the wars of the eighteenth century. In the later nineteenth century it was still widely held. Thus, in September 1885 Currie, after a visit to Friedrichsruh, reported to Salisbury a remark by Bismarck, to the effect that 'a Treaty with England was an uncertain thing, as with a change of Ministry it might no longer be considered binding'.[6] On 1 February 1887 Malet wrote from Berlin that the Chancellor had observed—rather more tactfully than on the occasion of Currie's visit—that he 'understood the difficulty which lay in the way of any Prime Minister in England who attempted to make a foreign alliance'.[7] It may be that Salisbury borrowed this argument and adapted it to his own purpose, stressing, however, not the instability of British governments, but the impossibility of knowing in advance whether a popularly elected House of Commons would permit a treaty obligation to be honoured.

At all events, on 23 February 1887 Salisbury sent Queen Victoria a brief memorandum, containing what he called 'a summary of the language which he has always held to Count Hatzfeldt when pressed by him to declare what the conduct of England would be in the eventuality of European war'.[8] 'No English Government can give definite pledges of military or naval cooperation in a future contingency': he explained, 'because it cannot be sure that Parliament would make such a promise good.'⁹ Three days later he wrote to Paget, now ambassador in Vienna, reporting a conversation with the Austro-Hungarian ambassador, who had informed him that his foreign minister, Count Kálnoky, 'was aware that no pledge of material cooperation could be given by a Parliamentary Government such as ours until the precise case had arisen in respect of which it was invoked'. 'I confirmed and emphasized the Ambassador's own statement', Salisbury added, 'with regard to the inability of a Parliamentary Government to give assurances of material support in case of events which had not yet arisen and whose precise character could not be foreseen.'¹⁰

It was, of course, by no means unknown for a minister, who wished politely to decline to involve his country in some proposed commitment, to plead the authority of the legislature as a reason. Bismarck, if we may believe Odo Russell, resorted to this device in December 1870.¹¹

There was also the example of the United States. The first article of the American constitution explicitly entrusts the power to declare war to the Congress, which does, therefore, in theory, possess an authority in regard to the choice between peace and war similar in some respects to that which Salisbury attributed to the British Parliament. On at least one occasion Salisbury was reminded of this convenient arrangement, behind which a United States administration, when confronted with an inadmissible request from a foreign power for a promise of cooperation by force of arms in a hypothetical contingency, could plausibly take refuge. In 1898 Pauncefote, the ambassador in Washington, after an unsuccessful *démarche*, passed on to Salisbury a message to the effect that 'the insurmountable difficulty in the way of any engagement by the Administration which would involve material support in certain contingencies, was the Provision of the Constitution which vested in Congress the power to declare War'.¹²

The theory of the insuperable obstacle placed in the path of all governments by Britain's 'popular constitution' evidently appealed to the man who in 1867 had resigned office because he felt unable to support the Conservative reform bill, and who still looked on his country's political institutions without enthusiasm. For a decade and a half Salisbury continued to resort to his constitutional argument when either pressed to involve Britain in some continental commitment or suspected of having already done so. He even expounded it, although not frequently, in the House of Lords.[13] His expositions of the working of what was, after all, the very moderately 'popular' system of government, obtaining in this country in the later nineteenth century, were assiduously reported to the Quai d'Orsay,[14] the Wilhelmstrasse[15] and the Ballhausplatz.[16]

For some years this theory enjoyed a certain vogue. In 1891 the *Spectator* endorsed the view that 'a policy planned in advance of facts is inconsistent with democratic institutions; that the English people in grave contingencies look first of all to the justice of the quarrel; and that their opinion on the war, when it broke out, would depend in a great degree on its objects and its cause'.[17] 'The constitutional form of government in England precludes her from entering into alliances with foreign Powers', wrote Loftus in the following year.[18] 'With our institutions and our system of Parliamentary government', declared Edward Dicey in the *Fortnightly Review* in 1896, 'any lasting general alliance with a foreign country is a practical impossibility.'[19] In the same year Goschen[20] and in 1901 Balfour both expressed themselves to similar effect.[21] No doubt Salisbury had on more than one occasion favoured them with his views on the subject.

(ii)

It would be interesting to know whether Salisbury really believed that 'in this country it was impossible to take any engagement involving an obligation to go to war'.[22] Did he, perhaps, merely find this theory a useful device, which enabled him to avoid time-consuming argument? Or did he believe that, although it was impossible for Britain to enter into such an engagement with a great power, there was no insuperable difficulty in the case of a small power?

At all events, in 1897 he concluded the Bangkok convention with Siam.

In 1899 he gave Spain a pledge that entailed an undeniable, although strictly limited, obligation to render that power armed assistance, should the need arise.

In the previous year Salisbury had expressed scepticism both as to the seriousness of the threat to Gibraltar, presented by the military works on the coast of the Bay of Algeciras, and as to the feasibility of obtaining from the Spanish government an undertaking to discontinue them.[23] As far as the latter point was concerned, he proved, for the time being, to be right.

Nevertheless, in the following year, after a change of government in Madrid, Silvela, the new prime minister and foreign minister, conscious, no doubt, of his country's weak position, informed Drummond Wolff that the Spanish government had decided to discontinue the military works, since they would serve no useful purpose. In return he asked for an assurance that Britain desired no further territory from Spain and would undertake to prevent any hostile landing in the Bay of Algeciras.[24] On 16 March 1899 Salisbury instructed Wolff to comply with this request. The British government, he wrote, had at no time entertained the idea of making the question at issue a ground for demanding further territorial acquisitions. They would be ready, if the occasion should arise, 'to give their military and naval assistance for preventing any hostile landing on coast of Bay of Algesiras [sic] or any attack by sea on that coast'.[25]

The area to which the pledge given by Salisbury applied was small. In any case, no British government that wished to retain Gibraltar could possibly have ignored an attack by a third power on the strategically vital coast of the Bay of Algeciras, whether or not Britain was bound to Spain by an explicit promise to defend it. Moreover, to provide armed assistance for the defence of this locality, situated so close to Gibraltar, would have been perfectly feasible.

Wolff asked Salisbury to ensure that the transaction be kept secret. It would, he wrote, if bruited abroad, greatly damage the standing of the Spanish government, and perhaps even that of the Queen Regent.[26] This was a precaution, concerning the wisdom of which Salisbury probably needed no urging. At all events, the agreement of March 1899 with Spain remained one of the best kept diplomatic secrets of his last administration.

Less than six months later, after the outbreak of the Boer War, Salisbury, in order to ensure that Portugal should not permit the South African Republic to import arms through Mozambique and should not proclaim her neutrality, signed the joint declaration with Soveral, the Portuguese minister in London, which not only reaffirmed the 'ancient treaties', but clarified the obligations that they entailed, leaving no doubt that Britain was pledged to defend, not only Portugal's European mainland, but her overseas possessions as well.[27] This transaction, too, was intended to be secret.

Nevertheless, whatever pledges he was prepared to give or reaffirm in the case of a small or weak or extra-European power, Salisbury may well have come to believe, not that it was impossible for any British government to enter into an engagement, involving an obligation to go to war in a contingency that might arise in the future, but that it was impossible to be sure that, should the contingency arise, such an engagement would be honoured.

Thus, on 15 January 1902, after Sanderson had passed on to him a copy of a letter, written by Holstein to Chirol of the *Times* and containing some highly uncomplimentary remarks about himself,[28] Salisbury replied:

I have always been Holstein's *bête noire*—I do not know why.

But our policies differ in this—that he believes the mutual conduct of nations can be arranged beforehand like a game of chess —whereas I believe that no one can foresee or predict what in any future contingency a democratic Parliament will do. Tell me what is the *casus belli* and I may be able to give a guess at the conduct which England will pursue. But without such information we not only cannot guess what England will do, but we cannot determine her course beforehand by any pledges or any arguments derived from general interests.[29]

Writing to Lascelles on the same day, Sanderson described Salisbury's comment on Holstein's letter as 'very characteristic'. 'Lord Salisbury', he observed, ' . . . is always singularly pessimistic as to the time which this Country would take in making up its mind for action in any emergency—and the disadvantages that would result.'[30]

Whatever time-saving device Salisbury may have employed on other occasions, he can hardly have wanted to pull the wool over the eyes of the permanent under-secretary at the Foreign

Office, to whom he had evidently explained his views more than once. Perhaps it was not a coincidence that in January 1902, when Salisbury wrote this letter to Sanderson, the agreement with Japan was under negotiation. Indeed, only a week previously the prime minster had criticized Lansdowne's proposals at some length.[31]

In any case, however genuine Salisbury's disbelief in the possibility of relying on a 'democratic Parliament' to permit a treaty obligation to be honoured, should the *casus foederis* ever arise, the House of Commons had no monopoly of unpredictability. The failure of the Tripartite Treaty of 1856, on which Salisbury often animadverted, had been the result, after all, not of the refusal of the House of Commons to (in his own words) 'acknowledge the obligations of an engagement made in former years',[32] but of the attitudes of the governments of all three of the signatory powers in circumstances that were very different from those prevailing at the time of the conclusion of the treaty. However, quite apart from any constitutional difficulty, real or imaginary, there was in the Salisbury era no compelling reason why Britain should enter into an alliance, in the sense of a pledge explicitly entailing the *casus belli* in a hypothetical contingency, with any of the great continental powers.

Few, if any, ministers can seriously have believed that Britain should conclude an alliance with either France or Russia—let alone with both of them. Her differences with these powers were long-standing and notorious. 'About the most unlikely thing in all political speculation is an English-French-Russian alliance', wrote Frederick Greenwood in the *Contemporary Review* in 1896.[33]

On the other hand, from the later 1880s onwards there was much talk of the possibility of Britain's adherence to the Triple Alliance.[34] Here the situation was more complicated. Salisbury set considerable store by what he called the 'alliance' with Austria-Hungary[35] and also that with Germany.[36] He was much less enthusiastic about the 'alliance' with Italy. 'To my mind the Italian alliance is an unprofitable, and even slightly onerous corollary on the German alliance', he wrote to Dufferin, the ambassador in Rome, in 1891. 'Germany and Austria are ery useful friends as regards Turkey, Russia, Egypt, and even rance', he added. He valued the 'Italian alliance', he ex-lained, for the sake of Germany and Austria.[37] Five years later e impressed on Lascelles his wish 'to lean to the Triple lliance without belonging to it'.[38] In 1898 he told Balfour that rance was acting as if she meant to drive Britain 'into a erman alliance'. This he regarded 'with some dismay'. He ought that Germany would 'blackmail us heavily'.[39]

Salisbury must also have been aware of the suspicion with hich any such involvement would be regarded by many iberals. In fact, during his fourth and last period as foreign cretary there was not a great deal in his attitude towards the lliances of the great continental powers of which the Opposi-on could complain. In 1896 the *Speaker* observed:

nglish Conservative newspapers had upheld the Triple Alliance, nd advocated our giving it support. The Liberal Government, aturally enough, maintained our isolation; . . . Lord Salisbury did kewise.[40]

Iarcourt put the matter differently. In 1897 he told the Eighty lub that no British government had 'ever dared to propose to in the Triple Alliance or the Dual Alliance'. Even Salisbury's overnment had 'kept a free hand'.[41]

In fact, at the time when the story of Britain's adherence to ie Triple Alliance was going the rounds, Salisbury himself had iven Robert Morier, the ambassador in St Petersburg, an xplanation of the considerations that governed Britain's iternational position. On 1 February 1888 he wrote:

I do not myself know for certain what the provisions of the triple liance are. But if popular rumour is correct they constitute a efensive alliance of the closest form; and therefore I cannot under-and how the idea has got about that we have joined it. No two owers are less fitted for a mutual defensive alliance than England nd Germany; for Germany's most dangerous enemy is almost ivulnerable to us.

At the same time it is necessary to insist that our policy is identical ith that of the Central Powers. England and Germany, and, to a reat extent Austria are 'satisfied' Powers. France and Russia are iungry' Powers. Italy, it is true, is eminently a hungry Power: but ie objects of her appetite are no great matter to us.[42]

CHAPTER XVII

'Policy of alliances'

(i)

The mid 1890s were marked by a succession of episodes tha were, from the British point of view, mortifying. There was th Rosebery government's abandonment in 1894, under pressur from France and Germany, of its treaty with the Congo State the conquest by France in the years of 1894–6 of Madagascar an island where British missionaries had been active and wher Britain enjoyed tariff advantages; the action of Russia, German and France in 1895 in dictating to Japan the terms of a settle ment with China; the Cleveland message to Congress of 1 December 1895; the Kruger telegram, which followed th Jameson Raid; Salisbury's failure to obtain any alleviation c the lot of the Armenians. It would be easy to prolong the list.

In retrospect some of these incidents now appear trifling others scarcely avoidable. At the time they produced a wide spread feeling of exasperation.

It happened that this series of vexations coincided with th gradual realization on the part of the public that France an Russia had come together, and that Britain, accordingly, ha been left as the one great power without an ally amongst th other five. There was much talk of the country's 'isolation' which to many contemporaries appeared to be the consequenc of a systematic policy, precluding any commitment of the kin in which the great continental powers were now involved. In a article in the *Contemporary Review* for June 1895 Frederic Greenwood blamed the country's 'isolation' on what he calle 'a policy of absolute abstention from binding alliances'.[1] Th next step in the argument was obvious. In a further article i the same review for February 1896 Greenwood declared tha what he called the 'policy of no alliances' contained muc 'obvious fallacy' and 'should be reconsidered'.[2] The *Saturda*

Review criticized Britain's 'historic policy of isolation'. 'We frankly can go no further alone', it acknowledged.[3] Even the *Spectator* admitted that people in Britain were being forced 'to consider the question of alliances very earnestly'.[4]

On 17 February 1896 there appeared in the *Morning Post* the first of a series of articles on Britain's international position by the military expert, Spenser Wilkinson, who shortly afterwards incorporated them in a book, published in the same year and entitled *The Nation's Awakening*.[5] Wilkinson strongly criticized what he regarded as the failure of both Liberal and Unionist governments to defend the country's rights. He also gave warning of the possibility of the formation of a new and potentially hostile combination of continental powers:

Thus at the present moment a fresh grouping of the Continental Powers is under consideration. If England holds aloof, her interests will be sacrificed to the peace of the Continent, and she will be confronted by a combination far stronger than her naval and military preparations will enable her to oppose with any probability of success. She will have to choose between the sacrifice of her interests without war, and the still greater sacrifices that must follow defeat.[6]

This situation, Wilkinson argued, although dangerous, nevertheless offered Britain an opportunity. The government should compose such of its differences with other powers as were merely temporary and accidental and take the lead in the formation of a new group, powerful enough to frustrate the designs of those powers that threatened her enduring interests.[7] This it should do by means of a system of alliances. There were to be treaties with Austria-Hungary, Italy, China and Japan for the defence of certain specified objects and a more general treaty with Germany. Britain and Germany were each to define their respective vital interests, an attack on which by either Russia, supported by France, or by France, supported by Russia, was to be *casus belli*. The aim of these treaties was to be 'the prevention of Russian aggression without war'.[8] As for the 'policy of isolation' or 'abstinence from alliances', its continuance Wilkinson argued, could only lead either to the sacrifice of British interests, or to the construction of vast armaments,

or to both.[9] Britain's true policy consisted in the prompt asser-
tion of her rights, which would 'bring the necessary alliances
along with it'.[10]

However, although the so-called policy was under attack by
some journalists, its wisdom had not as yet been questioned,
publicly at least, by any front-rank politician. On the contrary,
Goschen, the First Lord of the Admiralty, in a speech at Lewes
on 26 February 1896, declared his belief that the government
could at any time make such alliances as it chose, were it not
that to contract such obligations would be incompatible with
the country's 'democratic institutions'. The difficulty, Goschen
explained, lay 'in our Constitution'—an argument that, no
doubt, owed something to Salisbury's disquisitions on the
subject. Britain's 'isolation', about which so much had been
said and written recently, was, according to Goschen, 'deliber-
ately chosen'. It was 'the freedom to act as we choose in any
circumstances that may arise'. In short, it was, to quote a
Canadian politician of the period, 'splendid'.[11]

Several leading Liberals ridiculed the notion of 'splendid
isolation'.[12] Nevertheless, whatever their views concerning
Goschen's terminology, members of the Opposition wished to
see the country's freedom of action preserved. On 3 March
1896 Rosebery told the Eighty Club that he agreed with
Goschen that to enter into a 'system of alliances' was 'not
possible in our conditions', and that it was still less 'desirable'.[13]
A few months later Harcourt, in a speech to his constituents at
Ebbw Vale, declared that what Britain needed was an *entente
cordiale* with other powers, not 'an alliance which becomes
obsolete almost as soon as it is made'.[14] In the following year,
when he in his turn addressed the Eighty Club, he expressed
the Jeffersonian wish that 'this country should be the friend of
all States, but the instrument of none'. He was, he said,
'opposed to all engagements which bind England to dangerous
obligations with great military and despotic Powers'. 'England
ought always to keep a free hand for a free people', Harcourt
added.[15] 'We have no wish to pledge ourselves to interfere in
any Continental complications', wrote the *Speaker*, 'and we
prefer to retain freedom of action without pledging ourselves as
to conditions which have not yet arisen.'[16]

It should not be thought that in 1896 criticism of the so-called 'policy of no alliances' reached the dimensions of a nation-wide agitation. However, the controversy produced a catch-phrase, which took the fancy of some politicians and journalists—especially Liberals. The opposite of a 'policy of no alliances' was clearly a 'policy of alliances'.[17] A good deal was to be heard of this alternative policy before long.

Salisbury, meanwhile, continued to experience difficulties in the field of foreign affairs.[18] The Opposition accused him of pusillanimity.[19] The 'Tory upper rank and file' was, according to Harcourt, 'sulky and depressed'.[20] A succession of by-elections went against the Unionists. There were prolonged differences with France over the undemarcated territory between the British and French possessions in West Africa. In the early months of 1898 Russia's proceedings at Port Arthur and Talienwan created further problems.

Once again it was tempting to argue that the remedy for the government's apparent inability to defend the country's interests was to seek an ally. Ellis Ashmead Bartlett, a Conservative back-bencher, told the House of Commons that the reason why Britain had during the preceding five years been 'steadily pushed down-hill' was the existence of 'the great Russo-French combination'. Britain herself had not a single ally in Europe, and, until she returned to her 'ancient alliances', she could have no hope of success. She could not 'against an armed Europe, stand alone'.[21]

(ii)

There were, in fact, a number of powers, with which it was possible at least to contemplate cooperation in defence of common interests in the Far East.

On 7 March 1898, at the time of the Port Arthur episode, Balfour made an approach, through Pauncefote, the ambassador in Washington, to the United States. The British government, he telegraphed, were 'anxious to know whether they could count on the cooperation of the United States in opposing any action by foreign Powers which would tend to restrict the opening of China to the commerce of all nations'. Pauncefote was to ascertain confidentially whether the United States would be prepared to join with Britain 'in opposing such measures if the contingency should present itself'.[22]

It is unlikely that Balfour's *démarche* would in any circumstances have been successful. At all events, it was not well timed. Three weeks previously the *Maine* had been blown up in Havana Harbour. In March 1898 the United States was moving towards war with Spain. On 8 March Pauncefote saw President McKinley, Sherman, the secretary-of-state, being absent from the State Department because of illness, but was unable to obtain any positive response to his enquiry. Eventually, a week later, he saw Day, the assistant secretary-of-state, who, he reported, read him a written statement by the President to the effect that he did 'not see any present reason for the departure of the United States from its traditional policy respecting foreign alliances and as far as practicable avoiding any interference or connection with European complications'. To this statement Day added, according to Pauncefote, an allusion to the crisis over Cuba and a reminder that the 'celebrated warning against "entangling alliances" was looked upon as the Law of the Land'.[23]

Another apparently potential partner was Japan, which had demonstrated its military and naval efficiency in the war against China, four years previously. From about 1896 onwards there was recurrent talk of the possibility of collaboration with this rising Asian power. This was one theme of *The Nation's Awakening*.[24] In December 1897 both Curzon[25] and Chamberlain attempted to impress the possibility on Salisbury.[26] On 17 March 1898 Chamberlain had a conversation with Katō, the Japanese minister in London, without, however, achieving any immediate, positive result of importance.[27] In fact, Nishi, the Japanese foreign minister, was already negotiating with Rosen, the Russian envoy in Tokyo, with a view to a *modus vivendi* between their two countries in regard to Korea.[28]

(iii)

At some date, difficult to specify exactly, but perhaps early in March 1898, Spenser Wilkinson appears to have had a conversation with Joseph Chamberlain.[29] At all events, on 12 March of that year he sent the colonial secretary an encouraging letter, amplifying some remarks made previously. 'Everyone looks to you just now', he wrote, 'as the man who is standing up for England.' After giving a forceful warning of the probable attitude of the French, he enjoined Chamberlain to 'insist on the Cabinet's taking stock of its policy all round'.[30]

Whether Wilkinson's words had any influence on Chamberlain's actions in the weeks that followed can only be a matter for conjecture. They must, at least, have served to remind him of *The Nation's Awakening*, published two years before, its criticism of the so-called 'policy of isolation', its warning of the possibility of a combination of the great continental powers against Britain, its outspoken hostility towards Russia, and its plan for a system of alliances, based principally on a treaty with Germany.

On 28 March Salisbury left for the continent to convalesce from an illness.[31] On the following day Chamberlain had a conversation with the German ambassador.[32] 'Count Hatzfeld [*sic*], through Alfred Rothschild having expressed a desire to see me we met at the latter's house and had a long conversation', he recorded. According to his own account, Chamberlain told Hatzfeldt that Britain might abandon the policy, to which she had for many years adhered, of 'isolation' or 'non-entanglement in alliances', and went on to discuss the possibility of the establishment of 'an alliance . . . between Germany and Great Britain for a term of years'.[33] He subsequently had further talks both with the ambassador and with the over-zealous Freiherr von Eckardstein.[34]

Meanwhile, on 5 April the House of Commons debated foreign affairs. Sir Edward Grey gave warning of the disadvantages of 'isolation'.[35] Lord Charles Beresford, for his part, expressed the opinion that Britain should conclude an alliance with both Germany and Japan.[36]

On Salisbury's return to England Chamberlain reported at length on what he called his 'very curious conversations'. 'Recent experience seems to me to show that we are powerless to resist the ultimate control of China by Russia, and that we are at a great disadvantage in negotiating with France, as long as we retain our present isolation', he wrote, 'and I think the country would support us in a Treaty with Germany providing for reciprocal defence.'[37]

On 2 May Hatzfeldt called at the Foreign Office. 'His business was evidently to throw cold water', Salisbury observed to Chamberlain. The prime minister's own attitude towards his colleague's project was one of polite scepticism. 'I quite agree with you that under the circumstances a closer relation with Germany would be very desirable', he wrote, 'but can we get it?'[38] On 3 May Salisbury saw Chamberlain at the Foreign Office and later in the day returned to him his notes of his conversations with the German diplomats. 'They are very curious as well as interesting', Salisbury commented laconically.[39]

On 4 May Salisbury addressed the Primrose League at the Albert Hall. He expressed his conviction that Russia had made a great mistake in taking Port Arthur, reassured his audience as to Britain's future, and dismissed as 'jargon' the talk in which unnamed persons had recently indulged on the theme of the catch-word of the hour.[40] Nevertheless, criticism of his conduct of foreign affairs continued. 'The English people do not want to go to war', declared Harcourt at Cambridge on 7 May, 'but they do not like being snubbed all round the world.'[41]

On 11 May Salisbury wrote a dispatch to Lascelles, describing a conversation with Hatzfeldt, in which, he reported, the ambassador had dwelt on various matters that might be dealt with, not simply on their merits, but with a view to securing to Britain the friendship of Germany. Salisbury declined to recognize that Germany had any claim that Britain should purchase her support by concessions, to which, except for the consideration of that support, she would be averse. As far as any 'general alliance with Germany' was concerned, he observed that 'there might be much to be said for it so long as it dealt with general European interests'. On the other hand, with regard to the maintenance of the Ottoman Empire, 'this country was not in a condition to enter upon any further engagements'. This dispatch, Bertie noted, was seen by, amongst others, Chamberlain.[42]

On 13 May the government suffered another by-election reverse, when the announcement of the result of the poll in South Norfolk showed that a majority of over eight hundred had been turned into a minority of over thirteen hundred.

On the evening of that day the Birmingham Liberal Unionist Association held its annual meeting in the Town Hall, where, as was customary on such occasions, it was addressed by its president. Chamberlain could hardly do otherwise than answer the government's critics, more especially Harcourt. In the event he told his hearers that they had to consider a 'national question', warning them that before long the government—any government—might 'have to appeal to the patriotism of the people as a whole', and expressing the hope that, if that time should come, it would not find the nation wasting in party recrimination the energies that it would need 'for the defence of our national interests'. He displayed marked cordiality towards the United States, then at war with Spain, envisaging a situation, in which 'the Stars and Stripes and the Union Jack should wave together over an Anglo-Saxon alliance'. On the other hand, he made a strikingly hostile reference to Russia, quoting a proverb concerning the need, when supping with the devil, for a 'long spoon'.[43]

Chamberlain acknowledged that in the past Britain's 'policy of strict isolation' had been the right one. It had enabled the country to avoid 'entangling alliances'. On the other hand, he explained, in words that recall Spenser Wilkinson's warning, in recent years a new situation had arisen:

All the powerful States of Europe have made alliances, and as long as we keep outside these alliances, as long as we are envied by all, and suspected by all, and as long as we have interests which at one time or another conflict with the interests of all, we are liable to be confronted at any moment with a combination of Great Powers so powerful that not even the most extreme, the most hotheaded politician would be able to contemplate it without a certain sense of uneasiness.[44]

On the subject of alliances Chamberlain appealed to history, which, he claimed, showed that, unless Britain was allied to some great military power, as she had been in the Crimean War, she could not seriously injure Russia, although it might also be true that Russia could not seriously injure Britain either. If the 'policy of isolation' were to be continued in the future, he foretold, the fate of the Chinese Empire would probably be decided without reference to Britain's wishes and in defiance of her interests. On the other hand, Chamberlain declared:

If . . . we are determined to enforce the policy of the open door . . . we must not allow jingoes to drive us into a quarrel with all the world at the same time, and we must not reject the idea of an alliance with those Powers whose interests most nearly approximate to our own.[45]

This strange compound of alarmism, ingratiation, insult and confession of weakness had a mixed reception. Prices fell on a number of stock-exchanges[46] and what the *Economist* termed Chamberlain's 'indiscretion'[47] received much of the blame.[48] Some Unionist press comment was favourable.[49] On the other hand, the Liberal *Westminster Gazette* remarked that the 'Birmingham policy' was 'in reality, our old friend, the policy of alliances, put forward in the manner most disadvantageous to this country'.[50] The *Speaker* disavowed knowledge of any foreign adventures that were likely to tempt the country to depart from its 'traditional policy'; it did know, on the other hand, that 'alliances can only be bought at a price, and that not a light one'.[51]

In the House of Commons Harcourt referred briefly to the 'Birmingham Foreign Policy',[52] but did not ask for a debate or even put a question concerning what John Morley described indignantly as 'one of the most flagitious speeches ever made by an English minister'.[53] He thought it important, Harcourt explained, to know to what extent Salisbury was 'at the back of Chamberlain'.[54] In the House of Lords Kimberley, having asked a question about Weihaiwei, went on to complain about the colonial secretary's 'remarkable utterance', arguing that a situation of the sort that would warrant entering into a defensive alliance with another great power had not yet arisen.[55] Salisbury did not, however, allow himself to be drawn.[56] Further controversy was then silenced for the time being by the last illness and, on 19 May 1898, the death of Gladstone. Soon afterwards Parliament rose for the Whitsun recess.

On 8 June John Morley, in a speech at Leeds, replied to Chamberlain, affirming his faith in reliance on 'our own resources' and 'not upon alliances'.[57]

Soon after Parliament had reassembled Dilke initiated a debate in the House of Commons by proposing a reduction in the foreign secretary's salary.[58] Having first criticized Salisbury's handling of events in Madagascar, the Far East and elsewhere, he turned to the subject of Chamberlain's speech, observing that it constituted 'an invitation to this country to consider a system of permanent or standing alliances with . . . Germany'. Dilke declared both his disbelief in the possibility of obtaining an alliance with Germany against Russia and his opposition to the 'policy of alliances' in general. 'I believe', he told the House, 'it is far better for us to keep the control of our policy free from any of these connections with other Powers in time of peace.'[59]

Other Liberals, who followed Dilke, spoke to similar effect. Asquith asked what the people of Britain had done 'that we are now to go touting for allies in the highways and byways of Europe'. 'I am altogether opposed', he declared, 'as I believe the vast majority of our people are, to abandoning the free hand in these matters which we have always enjoyed.'[60] Harcourt dismissed the value of 'permanent alliances' as 'practically nothing'. 'If the interests exist, you will have the support of those whose interests are similar to your own, with or without alliances', he argued, 'if the interests have changed, you will not secure them by alliances which have no longer any binding force.'[61]

Chamberlain replied to his critics,[62] but his speech did not impress the fastidious parliamentary under-secretary for foreign affairs. Two days later Curzon relieved his feelings in a letter to his chief:

Chamberlain after some slashing hits at Harcourt and the other side, came terribly to grief over the effort to explain and defend, at the same time that he extenuated and minimised the Birmingham speech.

We suffered agonies on the front bench, as he proceeded to explain seriatim how we were not strong enough—without any ally—to stand up against Russia in the Far East, to preserve the independence of China, to exercise a controlling influence there, or even to maintain the 'open door'!

Conceive what play the Russian man will make with this at the next meeting of the Yamen.

... Meanwhile in all our minds was the reflection Que diable allait-il faire dans ce [*sic*] galère? Why this lamentable dissertation on the high principles of policy, from one not primarily responsible for their execution?

Of course I breathe not a word of this outside. But to you I may confess that that half hour was one to me of unmitigated gloom.[63]

Although the Birmingham, or, as it is often called, the 'long spoon', speech created a stir at the time, its real impact on public opinion appears to have been limited. 'Despite Mr Chamberlain', wrote Lucien Wolf in the *Fortnightly Review*, 'the English people are no more desirious to-day of contracting what President Jefferson called "entangling alliances" than they were twenty years ago.'[64]

In any case, before the end of 1898 the widespread feeling of frustration engendered by Salisbury's alleged 'policy of peaceful concessions'[65] had become a thing of the past. No one could possibly claim that the government had made a peaceful concession either to the Dervishes or to France. 'Khartoum and Fashoda', Harcourt prophesied, 'will rally the popular sentiment as much as Trafalgar and Salamanca.'[66] 'Lord Salisbury', commented that loyal Gladstonian, Edward Hamilton, in singularly un-Gladstonian language, 'deserves the thanks of the nation for having secured "Peace with honour" over the Fashoda difficulty.'[67] 'It is', declared Wolf, ' ... at Fashoda that Lord Salisbury has really retrieved himself.'[68] A power that has gained 'a victory for which ... there is no precedent in the relations of the great powers'[69] clearly did not need to go, in Asquith's phrase, 'touting for allies'.

In connexion with the controversy over the so-called 'policy of alliances' the comments of a young army officer of the period deserve quotation. In 1898 Captain William Robertson, of the Third Dragoon Guards, was taking a course at the Staff College, Camberley. His professor, Major G. F. R. Henderson, the distinguished military historian, set him an essay on the subject: 'What changes in the strategical relations between

Russia and England have been produced by the advance and recent acquisitions of Russia in the Far East?' Robertson's essay, dated 8 December 1898, was a model of lucidity and neatness:

We could doubtless bring more pressure to bear on Russia if we were allied to some Power who had access to her western land frontier, for it is in the reaching of her vulnerable points that our greatest difficulty lies. Still, as long as she confines herself to Asia, we cannot calculate on assistance from any European Power, with the possible exception of Turkey. In short, the Nation ought to be prepared to defend its possessions by its own exertions and resources. If it be unable or unwilling to do this, and relies on extraneous assistance, its downfall is merely a matter of time.[70]

In the autumn of the following year Edward Hamilton noted in his diary that 'this country wants no alliances', adding, however, that it was 'just as well that it should be on good terms with the most powerful man in Europe'.[71] When Hamilton recorded these opinions he was staying at Sandringham, where the Emperor William II had just spent a few days after a visit to Windsor, during which both he and Bülow had had talks with, amongst others, the colonial secretary. The South African War was in its second month.

On 29 November 1899 the German Emperor and his suite left for home. On the following day Joseph Chamberlain delivered a speech at Leicester, in which he expounded the advantages of 'a new Triple Alliance between the Teutonic race and the two great branches of the Anglo-Saxon race'.[72] Although Chamberlain qualified his remarks by explaining that it mattered little whether what was established was an 'alliance', which was committed to paper, or an 'understanding', which existed 'in the minds of the statesmen of the respective countries',[73] his speech was badly received.[74] 'Did you ever', Kimberley asked Spencer, 'read anything so ill judged as Chamberlain's second speech at Leicester?' 'He ought not to be allowed to open his lips on foreign affairs', he added.[75] The wisdom of delivering a public speech at any time on the desirability of an alliance or understanding with other powers is not obvious. Chamberlain could hardly have chosen a worse moment for a speech on this subject.

This fiasco marked the end of Chamberlain's efforts to promote an alliance by means of public speeches. They had, at all events, served to demonstrate the strength of what Lansdowne called 'the suspicion with which any entanglement in foreign alliances was regarded by a large part of the British public'.[76]

CHAPTER XVIII

'A pretty sudden shock'

(i)

Salisbury's own attitude to the problems of the Far East was not simply one of *laisser aller*. On 25 January 1898 he proposed an 'understanding' to Russia on the basis of a 'partition of preponderance', not only in the Chinese, but also in the Turkish, Empire.[1] Early in the following year he accepted a Russian proposal for a *modus vivendi* in China.[2] This was embodied in an agreement, signed on 28 April 1899, under which Britain was to seek no railway concessions to the north of the Great Wall of China, and Russia none in the basin of the Yangtse.[3] Salisbury's aim, in concluding the agreement of 16 October 1900 with Germany, providing for the maintenance of freedom of trade for the nationals of all countries in the ports of China,[4] was, according to a leading authority, 'not an alignment against Russia but an arrangement to bring Germany under a certain measure of control'.[5] There was nothing in all this of any *casus belli*.

(ii)

The following year saw the last attempts to promote an alliance with Germany. In January Eckardstein visited Chatsworth, where he talked with both his host and with Chamberlain.[6] In March and April he had interviews with Lansdowne at the Foreign Office.[7] In May Hatzfeldt himself called at the Foreign Office and, according to Lansdowne, put forward a proposal that Britain 'should join the Triple Alliance'.[8] Sanderson, after a conversation with Lansdowne, then drew up two drafts of a convention of alliance with Germany.[9] Finally, on 29 May, Salisbury, in what is probably the most celebrated of all his state papers, attacked what he called 'a proposal for including

England within the bounds of the Triple Alliance'. Such a bargain, he argued, would be a bad one for this country. Further, he maintained, as he had so often done in the past, the government was not competent to give a promise of the kind suggested. 'I do not see how, in common honesty', he wrote, 'we could invite other nations to rely upon our aids in a struggle, which must be formidable and probably supreme, when we have no means whatever of knowing what may be the humour of our people in circumstances which cannot be foreseen.'[10]

(iii)

Less than nine months after Salisbury's retirement from the foreign secretaryship MacDonald, the British minister in Tokyo, had unofficial conversations in London with Hayashi, his opposite number.[11] On 31 July 1901 Lansdowne himself saw Hayashi, to whom he suggested a discussion with a view to, in his own words, 'the possible establishment of an understanding between our two countries'.[12] In September of the same year Selborne, the First Lord of the Admiralty, impressed on the cabinet the desirability, on naval grounds, of an alliance with Japan.[13] On 5 November Lansdowne submitted a project for an agreement with Japan to the cabinet, the large majority of the members of which, according to Salisbury, favoured his proposal.[14]

Salisbury[15] and Balfour[16] both composed long memoranda in opposition to Lansdowne's project. Hicks Beach considered that Britain would be getting a poor bargain. 'I do not myself think', he wrote to Lansdowne, 'that we gain enough from the treaty to outweigh the serious objections to it.'[17]

However, although there were differences among the members of the cabinet as to the wisdom of the course recommended by the foreign secretary, there was a wide measure of agreement that it would constitute, not only an important move in the Far East, but also the abandonment of a long-established principle. Balfour wrote that he had hitherto understood that 'a policy of alliances was contrary to the traditions of this country' and, further, that 'it was scarcely possible for a Ministry to engage that, in certain contingencies, the country should go to war, since war was impossible without the support of Parliament, and when the critical moment came, that support might be withheld'. 'We have offered, in favour of Japan, to abandon our traditional policy', Balfour added, 'and we have proved in our own persons that a Ministry can promise to go to war in remote contingencies and over quarrels at present unforeseen.'[18] Hicks Beach thought that what was proposed was 'really a new departure in our foreign policy'.[19] Indeed, Lansdowne himself acknowledged that it would be 'an entirely new departure'.[20]

When the conclusion of the agreement was announced the verdict of a large section of the press was that it marked the end of that freedom in its foreign relations that, under various names, the country had so long enjoyed, and of the policy of which that freedom was the product. 'All we can say at the moment is that our magnificent isolation has come to an end with a pretty sudden shock', commented the *Daily News*.[21] The *Saturday Review* remarked that the agreement represented 'a radical change in British ideas of the value of a "free hand" '.[22] The *Spectator* deplored the abandonment of 'our old policy of doing without alliances, and the splendid freedom of action which that policy secured to us'.[23] 'We have passed, at a stroke of the pen', commented a contributor to the *Fortnightly Review*, 'from splendid isolation to splendid complication.'[24]

On 13 February 1902 both Houses of Parliament debated the agreement. Unionists and Liberals, whatever their differences of opinion as to its merits, agreed that it marked a break with the past. It constituted, according to Henry Norman, who opened the debate in the House of Commons, 'a momentous departure from the time-honoured policy of this country'.[25] Percy, the parliamentary under-secretary for foreign affairs, acknowledged that the present was the first occasion on which Britain had 'contracted a Treaty Alliance with a great military and naval power'. 'If ever there was a Treaty which justified us in departing from our traditional policy', he declared, 'it is this Treaty.'[26]

The most nostalgic evocation of the past on this occasion came from the champion of the principle of 'a free hand for a free people'. According to Harcourt the agreement marked 'the departure from principles which have been consecrated by the traditions of nearly a century'.[27] 'We have maintained without these alliances now, for the greater part of the century, a great and potent influence in Europe', he told the House of Commons, 'and now we are going to abandon that policy and embark upon a future which no man can foresee.'[28]

The reaction of the press and of Parliament to Lansdowne's move in the Far East is understandable. The agreement with Japan was undoubtedly an important innovation. Although it was not as unprecedented as some contemporaries thought, it did embody the first pledge, entailing the *casus belli*, of which Parliament and the public had been informed, given by Britain to any power in any part of the world for more than twenty years. It embodied the first pledge, explicitly entailing the *casus belli* in circumstances that were not merely temporary, given by Britain to any great power for more than forty years. It embodied the first alliance, entailing the *casus belli*, ever concluded by Britain with a non-European power on a basis of co-equality. Whether it would also, as Rosebery prophesied,[29] lead to further commitments elsewhere was a question for the future to decide.

CHAPTER XIX

'Still in force'

(i)

Implicit, and sometimes explicit, in much that was said and written at the time of the conclusion of the agreement with Japan was the assumption that Britain had hitherto enjoyed complete freedom of action in her relations with other powers.[1] The claim that Britain was free from all commitments had been made more than once previously, notably by Goschen in 1896.[2] But it is doubtful whether this supposed freedom was ever so much talked about as when, in the opinion of many contemporaries, it had been sacrificed. Some of those who spoke or wrote in this way were probably thinking primarily in terms of freedom from any alliance with a great power. Nevertheless, through either ignorance or carelessness in their choice of words, some contemporaries used language that implied that Britain had not hitherto been bound by any pledge whatever entailing the *casus belli*. To do so was to overlook the not inconsiderable contents of the Foreign Office's treaty-safe.[3]

(ii)

In the last quarter of the nineteenth century the vicissitudes of the Ottoman Empire repeatedly raised the question of the obligation entailed by the Tripartite Treaty of 1856. In 1876 the fifteenth Earl of Derby acknowledged in the House of Lords that it was still in force.[4] However, in the following year the approach of the Russo-Turkish War was the occasion for his explanation that it did not bind Britain to the Porte, but only to Austria-Hungary and France, neither of which was likely to invoke it.[5] When, soon afterwards, war broke out, all three guarantors refrained from invoking the treaty.[6]

By the later 1870s the once established British policy of the maintenance of the independence and integrity of the Ottoman Empire, of which the Tripartite Treaty had been the expression, had, in fact, ceased to be a practical proposition. Salisbury had recognized this at the time of the agitation against the massacres in Bulgaria.[7] Soon after succeeding Derby at the Foreign Office he impressed the point on Layard.[8]

In 1896 Curzon acknowledged in the House of Commons that Britain was still bound by the 'Special', that is, the Tripartite, Treaty.[9] However, by the later 1890s the Ottoman Empire had largely forfeited what respect it had previously enjoyed in this country.[10] In 1897 Salisbury told the House of Lords that, in not accepting the Czar Nicholas I's celebrated overture nearly half a century earlier, 'we put all our money upon the wrong horse'.[11] In the same year Harcourt declared that no government that held itself bound to go to war under the Tripartite Treaty would continue to occupy the Treasury Bench for twenty-four hours. When, in response to a request made in the House of Commons on 15 July 1898 by a Scottish Liberal back-bencher, Thomas Hedderwick, for details of 'all Treaties and Conventions now existing and still obligatory as contain a specific engagement or guarantee entered into by the Government of this Country in relation to the Territory or Government of any other Power',[13] a new return was in February 1899 laid before Parliament,[14] it did not, unlike its two predecessors, contain the text of the Tripartite Treaty, his poor opinion of which Salisbury had long since made clear.[15]

On the other hand, the return did include certain articles of the Treaty of Paris, including the seventh, under which Britain, together with five other powers, undertook to respect the independence and integrity of the Ottoman Empire and guaranteed in common the observance of this engagement. However, on 8 February 1877 Derby had pointed out to the House of Lords that the treaty contained no promise to make the non-observance of this engagement a *casus belli*; so far as the Treaty of Paris was concerned, therefore, Britain was 'in no sense bound by a promise to fight for Turkey'.[16] In his dispatch to Loftus of 1 May 1877, denying Britain's approval of Russia's action against Turkey, Derby quoted article vii of the Treaty of Paris, but made no reference to the guarantee.[17]

There still remained Britain's interest, real or supposed, in ensuring that Constantinople and the Straits should not fall into the hands of Russia. In 1885 Currie reported having told Bismarck, while at Friedrichsruh, that ever since he had been at the Foreign Office, Constantinople had been regarded as one of two questions—Belgium being the other—about which Britain would fight, and that although she might not now be prepared, unsupported, to go to war with Russia, she would no doubt do so, if other powers were ready to join her.[18]

It was also possible to argue that Britain was under a moral obligation in regard to the Straits, not, indeed, to the Ottoman Empire, but to Austria-Hungary.

In September 1896 Salisbury recorded that the Czar Nicholas II, in the course of an important conversation at Balmoral, had advanced the view that the Straits should be under Russian control. Salisbury, in reply, had acknowledged that Britain's interest in the matter, which arose out of her presence in Malta and Egypt, was purely maritime and was less than that of some other powers; the theory that Turkish rule at Constantinople was a bulwark of Britain's Indian Empire could not be maintained. He had explained, however, that there was a more serious objection to Russian control of the Straits, namely the one that came from Austria-Hungary, who 'could not allow herself to be surrounded by Russia'. 'I expressed in strong language my sense of the importance to Europe of the existence of Austria', wrote Salisbury, 'and my feeling that after having pursued this policy by her side for so many years there would be something of "*bassesse*" in our conduct if we left her in the lurch.'[19]

The Foreign Office's new return also contained the text of the Constantinople convention of 1878. Indeed, Salisbury could scarcely have omitted this product of his own early diplomacy, which constituted Britain's title as occupying power in Cyprus. However, the convention had not only from the time of its publication been bitterly attacked by the Liberals and by the former Conservative foreign secretary; it had also soon come to be regarded by the Porte as a bad bargain.[20] In 1879 Harcourt had told Hartington that British influence in Constantinople was '*nil*' and that the convention was a 'dead letter'.[21] In the following year Hartington incorporated the latter opinion in his election address.[22] By the mid 1890s it had become apparent that the reforms in Turkey-in-Asia, which Salisbury had made a condition of Britain's pledge of military assistance, were not going to materialize. In 1896 Curzon informed the House of Commons that, since the Sultan had not performed his part of the bargain, the British obligation had lapsed.[23] There cannot have been many people in Britain at the end of the nineteenth century who believed that their country was solemnly pledged to go to war with Russia, should the latter invade Turkey-in-Asia.

The return contained much on which it would be pointless to linger. There was article xvii of the Treaty of Vienna. There was the Swiss act of guarantee, the continued validity of which had not in 1872 worried even Sir Wilfrid Lawson.[24] There were the various treaties and conventions relating to Greece, whose problems had by this time ceased to be the concern only of the three original 'protecting powers'. There was the convention of 1846 with China, relating to, amongst other matters, Chu Shan. There was the Stockholm treaty of 1855, which had clearly no relevance to a world in which France and Russia were allies, although it was still theoretically in force and was not formally abrogated until 1907–8,[25] after the dissolution of the kingdom of Sweden and Norway. As for the Luxemburg treaty of 1867, the collective guarantee in its second article could scarcely be said to have become any more stringent with the lapse of time.

The treaties with Portugal, on the other hand, were in an altogether different category. In 1873 Granville sent dispatches to both Madrid and Lisbon acknowledging Britain's treaty engagements.[26] Even the clash between Britain and Portugal in south-eastern Africa and the resulting pressure brought to bear by Salisbury on the Lisbon government in the years 1890–1 did not bring about the formal denunciation of the 'ancient treaties'.[27] Hammond, now in retirement, having expressed doubts to Currie, his successor at one remove, as to whether Britain's resort to what he called 'coercion' could be reconciled with her obligations as an ally,[28] Currie assured him that Britain's treaty obligations to Portugal had not in the past been regarded as debarring the government from taking measures to enforce redress of grievances. 'I hope you will consider that we acted according to diplomatic forms and precedents', wrote Currie, some two weeks after the steps ordered by Salisbury had brought about the fall of the Portuguese government.[29]

At all events, politicians in London showed their willingness to let bygones be bygones. When, in the later 1890s, Britain's relations with the Boers deteriorated, the fact that the South African Republic's only outlet to the sea, other than through British territory, was that through Lourenço Marques on the coast of Mozambique gave added significance to the 'ancient treaties'.[30] In 1897 Chamberlain, according to his own account, told Soveral that the British government was 'animated by the most friendly feelings to the Portuguese nation and Government'. 'We were influenced by the recollection of our traditional alliance', he added, 'by our commercial interests, and by our sense of the importance to us as a naval Power of good relations with a country whose geographical position made her a valuable ally.'[31] In the following year Salisbury informed the British minister in Lisbon that he had told Soveral that the British government recognized the validity of the treaties with Portugal, allowing for such alterations as the lapse of time and change of circumstances would involve. 'We took up the same position with regard to them', Salisbury explained, 'as that assumed by Lord Granville twenty-five years ago.'[32]

The agreement—it actually comprised two separate conventions and a note—with Germany concerning Mozambique, Angola and Portuguese Timor, concluded by Balfour on 30 August 1898,[33] was a transaction, the compatibility of which with Britain's treaty obligations to Portugal is not immediately apparent. Salisbury, who was on the continent at the time, wrote to Balfour to say that the 'German Convention' was 'quite satisfactory'. 'I only hope', he added, 'that it will not come into use for a long time.'[34]

In the following year as the Foreign Office included in its new return not only, as in 1859 and 1871, the texts of the 'ancient treaties', but also an extract from the dispatch, acknowledging the British obligation to Portugal, which Granville had sent to Madrid in 1873.[35] On the eve of the outbreak of war in South

Africa, a few months later, Salisbury, in order to ensure that the Boers should not be able to import munitions through Lourenço Marques, invoked Portugal's obligations under the treaty of 1642.[36] Any possible doubt as to whether the 'ancient treaties' were still in force and as to whether the British obligation applied to Portugal's overseas possessions was removed by the joint declaration of 14 October 1899.[37]

In the early twentieth century the argument that the alliance with Portugal corresponded with Britain's own interests was still plausible. Indeed, it had been strengthened by recent events in southern Africa. Thus, in January 1902 Lieutenant-Colonel (formerly Captain) Robertson, now head of the foreign section of the Intelligence Division of the War Office, drew up a memorandum on Britain's 'Military responsibilities with regard to Belgium, Holland, Norway, Sweden and Portugal',[38] which his superior officer, Lieutenant-General Sir William Nicholson, the Director of Military Intelligence, submitted on 5 March to Sanderson.[39]

Robertson was evidently unaware of the existence of the Salisbury-Soveral declaration, but he knew of the treaties of 1703 and 1815, which, he wrote, still, as far he knew, held good. He also stressed Britain's interests, based on strategic considerations. The *status quo* in Portugal should be maintained, since her ports, if allowed to fall into the hands of another first-class naval power, might be used for attacks on trade routes. It was also in Britain's interest that Portugal's colonies, especially Mozambique, should not fall into other hands.[40]

Sanderson did not inform the Intelligence Division of Salisbury's renewal, less than three years previously, of the 'ancient treaties'. However, he minuted that the treaties specified by Robertson were 'admitted by us to be virtually in force'.[41] Lansdowne, too, acknowledged that they were 'still in force' and that Britain would 'certainly have to assist Portugal'.[42]

There remained the five power treaty with Belgium of 19 April 1839, the continued binding force of which Granville's treaties of August 1870 with Prussia and France had explicitly acknowledged.[43]

On 5 August 1870 Lumley had reported to Granville from Brussels that Gramont objected to his proposed arrangement, on the ground that it would 'weaken and throw doubt on the value of the original Treaty'.[44] Subsequent events showed that this objection contained some truth. Less than two years later Sir Wilfrid Lawson told the House of Commons that the treaties of 1870 constituted a proof that that of 1839 was 'unsatisfactory'.[45]

Nevertheless, it was undeniable that Britain was still bound by Palmerston's treaty, although the precise nature of the obligation that it entailed was far from clear. In 1874 Derby reported having told Münster that 'the maintenance of the territorial integrity and independence of Belgium was a principle to which successive Administrations in this Country had again and again pledged themselves'. The national honour was 'bound up with the observance of these promises'.[46]

In the later 1880s a new danger seemed to threaten Belgium. Once again, there was fear of a war between France and Germany. In an anonymous article, published in the *Fortnightly Review* in January 1887, Dilke pointed out that the fortifications on both sides of the Franco-German frontier were now so strong that, should there be another war between the two powers, each belligerent would find it difficult to invade the other's territory directly. On the other hand, Belgium's frontiers were poorly fortified and her army was small. In the event of a conflict, a German invasion of France through Belgium was, he considered, highly probable. Was it quite certain, he asked, that in such a contingency any of the other powers would think of coming to Belgium's assistance? Would they not excuse themselves on the ground that the treaty of 1839 was not in the most modern form, and that in 1870 special, temporary treaties had been thought necessary? Even the fact that Britain was bound by treaty to defend Belgium would hardly, Dilke suggested, be a sufficient argument to induce Parliament to contemplate single-handed intervention.[47]

On 4 February 1887 there appeared in the *Standard*, a morning newspaper, with which Salisbury had and was known to have a connexion, a letter, signed 'Diplomaticus', that is, Alfred Austin. Diplomaticus, too, stressed the possibility, in the event of a Franco-German war, of a German invasion of France through Belgium. He recalled the fact that Belgium's neutrality was 'protected by European guarantee' and that

Britain was 'one of the guarantors'. However, he maintained, Britain could not take France's side against Germany, even were the latter to attempt to turn the French flank by an advance through the Belgian Ardennes, without damaging her own interests all over the world. To the question whether Britain must not honour her signature he replied that her foreign minister ought to be equal to the task of meeting this obligation, without committing the country to war. 'The temporary use of a right of way', he added, 'is something different from a permanent and wrongful possession of territory.' In its leading article of the day the *Standard* commented favourably on this contribution by a correspondent who spoke 'with high authority'.[48]

The argument advanced by Diplomaticus went far beyond that put forward, however incautiously, by Dilke, who subsequently expressed his abhorrence of the doctrine enunciated in the *Standard*'s correspondence column.[49] Nevertheless, on the evening of 4 February the *Pall Mall Gazette* went even further, publishing under the head-line, 'There is no guarantee', an article asserting, needless to say, erroneously, that the five-power guarantee of 1839 had been given only to the Netherlands, and not to Belgium.[50] Even the *Morning Post* of the following day suggested only that, if either France or Germany were to march an army across Belgium, Britain should 'protest'.[51]

On 7 January 1887 Vivian, the minister in Brussels, wrote a dispatch to Iddlesleigh, describing the impact on the Belgian press of the *Fortnightly Review* article, the author of which he correctly identified.[52]

After Salisbury's return to the Foreign Office Vivian sent him a succession of dispatches, reporting conversations with the Prince de Chimay, the Belgian foreign minister, and with Beernaert, the president of the council of ministers, on the subject of Britain's probable action in the event of a threat to their country's neutrality, but without eliciting a reply.[53] On 1 February he wrote privately to Salisbury, stressing the anxiety felt in Brussels on the subject of the danger to which Belgium would be exposed in the event of a war between France and Germany, which was 'believed to be inevitable'. 'In the absence of instructions', Vivian added, 'I have not felt myself authorized to give the Belgian Government the assurance for which they are evidently anxious, that they may rely on our support in case of need.'[54]

After the publication in the *Standard* of Diplomaticus's letter Vivian sent Salisbury another dispatch, reporting that he had advised de Chimay not to attach any importance to a newspaper article, as it was a mistake to suppose that the *Standard*, or any other paper, was the official, or even the inspired, organ of the British government.[55] To this dispatch Salisbury replied briefly, approving the minister's language.[56] Eventually, on 26 February, Vivian wrote, telling Salisbury that he understood from his silence that the British government considered it inopportune or inexpedient to express any opinion concerning the guarantee of the neutrality of Belgium or to commit itself in any way as to its future policy.[57]

Salisbury's reticence on this occasion is easily intelligible. To have authorized Vivian to give de Chimay or Beernaert an assurance of British armed assistance, in anticipation of a contingency of the kind envisaged by Dilke and by Diplomaticus, would have been to impair the British government's freedom to decide its own course of action, if the need should arise. It would be rash to interpret his attitude as implying that in his eyes the guarantee, contained in the treaty of 19 April 1839, had ceased to be binding.

That the treaty was still in force was, of course, merely confirmed by its inclusion in the Foreign Office's new return. Moreover, since Belgium was a party the King of the Belgians was entitled to invoke the treaty, just as in 1832 Leopold I had invoked that of 1831.[58]

On the other hand, there remained the question, raised by Clarendon in 1867, of how far the treaty bound Britain to act in the event of one or more of her co-guarantors being unwilling to do so.[59] In 1892 Loftus coupled the Belgian guarantee with that relating to Switzerland. He considered that in each case Britain's obligation was dependent on the fulfilment of their obligations by the other guarantors.[60] The views of Sanderson on this point, although expressed six years after the publication of the return, are also of interest. In 1905 he explicitly stated, in his letter to Sir George Clarke, that the 'guarantee of the Belgian State and its neutrality' was 'collective'. This did not mean that he endorsed the 'Derby doctrine', which he, in fact, repudiated. However, although he considered that a 'collective guarantee of all the Great Powers' was 'sufficient as a rule for protection against risk of attack by minor Powers', he acknowledged that 'the main danger' lay in 'the possible defection of one or more of the Guarantors'.[61]

Quite apart from any question of treaty obligation, however, the view continued to prevail that the independence of Belgium was a matter in which Britain had a vital interest. In 1874 Derby, in a letter to Odo Russell, gave, as one reason why Britain ought to look to Germany as the power with which she had most in common, the fact that 'Germany does not threaten Belgium'.[62] Indeed, no British government that took seriously its responsibility for the maintenance of national security could afford to remain indifferent to any threat by a great power— more especially a great naval power—to either of the two small kingdoms that made up the geographical region known as the Low Countries. 'From the point of view of British interests it is manifestly desirable to maintain the status quo in both Belgium and Holland', wrote Robertson in 1902. The future Chief of the Imperial General Staff stressed in particular the strategic importance to Britain of the latter country. 'The coast line between the Texel and the Scheldt offers splendid facilities for the establishment of naval works', he pointed out, 'and it has always been our aim to prevent this formidable maritime position from falling into the hands of a Power capable of using it against us.'[63]

Although there was sometimes talk of the possibility of a German attack on the Netherlands, the danger to Belgium was more apparent. The proviso made by Clarendon in 1852, that Britain could not be expected to defend Belgium single-handed, still, of course, held good. In 1885 Currie reported to Salisbury, after his visit to Friedrichsruh, that, in reply to a question by Bismarck, as to whether Britain would fight in the event of an attack on Belgium, he had replied that, no doubt, she would— 'if she had an ally'.[64] On the other hand, if the outbreak of a war between France and Germany were to result in the violation by either side of the neutrality of Belgium—or of that of both Belgium and the Netherlands—the requisite ally would automatically be forthcoming.

Moreover, should such a conflict occur, other great continental powers would, in all probability, also be involved, in which case the theatre of war would not be confined to Belgium. Lansdowne appreciated this point. 'The belligerents', he minuted in 1902, apropos of Robertson's memorandum, 'will hit one another wherever they can do so with the best prospect of success and the best means of helping a weak ally will not be found in sending small expeditions to assist him in defending his own territory, but in waging war upon his assailants wherever we can find a weak point in their armour.'[65]

There was one further consideration that might be expected to play at least some part in deciding the course to be adopted by the government of the day in the event of an invasion of either Belgium or the Netherlands by a great power. An attack on a small country, situated close to Britain's own coast and enjoying a constitutional form of government, could be expected to raise the sort of moral issue, to which Gladstone had appealed in his correspondence with Bright in August 1870. Concern for a moral issue can, no doubt, be dismissed as sentimental, but it would be rash to assume that such concern never in any circumstances influences any member of a cabinet that has to make a choice between peace and war.

On the other hand, as far as Belgium was concerned, an issue of this kind might have exercised only a limited influence in the years when Leopold II's business activities were attracting so much adverse publicity. In 1887 Dilke was of the opinion that the 'Congo business' had robbed Belgium of some sympathy.[66]

In any case, whatever argument was employed in favour of intervention in the event of an invasion of either Belgium or the Netherlands, its plausibility was bound to depend, to some extent, on whether the victim resisted the attack.

(iii)

A survey of Britain's commitments at the beginning of the twentieth century would be incomplete without reference to certain transactions, of which the return of 1899 made no mention.

Lepel Griffin's letter to Abdul Rahman had been laid before Parliament at the time. Not being either a treaty or a convention it did not, strictly speaking, fall within the terms of reference given by Hedderwick to the Foreign Office.

Nor had the agreements of 1887 with Italy and Austria-Hungary been embodied in formal treaties or conventions. Their omission could also be justified on the grounds that they had not entailed the *casus belli* and were no longer in force—at least, not indubitably.

The omission of the Bangkok convention of 1897 is less easy to justify.

The conventions of 30 August 1898 with Germany were signed some six weeks after Hedderwick made his request in the House of Commons. In any case, whatever their possible implications, they did not stipulate any *casus belli*.

It so happened that it was only a few weeks after this return had been laid before Parliament that Salisbury gave his undertaking to Spain in regard to the Bay of Algeciras. His reaffirmation of the 'ancient treaties' with Portugal followed later in the same year. On neither of these two occasions did the government lay the relevant papers before Parliament. Indeed, it would be interesting to know whether Salisbury consulted even the cabinet concerning some of the transactions of his fourth foreign secretaryship. It is, at least, not certain that the prime minister, who was also the foreign secretary, invariably took the entire cabinet into his confidence. In fact, the popular belief that Britain enjoyed complete freedom of action in her foreign relations was probably to some extent the result of lack of information.

(iv)

Some reference should also be made to certain regions where Britain had an interest in the maintenance of the existing situation, even though that interest was not expressed in a formal alliance or in a guarantee of independence, neutrality or territorial integrity. The case of the Netherlands has already been mentioned. Britain's presence in India gave her an interest in ensuring that Persia should not be annexed or dominated by Russia.[67] Her presence in Gibraltar gave her an interest in ensuring that the coast of Morocco, including the Spanish town of Ceuta, should not pass into the hands of France.[68] It would be easy to name other areas, where for similar reasons, Britain was concerned to ensure the continuance of the existing state of affairs.

The balance of power, as defined by Palmerston,[69] was another vital interest. The principle that, at least in western Europe, no one power should gain such preponderance, as to endanger the security of the remainder, was one to which any British government was virtually bound to subscribe.

(v)

To resume. At the beginning of the twentieth century Britain was bound by her recently reaffirmed treaties with Portugal; was a party to a number of 'formal' guarantees, including that of the independence and neutrality of Belgium; had, together with France, a treaty obligation, which was still theoretically valid, to Sweden; was under a secret and minor obligation to Spain; had commitments of varying stringency in Asia. Most, although not all, of these obligations corresponded with her interests, real or supposed, and related to areas, the geographical situation lent itself to the use of sea-power.

On the other hand, Britain had no commitment that was really comparable with the Austro-German, the Triple or the Franco-Russian alliance. She enjoyed far more liberty of action in Europe than did any of the great continental powers.

CHAPTER XX

'Semi-detached policy'

(i)

It is evident that many of the generalizations cited in the first chapter of this book do not bear scrutiny so far as the early and middle years of the nineteenth century are concerned. Equally, it is a fact that at the beginning of the twentieth century it was more than forty years since Britain had last given another great power an unequivocal pledge entailing the *casus belli*, otherwise than in circumstances that were merely temporary. In Europe Britain enjoyed a comparatively free hand. The question is, therefore, whether this state of affairs should be regarded as the result of a 'traditional policy', of adherence to a principle, or even of a constitutional impediment. Or should we look for some other explanation?

(ii)

There was, of course, no statement of the British attitude towards alliances and other involvements comparable, so far as popular fame was concerned, with Washington's Farewell, or Jefferson's First Inaugural, Address. On the other hand, there can be no doubt of the existence of what J. L. Hammond called 'the traditional British distrust of foreign commitments'.[1] This distrust found expression in Cobden's principle of 'non-intervention' in the affairs of the continent, the corollary of which was the avoidance of any pledge that would render such intervention a duty. Some Liberals continued for many years to uphold this principle. Indeed, for a time it was often said that the government was about to adopt, or even that it had adopted, the principle of 'non-intervention'—a view to which Stanley's speeches lent plausibility. However, it would be rash to accept at their face-value contemporary assertions that the conduct of foreign affairs by any British government—even that of 1866—was based on the principles of the Manchester School.

(iii)

The comparisons sometimes made at the time between the British and the American attitudes towards foreign commitments were clearly misplaced. Britain's geographical situation and her imperial interests, real or supposed, rendered difficult, if not impossible, the detachment from European involvements that at this period was still feasible for the United States. Mountague Bernard saw this in 1865. Britain, he pointed out, was separated from 'the traditional friendships and enmities and the restless politics of Europe' not by 'three thousand miles of sea', but merely by 'a little strait'.[2] Twenty years later the fifteenth Earl of Derby spoke at Blackburn to similar effect. 'We are not', he declared, 'in the happy position of the United States, who can afford to have no foreign policy. We cannot absolutely seclude ourselves from the affairs of Europe.'[3]

Salisbury's argument that, because of the popular and parliamentary nature of the constitution, no British government could enter into an engagement entailing an obligation to go to war in a contingency that might arise in the future, although, no doubt, very useful as a time-saving device, admitted in practice of some striking exceptions. More plausible was his view that there was no certainty that, should the *casus foederis* arise, a 'democratic Parliament' would allow the government of the day to honour the pledge. Even so, the unpredictability, of which Salisbury made so much, was not peculiar to Parliament. In any case, Parliament in the Salisbury era was a good deal less democratic than the pronouncements of many contemporaries would lead one to suppose.

Salisbury did not lack other arguments of a general nature to justify the negative attitude that he so often adopted towards approaches from other powers. Quite apart from any constitutional difficulty, real or imaginary, or any general principle, however, he appears to have held quite simply, that it was not in Britain's interest to become involved in a formal alliance, in the sense of a long-term pledge entailing the *casus belli*, with any member of the *Triplice*, let alone with all three. As to entering into such a relationship with either France or Russia, or with both of them, it is doubtful whether he often had occasion to consider the possibility. The Liberal leaders' view of Britain's interests in these matters was clearly similar to Salisbury's.

On the other hand, Salisbury appears to have felt in no way inhibited, if he considered such a step necessary, from giving a pledge of armed support to a small or weak power, provided that its geographical situation lent itself to the use of sea-power. In his later years he preferred to keep such pledges secret. Whether a Liberal government would have been willing to enter into the commitments to Siam and Spain, undertaken by Salisbury during his fourth foreign secretaryship, must remain a matter for speculation.

As for those 'formal' guarantees, about which Queen Victoria wrote to Russell in 1861, the contrast between the record of the Palmerstonian era and that of the later nineteenth century is certainly striking. In the light of the numerous, although abortive, projects of the 1880s and 1890s, the objection to pledges of this type cannot be said to have been universal. Nevertheless, the governments of the later nineteenth century do appear to have been less ready to give 'formal' guarantees than some of their predecessors. The fact that the guarantee of 1867 proved to be the last given by any British government in the nineteenth century in connexion with the territory or institutions of a foreign country and under an article of a treaty convention or act was not merely fortuitous.

(iv)

Quite apart from the alleged constitutional impediment so often invoked by Salisbury, there were also certain strategic factors in operation in the later nineteenth century that would have rendered it difficult and probably impossible for any British government, even if it had so desired, to enter into an alliance with a great European power, comparable with, for example, the *Triplice*.

The ability of a power to honour its obligations under such an alliance depended on its possession of a large army that could be rapidly mobilized. By the end of the eighth decade of the nineteenth century every great continental power had adopted a system of conscription.

By continental standards Britain had only a minute army on her own territory. In 1870, for example, Cardwell informed Gladstone that the army 'at home' numbered 83,695; it was 'in view of Continental Armies an extremely small one'; in fact, it was 'a Garrison for these two islands'.[4] From Paris Lyons warned Granville that a declaration by the British government that it would send an expeditionary force to Belgium 'would be only laughed at', unless it also 'prepared armaments on a continental scale'[5]—an operation that would take time. In 1887 Dilke pointed out that Britain, 'being unable to rapidly mobilise large forces, could do nothing in the first months of a Continental conflict'.[6] The corollary of this state of affairs must have been apparent to any well informed observer.[7] A long-term pledge to a great continental power, entailing an obligation, if the *casus foederis* should arise, to dispatch a large army to the continent immediately after the declaration of war, was not within the range of practical politics.

In particular, the alliance with Germany, envisaged by Chamberlain, was not feasible. It was, in Dilke's words, a 'will-of-the-wisp'.[8] Chamberlain's suggestion was clearly unacceptable to the German government. Bülow could not be expected, by committing Germany to the joint defence of matters of common interest in the Far East, to expose his country to invasion by Russia, especially in view of the fact that the latter was allied with France. There was no answer to the German Emperor's question, as reported by Lascelles: 'Where should I be then and how could you help me[?]'[9]

Little more than a year after this question was put Britain found herself at war in South Africa. The events of 1899–1902 did nothing to increase Britain's eligibility as an ally, so far as the great powers of Europe were concerned.

(v)

Can anything be said to be left of the explanations of Britain's international position given by numerous contemporaries and endorsed by a large body of distinguished historians? Should one perhaps accept the verdict of the French observer, Francis de Pressensé, of *Le Temps*, who in 1896 wrote sarcastically of this country's 'semi-detached policy'?[10] At all events, it may be of interest to enquire whether it is possible to formulate the British attitude during the period under review towards 'foreign commitments' in positive terms.

(vi)

Successive British governments considered that this country had an interest in ensuring the maintenance of the independence of Portugal. Towards the end of the nineteenth century the government also had reasons for wishing to ensure that Mozambique should not fall into the hands of another great power. The 'ancient treaties', which Castlereagh renewed and the obligations entailed by which Canning, Palmerston, Granville and Salisbury all acknowledged, were the expression of this interest. Strategically Britain was in a good position both to defend her interests and to honour her obligation.

The alliance with Portugal did not, of course, rest on a basis of co-equality. Moreover, the British government's conduct during Salisbury's second administration and in 1898 was difficult to reconcile with the obligations stipulated in the 'ancient treaties'. Nevertheless, the declaration of 14 October 1899 left, at least so far as the Foreign Office was concerned, no ground for questioning their continued validity.

In the past, when Britain had made war on the continent of Europe against a great power, she had usually collaborated with one or more other great powers. She did so in the wars against revolutionary France and against Napoleon. During the Crimean War she did so again. Indeed, Britain could scarcely hope to be able to conduct a successful continental war single-handed against a great power, except, perhaps, in a remote area that was both easily accessible by sea and relatively inaccessible by land.

When there was a possibility of having to take part in a continental war that was likely to break out in the near future, or had broken out already, the government of the day could be expected to enter, or, at least, to propose entering, into whatever engagements it considered necessary in the circumstances, as Russell's approaches to France at the time of the Schleswig-Holstein crisis illustrate. The treaties concluded by Granville with Prussia and France in August 1870 arose out of the fear of a peace settlement, at which Belgium would be sacrificed. Their wisdom was questioned at the time by some professional diplomats.

On two occasions in the course of the nineteenth century Britain participated, as a member of a victorious war-time coalition, in a peace settlement, imposed on a vanquished great power. On each occasion the government of the day gave certain pledges, intended to ensure the durability of the settlement.

The principal pledges given by Castlereagh with this object in view after the defeat of Napoleon were those embodied in the three treaties of 20 November 1815 with, respectively, Austria, Prussia and Russia. These treaties, although they proved ultimately to be dead letters, were initially intended to entail serious obligations.

The Stockholm treaty of 21 November 1855, although signed more than four months before the end of the Crimean War, was, as Palmerston explained at the time, designed to achieve part of the main purpose of the war, namely the containment of Russia. It remained in force, theoretically at least, after the conclusion of peace. As for the Tripartite Treaty of 15 April 1856, it was specifically framed to ensure respect for the Treaty of Paris. On the other hand, after the Crimean War Britain was at peace, as far as the rest of Europe was concerned, for over half a century. The question of a new pledge, intended to ensure the durability of a peace settlement that had been imposed on a defeated power did not, therefore, arise.

On a number of occasions the government of the day entered into an agreement with one or more other great powers, providing for the use of armed force, but only for the limited and more or less clearly defined purpose of dealing with a situation that already existed, without formal declaration of war, and not against a great power. A well known example of such an engagement was that embodied in the London treaty of 6 July

1827 with France and Russia, intended to bring about a settlement of the conflict between the Turks and the Greeks. Another
was the convention of 15 July 1840, directed against Mehemet Ali.

Successive foreign secretaries, notably Palmerston, drew a
sharp distinction between such limited engagements, designed
to deal with immediate problems, and those that, being
'prospective', were open to objection.

Britain also had an interest in ensuring that Gibraltar should
not be subject to any threat from neighbouring Spanish territory
and that the territory in question should not come under the
control of a potentially hostile great power. A promise to assist
Spain in preventing the latter contingency from occurring did
not commit Britain to do more than she would have done in
any case, even if bound by no pledge at all. Moreover, to
provide armed assistance for the defence of the coast of the Bay
of Algeciras posed no insoluble strategic problem. Such a
pledge had, however, for obvious reasons, to be kept secret.
Salisbury appreciated that no Spanish government that was
known to have given the undertaking conceded by Silvela in
1899 would have survived for long.

It had for many years been the practice of British governments to give guarantees in connexion with a variety of matters.
In committing Britain in 1815 to guarantees of Prussia's possession of her acquisitions from Saxony, of the integrity and
inviolability of the territory of Switzerland, and of the neutrality
of northern Savoy, Castlereagh was, therefore, acting in accordance with established practice. Even Canning was willing to
guarantee a settlement of the conflict between Brazil and
Buenos Aires and to participate in a quintuple guarantee of the
eventual Greek settlement. Palmerston joined with the other
great powers in guaranteeing the execution of the first twenty-
four articles of the Belgian treaty of 15 November 1831. Thereafter successive British governments continued to participate in
guarantees, given in conjunction with two or more other great
powers and relating to the territory or internal institutions of
various foreign countries, down to the time of the third Derby
administration. However, in 1867 Stanley did not wish to
involve Britain in a guarantee of the neutrality of Luxemburg
and only consented to do so under pressure.

Not all the guarantees of the mid-nineteenth century were the result of peaceful collaboration between the great powers. The Treaty of Paris of 1856, with its four guarantee articles, was, in Sanderson's words, 'accepted by Russia as the result of defeat'.[11] The Tripartite Treaty, with its additional guarantee of the independence and integrity of the Ottoman Empire, was obviously directed against Russia.

Although Britain did not once in this period give a 'sole' guarantee in connexion with the territory or institutions of a foreign country, on a number of occasions ministers showed their willingness to give such a pledge.

Britain also entered, either through the Foreign Office or through the government of India, into a number of engagements with the rulers of various territories in Asia.

Successive British governments were especially concerned at the threat posed by Russia's expansion across Asia. The Constantinople convention of 1878 was designed to frustrate any possible future Russian design against Turkey-in-Asia. The Treaty of Gandamak of 1879 and Lepel Griffin's less formal pledge of the following year were both intended to prevent Russian penetration into Afghanistan, or, at least, into that part of the country that the British government cons dered strategically vital from the point of view of the defence of India.

That Britain did not in the era of 'Beaconsfieldism' enter into an alliance with a great power to check Russia's expansion in Asia was, presumably, chiefly owing to the fact that there was no other great power with territory in those parts of Asia into which Russia was expanding. The Ottoman Empire in Asia might, indeed, with luck be turned into a major power. In 1878 Layard wrote to Lytton that 'we may still do something with Turkey as an Asiatic Power, check Russia, and secure a powerful and useful ally in Asia'.[12] In the event, this hope proved to be vain.

However, in the last decade of the nineteenth century a different situation arose. The principal field of Russia's expansion was now the Far East. This was the very area that saw in the 1890s the emergence of a new great power. It was not long before observers in Britain came to regard Japan as a potential ally against Russia.

In India Britain had a considerable army with a long tradition of active service, outside as well as in the sub-continent,
and with almost inexhaustible reserves.[13] British land forces
could be moved to a potential theatre of war in the Far East as
quickly as, or quicker than, those of most other European
powers. The navy could be expected to play a decisive role in
any campaign fought in a region that was accessible by sea.
Thus, the factors that limited Britain's eligibility as an ally in
Europe did not apply to the Far East. Whether the Unionist
government was wise to enter into an alliance with Japan is
another matter. Twelve years later Lord St Aldwyn—as Hicks
Beach had now become—recorded his opinion that, if Salisbury
had still been foreign secretary at this period, the alliance would
not have been concluded.[14]

(vii)

It is seldom wise for any government, whatever the constitutional basis on which it rests, to commit itself to pursuing an
arduous, expensive and possibly sanguinary course of action in
a hypothetical contingency that may arise in the distant future
and, therefore, in circumstances, the nature of which it cannot
possibly foresee. If an attack is made on what a power regards
as a matter of vital interest to itself, it will in all probability
defend that interest, whether or not it is bound by treaty to do
so. If, on the other hand, the object attacked is not a matter of
vital interest to itself, no power is likely to consider itself bound
by any treaty, however strongly worded, to resort to force of
arms in its defence. One does not have to be a professional
diplomatist to appreciate these points, which contemporaries
made more than once in the course of the nineteenth century.
    Nevertheless, wisely or unwisely, successive British govern-
ments, influenced by a variety of considerations, entered into
'prospective engagements' with a number of powers, both great
and small, that unequivocally entailed the *casus belli*. These
engagements related to parts of both Europe and Asia. They
also gave certain other pledges, that, although not unequivocally entailing the *casus belli*, could be understood as so doing.
In so far as these pledges corresponded with what were looked

on as vital British interests and in so far as it was strategically possible to implement them, they were liable to be considered, in the event of an emergency, as binding the country to go to war. Even though Britain in the later nineteenth century under-took no new 'formal' guarantee, relating to the territory or institutions of a foreign country, the binding force of at least some of those given in earlier periods was not open to question.

The fact that at no time in the later nineteenth century did Britain enter into an engagement comparable with the Austro-German, the Triple or the Franco-Russian alliance calls for no elaborate explanation. There was really no need to do so. Whether the abstention of both Conservative and Liberal governments from involvement in any such European alliance should be regarded as a 'policy' depends largely on how one understands that elastic and hard-worked term.[15] In so far as Britain had such a 'policy', it was clearly not brought to an end by the 'new departure' of 30 January 1902.

NOTES

'Freedom from all entanglements'

1 Hansard, 3, ccxxiv, col. 1099, 31 May 1875.
2 *The Writings of George Washington* (ed. J. C. Fitzpatrick), xxxv, p. 234.
3 *The Writings of Thomas Jefferson* (ed. P. L. Ford), viii, p. 4.
4 *F.B.F.P.*, p. 517.
5 Lord Strang, *Britain in World Affairs* (London, 1961), p. 218.
6 *E.H.R.*, lxvii (1952), p. 356.
7 K. Bourne, *The Foreign Policy of Victorian England 1830–1902* (Oxford, 1970), p. 179.
8 *T.R.H.S.*, 4, xxv (1943), p. 125.
9 A. J. Grant and H. Temperley, *Europe in the Nineteenth Century* (London, 1927), p. 422.
10 *History*, liv (1969), p. 392.
11 R. Albrecht-Carrié, *Diplomatic History of Europe since the Congress of Vienna* (London, 1958), p. 232.
12 F. S. Northedge and M. J. Grieve, *A Hundred Years of International Relations* (London, 1971), p. 80.
13 S. B. Fay, *The Origins of the World War* (New York, 1948), i, p. 124. There are many other examples of this view.
14 Cf. most of the works cited above.
15 *T.R.H.S.*, 4, xxv (1943), p. 125.
16 *T.R.H.S.*, 4, xxix (1947), p. 63.
17 M. Baumont and others, *L'Europe de 1900 à 1914* (Paris, 1966), p. 21; Grant and Temperley, op. cit., p. 422; *F.B.F.P.*, p. 521.
18 Northedge and Grieve, op. cit., p. 80. There have been many other expressions of this view.
19 F. Gosses, *The Management of British Foreign Policy before the First World War* (Leyden, 1948), p. 98.
20 See below, ch. II.
21 See below, chs. XVII, XVIII and XIX.
22 See C. Howard, *Splendid Isolation* (London, 1967), ch. II. This phrase had, of course, other meanings besides the one mentioned here.
23 Lord Augustus Loftus, *Diplomatic Reminiscences 1837–1862* (London, 1892), i, p. 272.
24 *Globe* (Toronto), 16 Jan. 1896.
25 Howard, op. cit., ch. III.
26 *Speaker*, 15 Feb. 1902.
27 See below, chs. III and XIV.
28 Hansard, 4, lviii, col. 1432, 10 June 1898.
29 See below, ch. XVII.
30 Chamberlain, memorandum, 29 March 1898, Garvin, *Joseph Chamberlain*, iii, p. 260.
31 Hansard, 4, lvii, col. 1512, 17 May 1898.

32 *Quarterly Review*, cxcvi (1902), p. 664.
33 Speech at Birmingham, 13 May 1898, *Times*, 14 May 1898.
34 Hansard, 4, cii, col. 1301, 13 Feb. 1902.
35 See below, chs. xvii and xviii.
36 See below, ch. xviii.
37 See below, ch. xvi.
38 See below, chs. iv, viii, xii and xix.
39 See below, chs. ii and xiv.

II 'Prospective engagements'

1 Felix Gilbert, *To the Farewell Address* (Princeton, N.J., 1961), ch. ii.
2 *Parliamentary History of England*, xv, col. 653, 10 Dec. 1755, quoted Gilbert, op. cit., p. 27.
3 Jeremy Bentham, 'Plan for an Universal and Perpetual Peace', Essay IV of 'Principles of International Law', *Works*, ed. J. Bowring (London, 1843), ii, p. 549.
4 See below, ch. ix.
5 Hansard, 3, clxxxiv, col. 736, 9 July 1866.
6 See below, chs. v, vii, xiii, xv, xvi and xvii.
7 Hansard, 3, cccxiii, col. 38, 31 March 1887.
8 Hansard, 3, cvii, col. 808, 21 July 1849.
9 Speech at Ebbw Vale, 5 Oct. 1896, *Times*, 6 Oct. 1896.
10 Lascelles to Lansdowne, 25 Aug. 1901, *B.D.*, ii, no. 90.
11 Canning to Ward, 14 Oct. 1825, *B.I.L.A.*, i, no. 259.
12 Palmerston to 1st Earl Granville, 7 Jan. 1834, Granville Papers, P.R.O. 30/29/415.
13 Palmerston to Clanricarde, 11 Jan. 1841, *F.B.F.P.*, no. 33.
14 Russell to Queen Victoria, 7 Sept. 1859, *L.Q.V.*, i, iii, p. 472.
15 Gladstone to Rosebery, 12 July 1891, Rosebery Papers, Box 19.
16 Palmerston to 1st Earl Granville, 7 Jan. 1834, Granville Papers, P.R.O. 30/29/415.
17 Russell to Queen Victoria, 29 Dec. 1851, *L.Q.V.*, i, ii, p. 427.
18 Mountague Bernard, *Four Lectures on Subjects connected with Diplomacy* (London, 1868), pp. 92–4. Bernard delivered the lecture here quoted in 1865.
19 Hansard, 4, lviii, cols. 1338–9, 10 June 1898.
20 Monson to Salisbury, 8 Sept. 1898, *B.D.*, i, no. 187.
21 *Selections from Speeches of Earl Russell 1817 to 1841 and from Despatches 1859 to 1865* (London, 1870), ii, p. 240.
22 Gladstone, speech at West Calder, 2 April 1880, *P.S.S.*, 2, p. 352.
23 *M.E.T.*, iii, nos. 427–8.
24 See below, ch. xi.
25 *M.E.T.*, i, no. 136.
26 Protocol of 12 July 1827, with annexed instruction, Stratford Canning Papers, F.O. 352/19, pt. 1 (1).
27 Palmerston to Lamb, 15 Nov. 1827, Melbourne Papers, R.A. Box 11/1.
28 *M.E.T.*, ii, no. 162.
29 *M.E.T.*, ii, no. 171.
30 *M.E.T.*, ii, no. 173.
31 *M.E.T.*, ii, no. 190.
32 For the Concert see W. N. Medlicott, *Bismarck, Gladstone and the Concert of*

Europe (London, 1956), pp. 1, 17; C. Holbraad, *The Concert of Europe* (London, 1970).
33 Speech at Guildhall, 9 Nov. 1896, *Times*, 10 Nov. 1896.
34 Speech at West Calder, 27 Nov. 1879, *P.S.S.*, i, p. 115.
35 Granville to Lyons, 1 May 1880, F.O. 27/2421, no. 447.
36 Speech at Guildhall, 9 Nov. 1895, *Times*, 11 Nov. 1895.
37 Cecil, *Salisbury*, i, p. 306.
38 Russell to Paget, 9 March 1864, F.O. 22/311, no. 59.
39 *A.P.*, 1864, lxv, no. 1140, p. 172.
40 Hansard, 3, clxxvi, col. 1170, 8 July 1864.
41 Hansard, 3, clxxii, col. 1246, 23 July 1863.
42 Ibid., col. 1252.
43 *M.E.T.*, ii, no. 230.
44 Palmerston to Russell, 5 April 1860, Russell Papers, P.R.O. 30/22/21.
45 Manderström to Wachtmeister, 19 July 1863 (copy), R.A. I. 90/23. See also W. E. Mosse, *The European Powers and the German Question 1848–1871* (Cambridge, 1958), p. 152, to which I owe the reference.
46 Hansard, 3, clxxii, col. 1252, 23 July 1863.
47 Hansard, 3, clxxvi, col. 815, 4 July 1864.
48 *B.D.*, viii, no. 1.
49 Salisbury to Queen Victoria, 5 Feb. 1887, *L.Q.V.*, 3, i, p. 271.
50 Salisbury to Queen Victoria, 10 Feb. 1887, *L.Q.V.*, 3, i, p. 272.
51 Salisbury to Paget, 9 Feb. 1887, Paget Papers, B.M. 51,229.
52 Salisbury to Malet, 15 Feb. 1887, Malet Papers, F.O. 343/2.
53 Salisbury, memorandum, 23 Feb. 1887, R.A. H. 34/42.
54 *B.D.*, viii, no. 2.
55 Sanderson, memorandum, 22 Jan. 1903, *B.D.*, viii, no. 2.
56 Cecil, *Salisbury*, ii, pp. 264–72.
57 *M.E.T.*, iv, no. 524.
58 Sandon, cabinet journal, 23 May 1878, Ryder Papers, 407.
59 Speech at Southwark, 20 July 1878, *Times*, 22 July 1878. On 18 July 1878 Derby had employed the same adjective in connexion with the convention. (Hansard, 3, ccxli, col. 1804.) Gladstone kept a note of the relevant passage from Derby's speech. (Gladstone Papers, B.M. 44, 141.)
60 *B.F.S.P.*, lxx, p. 49.
61 Lytton to Cranbrook, 22 May 1879, Cranbrook Papers, H.A. 43. T. 501/32.
62 Griffin to Sirdar Abdul Rahman, 14 June 1880, *A.P.*, 1881, lxx, p. 85.
63 *B.F.S.P.*, lxxiv, p. 367.
64 L. Mallet, Memorandum respecting Siam, 9 Jan. 1902, F.O. 69/236.
65 *B.D.*, i, no. 91.
66 Balfour, memorandum, 5 Sept. 1898, Salisbury Papers, A/96.
67 *D.E.W.H.*, i, p. 352.
68 Labouchere to Chamberlain, 15 Dec. 1883, Joseph Chamberlain Papers, J.C. 5/50/16.
69 *M.E.T.*, iii, p. 2057.
70 See below, chs. VIII and XIX.
71 *M.E.T.*, i, no. 44.
72 Wellington, *Supplementary Despatches, Correspondence and Memoranda*, xii, p. 836.
73 Ibid., p. 835.
74 Palmerston to Grey, 'Monday evening' (probably 22 Feb. 1831), Grey of Howick Papers, 44/34.
75 William IV to Palmerston, no date, c. 1831–3, Palmerston Papers, RC/A/10

76 J. Duhamel, *Louis-Philippe et la première entente cordiale* (Paris, 1951), p. 115.
77 Hammond, 'Memorandum of the state of Foreign Relations at the close of the
   year 1858', 1 Jan. 1859, Papers of the 14th Earl of Derby, 144/2.
78 *B.D.*, viii, nos. 1 and 2.
79 Granville to Buchanan, 16 Jan. 1872, F.O. 7/796, no. 13.
80 Aberdeen to Bagot, 3 Sept. 1830, Bagot Papers.
81 Aberdeen to Bagot, 15 Oct. 1830, Bagot Papers.
82 See below, ch. VII.
83 See below, chs. III, VI and VII.
84 See below, ch. XIV.

III 'A dangerous game to play'

1 See above, ch. I.
2 Canning to à Court, 18 Sept. 1823, F.O. 185/91, no. 54. The greater part of
   this dispatch is printed in Harold Temperley, *The Foreign Policy of Canning
   1822–1827* (London, 1966), p. 539.
3 *Times*, 13 April 1872.
4 Russell, circular dispatch, 19 April 1861, F.O. 65/571, no. 46; copy in R.A.
   I. 36/13.
5 Napier to Russell, 4 May 1861, F.O. 181/387, no. 96; copy in R.A. I. 36/13.
6 Confidential print, 14 May 1861, R.A. I. 36/13.
7 Queen Victoria to Russell, 20 May 1861 (draft in the Prince Consort's hand-
   writing), R.A. I. 36/33, printed, *L.Q.V.*, 1, iii, p. 561.
8 See below, ch. VI.
9 D. B. Horn, *Great Britain and Europe in the Eighteenth Century* (Oxford, 1967),
   p. 123.
10 *M.E.T.*, i, no. 27.
11 *M.E.T.*, i, no. 43.
12 *M.E.T.*, ii, no. 153.
13 *M.E.T.*, ii, nos. 183–5.
14 *M.E.T.*, ii, no. 159.
15 *M.E.T.*, ii, no. 255.
16 *M.E.T.*, ii, no. 264.
17 *M.E.T.*, ii, no. 270. For French text see *B.F.S.P.*, xlvi, p. 25.
18 *M.E.T.*, ii, no. 286.
19 *M.E.T.*, ii, no. 347.
20 *M.E.T.*, iii, no. 405.
21 Hansard, 3, cciv, col. 1361, 6 March 1871.
22 Speech at Edinburgh, 17 March 1880, *P.S.S.*, 2, p. 31.

IV 'An undertaking to defend'

1 See above, ch. III.
2 Palmerston to Cowley, 2 Feb. 1859, Cowley Papers, F.O. 519/292.
3 Russell to Fane, 14 Sept. 1859, F.O. 7/564, no. 74.
4 Napier to Russell, 4 May 1861, F.O. 181/387, no. 96.
5 J. Headlam-Morley, *Studies in Diplomatic History* (London, 1930), p. 121.
6 M. R. D. Foot, 'Great Britain and Luxemburg 1867', *E.H.R.*, lxvii (1952),
   p. 371.

7　E. V. Gulick, *Europe's Classical Balance of Power* (Ithaca, N.Y., 1955), p. 281.
8　R. C. K. Ensor, *England 1870–1914* (Oxford, 1936), p. 491.
9　E. von Vattel, *Le droit des gens* (repr. Washington, D.C., 1916), i, p. 445.
10　G. F. von Martens, *Précis du droit des gens moderne de l'Europe* (Göttingen, 2nd ed. 1801), p. 496.
11　Bernard, op. cit., p. 199.
12　Canning to à Court, 18 Sept. 1823, F.O. 185/91, no. 54. For the events that occasioned this dispatch see Temperley, op. cit., p. 93.
13　Napier to Russell, 4 May 1861, F.O. 181/387, no. 96; copy in R.A. I. 36/13.
14　Queen Victoria to Russell, 27 May 1861, R.A. I. 36/33.
15　See below, ch. v.
16　For Russell's plan see his circular dispatch of 19 April 1861, F.O. 65/571, no. 46. For Gorchakov's objection see Napier to Russell, 4 May 1861, F.O. 181/387, no. 96. For Queen Victoria's objection see her letter to Russell, 27 May 1861 R.A. I. 36/33.
17　*Times*, 13 April 1872.
18　Hansard, 3, ccxli, col. 1796, 18 July 1878.
19　See below, ch. xii.
20　See below ch. xiv.
21　See below, ch. x.

v　'In this instance'

1　Speech at Eighty Club, 13 April 1897, *Times*, 14 April 1897.
2　See above, ch. iv.
3　Yandiola to à Court, 23 Aug. 1823, Heytesbury Papers, B.M. 41,544.
4　À Court to Yandiola, 27 and 31 Aug. 1823, *B.F.S.P.*, x, pp. 992–4.
5　Angoulême to à Court, 28 Aug. 1823; Eliot to à Court, 30 Aug. 1823, Heytesbury Papers, B.M. 41,544.
6　À Court to Canning, 31 Aug. 1823, Canning Papers, 118.
7　Canning to à Court, 18 Sept. 1823, F.O. 185/91, no. 54.
8　Canning to à Court, 3 Oct. 1823, F.O. 185/92, no. 58.
9　Canning to Ponsonby, 18 March 1826, *B.I.L.A.*, i, no. 45.
10　*B.I.L.A.*, i, pp. 68-70.
11　Canning to Wellington, 10 Feb. 1826, *D.C.M.*, iii, p. 93.
12　*M.E.T.*, i, no. 129; *B.F.S.P.*, xiv, p. 632.
13　Canning to Liverpool, 22 Dec. 1826 (copy), Canning Papers, 72.
14　Liverpool to Canning, 22 Dec. 1826, Canning Papers, 72.
15　Dudley to Stratford Canning, 14 July 1827, Stratford Canning Papers, F.O. 352/19, pt. 1 (1).
16　*M.E.T.*, i, no. 136.
17　Aberdeen to Bagot, 20 Nov. 1829, Bagot Papers.
18　*M.E.T.*, ii, no. 149.
19　Wellington, memorandum, 17 Feb. 1830, *D.C.M.*, vi, p. 518.
20　See above, ch. ii.
21　Dudley to 1st Earl Granville, 31 Aug. 1827, Granville Papers, P.R.O. 30/29/ 14/4.
22　Stratford Canning to Codrington, 1 Sept. 1827, S. Lane-Poole, *Life of Stratford Canning* (London, 1888), i, p. 449.
23　Palmerston to Lamb, 15 Nov. 1827, Melbourne Papers, R.A. Box 11/1.
24　Hansard, 2, xviii, col. 3, 29 Jan. 1828.

25 Canning to à Court, 3 Oct. 1823, F.O. 185/92, no. 58.
26 Canning to à Court, 31 March 1824, *B.I.L.A.*, ii, no. 555.
27 Canning to à Court, 2 April 1824, *B.I.L.A.*, ii, no. 556.
28 Canning to à Court, 3 April 1824, F.O. 185/95, no. 15.
29 À Court to Canning, 3 May 1824, *B.I.L.A.*, ii, no. 557.
30 Canning to à Court, 2 April 1824, *B.I.L.A.*, ii, no. 556; Canning to Bagot, 29 May 1824, Bagot Papers.
31 Canning to Bagot, 29 May 1824, Bagot Papers.
32 Canning to 1st Earl Granville, 21 June 1825, Granville Papers, P.R.O. 30/29/8/8.

VI 'The strongest and most refined guarantees'

1 E.g., in his letter to William Temple, 18 Jan. 1828, Palmerston Papers, GC/TE/194. There are many other examples.
2 *B.F.S.P.*, xviii, p. 760.
3 Palmerston to Grey, 'Thursday evening', Grey of Howick Papers, 45/23. 20 Jan. 1831 was a Thursday.
4 *M.E.T.*, ii, no. 153.
5 Hansard, 3, ix, col. 847, 26 Jan. 1832.
6 *M.E.T.*, ii, no. 159.
7 Palmerston to Clanricarde, 12 March 1841 (copy), Palmerston Papers, GC/CL/88.
8 *M.E.T.*, ii, no. 193.
9 Palmerston to Russell, 26 June 1849, Russell Papers, P.R.O. 30/22/7F.
10 *M.E.T.*, ii, no. 222.
11 Palmerston to Westmorland, 10 May 1850 (copy), Palmerston Papers, GC/WE/197.
12 *M.E.T.*, ii, no. 230.
13 See above, ch. III.
14 Palmerston to Clarendon, 22 July 1855, Clarendon Papers, C. 31.
15 Palmerston to Clarendon, 13 Dec. 1855, Clarendon Papers, C. 31.
16 Palmerston to Cowley, 13 Aug. 1863, Cowley Papers, 519/292.
17 Earl Russell, *The Foreign Policy of England 1570–1870* (London, 1871), p. 81.
18 Hansard, 3, ccx, col. 1178, 12 April 1872.
19 Hansard, 3, ccxxxii, cols. 475–6, 16 Feb. 1877.
20 Hansard, 3, ccxl, col. 1409, 13 June 1878.
21 Gladstone to Granville, 19 Oct. 1882, *G.G. 1876–86*, i, no. 871.
22 Hansard, 3, ix, col. 1274, 3 Feb. 1832.
23 Palmerston to Westmorland, 10 March 1848, F.O. 64/282, no. 44.
24 Ibid. See also Palmerston to Westmorland, 14 March 1848, F.O. 64/282, no. 50.
25 Van Zuylen van Nijevelt to van Hall, 9 Nov. 1854, Algemeen Rijksarchief, The Hague, Buitenlandse Zaken, inv. nr. 2773, exh. 23 Nov. 1854, nr. 172. See also *F.B.F.P.*, no. 36, to which I owe this reference.
26 Memorandum, 6 March 1848, enclosed with van Zuylen van Nijevelt's dispatch of 9 Nov. 1854, ibid. French as in the original.
27 Palmerston to Russell, 26 June 1849, Russell Papers, P.R.O. 30/22/7F.
28 Palmerston to Clarendon, 24 July 1855, Clarendon Papers, C. 31.
29 *M.E.T.*, ii, no. 262.
30 *M.E.T.*, ii, no. 153. For Palmerston's handling of the Belgian question see

Charles Webster, *The Foreign Policy of Palmerston 1830–1841* (London, 1951), i, pp. 104, 514; Jasper Ridley, *Lord Palmerston* (London, 1970), p. 122.

31 Matuszewic to Nesselrode, 3/15 Nov. 1830, F. Martens, *Receuil des traités et conventions conclus par la Russie avec les puissances étrangères*, xi, p. 442.

32 *B.F.S.P.*, xix, p. 258.

33 Palmerston to Bagot, 16 Nov. 1831, Bagot Papers.

34 King Leopold I to Palmerston, 11 March 1832, Palmerston Papers, RC/M/58.

35 Palmerston to Bagot, 13 March 1832, Bagot Papers.

36 Palmerston to Heytesbury, 15 March 1832, Heytesbury Papers, B.M. 41,563.

37 Palmerston to Heytesbury, 1 June 1832, Heytesbury Papers, B.M. 41,563.

38 Ibid.

39 Palmerston to Grey, 5 June 1832, Grey of Howick Papers, 45/237.

40 Palmerston to Matuszewic, 6 June 1832 (copy), Palmerston Papers, GC/MA/320. There is a French version of this document in *Lettres et papiers du Chancelier Comte de Nesselrode* (Paris, 1908), vii, p. 222. It appears, however, to be a translation of Palmerston's letter, not a French original.

41 King Leopold I to Palmerston, 17 July 1832, Palmerston Papers, RC/M/69.

42 Palmerston, memorandum for King William IV, 1 Oct. 1832 (copy), Grey of Howick Papers, 45/300.

43 Palmerston to Grey, 2 Oct. 1832, Grey of Howick Papers, 45/302.

44 Palmerston to Grey, 14 Oct. 1832, Grey of Howick Papers, 45/316.

45 Palmerston, memorandum for King William IV, 1 Oct. 1832 (copy), Grey of Howick Papers, 45/300.

46 *M.E.T.*, ii, no. 162.

47 Aberdeen to Peel, 25 Jan. 1833, Peel Papers, B.M. 40,312.

48 *M.E.T.*, ii, nos. 183–5.

49 Hansard, 3, x, col. 278, 13 Feb. 1832; col. 480, 17 Feb. 1832.

50 Hansard, 3, lii, col. 454, 21 Feb. 1840; col. 1081, 9 March 1840.

51 Palmerston to Melbourne, 8 June 1838, R.A., Z. 501/39.

52 Palmerston to Matuszewic, 6 June 1832 (copy), Palmerston Papers, GC/MA/320.

53 Ibid.

54 Grey to Palmerston, 20 Dec. 1830, Palmerston Papers, GC/GR/1943.

55 Grey to Princess Lieven, 30 Jan. 1831, *Correspondence of Princess Lieven and Earl Grey*, ed. G. le Strange (London, 1890), ii, p. 150.

56 Palmerston to 1st Earl Granville, 26 Dec. 1831, Granville Papers, P.R.O 30/29/404.

57 Palmerston to Clarendon, 13 June 1859, Clarendon Papers, C. 524.

58 *B.F.S.P.*, xix, p. 35.

59 Headlam-Morley, op. cit., p. 132.

60 Palmerston to Beauvale, 10 May 1841, *F.B.F.P.*, no. 32.

61 For the convention of 7 May 1832 see also Douglas Dakin, *The Unification of Greece 1770–1923* (London, 1972), p. 64.

62 Protocol of 21 April 1855, *B.F.S.P.*, xlv, p. 99.

63 Protocol of 26 April 1855, *B.F.S.P.*, xlv, p. 111.

64 *M.E.T.*, ii, no. 264.

65 For the origins of this treaty see W. E. Mosse, *The Rise and Fall of the Crimean System 1855–71* (London, 1963), ch. II. I am indebted to Professor Mosse's book for a number of references.

66 See below, ch. VII.

67 Russell to Clarendon, 23 April 1855, Clarendon Papers, C. 30.

68 Buol and Bourqueney, joint memorandum, 14 Nov. 1855 (copy), R.A. G. 40/8

69 Clarendon to Cowley, 19 Nov. 1855, F.O. 27/1059, no. 1338.
70 Clarendon to Palmerston, 24 March 1856, Palmerston Papers, GC/CL/838.
71 Clarendon to Palmerston, 31 March 1856, Palmerston Papers, GC/CL/847.
72 Palmerston to Clarendon, 1 April 1856, Clarendon Papers, C. 49.
73 Palmerston to Clarendon, 2 April 1856, Clarendon Papers, C. 49.
74 Clarendon to Palmerston, 12 April 1856, Palmerston Papers, GC/CL/862.
75 *M.E.T.*, ii, no. 270.
76 Palmerston to Clarendon, 2 April 1856, Clarendon Papers, C. 49.
77 Clarendon to Delane, 27 April 1856, Delane Papers, 7/43.
78 Stratford de Redcliffe to Clarendon, 24 April 1856, Clarendon Papers, C. 61.
79 Clarendon to Palmerston, 31 March 1856, Palmerston Papers, GC/CL/847.

VII 'Inkshed'

1 Palmerston to 1st Earl Granville, 7 Jan. 1834, Granville Papers, P.R.O. 30/29/415.
2 Hansard, 3, xcvii, col. 122, 1 March 1848.
3 Palmerston to Grey, 24 Nov. 1833, Grey of Howick Papers, 45/469.
4 Grey to Palmerston, 5 Dec. 1833, Palmerston Papers, GC/GR/2279.
5 Grey to Palmerston, 13 Dec. 1833, Palmerston Papers, GC/GR/2282.
6 Palmerston to Grey, 14 Dec. 1833, Grey of Howick Papers, 45/474.
7 *M.E.T.*, ii, no. 171.
8 Palmerston to 1st Earl Granville, 11 April 1834, Granville Papers, P.R.O. 30/29/415.
9 Palmerston to William Temple, 21 April 1834, Palmerston Papers, GC/TE/219.
10 Palmerston to Grey, 25 April 1834, Grey of Howick Papers, 45/498.
11 Palmerston to 1st Earl Granville, 8 Dec. 1835, Granville Papers, P.R.O. 30/29/421.
12 Palmerston to 1st Earl Granville, 9 Feb. 1836, Granville Papers, P.R.O. 30/29/421.
13 Palmerston to Melbourne, with enclosures, 7 and 14 Jan. 1836, Melbourne Papers, R.A. Box 11/31–34.
14 Palmerston to Melbourne, 14 Jan. 1836, Melbourne Papers, R.A. Box 11/33.
15 Palmerston to 1st Earl Granville, 9 Feb. 1836, Granville Papers, P.R.O. 30/29/421.
16 Palmerston to 1st Earl Granville, 8 March 1836, Granville Papers, P.R.O. 30/29/421.
17 For an account of this negotiation see *B.D.*, viii, no. 81.
18 Palmerston, minute, 3 June 1855, *B.D.*, viii, no. 81.
19 Clarendon to Palmerston, 3 June 1855, Palmerston Papers, GC/CL/647.
20 Clarendon to Palmerston, 19 July 1855, Palmerston Papers, GC/CL/670.
21 Palmerston to Clarendon, 22 July 1855, Clarendon Papers, C. 31.
22 Palmerston to Clarendon, 24 July 1855, Clarendon Papers, C. 31.
23 Palmerston to Clarendon, 26 July 1855, Clarendon Papers, C. 31.
24 Argyll to Clarendon, 13 Aug. 1855, Clarendon Papers, C. 29.
25 Palmerston to Clarendon, 25 Sept. 1855, Clarendon Papers, C. 50.
26 Ibid.
27 Ibid.
28 *M.E.T.*, ii, no. 262.
29 Palmerston to Clarendon, 17 Dec. 1855, Clarendon Papers, C. 31.
30 Palmerston to Clarendon, 29 May 1856, Clarendon Papers, C. 49.

31 Palmerston to Clarendon, 2 April 1856, Clarendon Papers, C. 49.
32 Hansard, 3, cxlii, col. 127, 6 May 1856.
33 Hansard, 3, cxlii, col. 135, 6 May 1856.
34 Nassau Senior, *Historical and Philosophical Essays* (London, 1865), i, p. 90.
35 Palmerston to 1st Earl Granville, 5 May 1834, Granville Papers, P.R.O. 30/29/415.
36 Palmerston to Clarendon, 2 May 1856, Clarendon Papers, C. 49.
37 As recorded by Chichester Fortescue, diary, 14 July 1860, Carlingford Papers, H. 358/4.

VIII 'Still obligatory'

1 Hansard, 3, clii, col. 42, 3 Feb. 1859.
2 *A.P.*, 1859 (2), xxxii, p. 593. For the provenance of this 'blue-book' see Lillian M. Penson, 'Obligations by Treaty: Their Place in British Foreign Policy, 1898–1914', in *Studies in Diplomatic History and Historiography in honour of G. P. Gooch*, ed. A. O. Sarkissian (London, 1961), p. 77.
3 For the attitudes of Castlereagh and Canning and for the events of 1826 see Temperley, op. cit., pp. 193–8 and 365–89.
4 Palmerston to 1st Earl Granville, 10 June 1831, 10 and 11 April 1834, Granville Papers, P.R.O. 30/29/14/6 and 30/29/415.
5 Granville to Howden, 7 Feb. 1852 (copy), Granville Papers, P.R.O. 30/29/20.
6 Wellington, 'Observations on the King of France's Speech', July 1831, *D.C.M.*, vii, p. 477.
7 Palmerston to King William IV, 25 June 1832 (draft), Palmerston Papers, RC/AA/34.
8 Canning to Bagot, 24 July 1824, Bagot Papers; Granville to Howden, 7 Feb. 1852 (copy), Granville Papers, P.R.O. 30/29/20. In 1840 the point was raised in the House of Commons. See Hansard, 3, lii, col. 464, 21 Feb. 1840.
9 Aberdeen to Morier, 11 Feb. 1845, F.O. 100/43, no. 1.
10 J. B. Conacher, *The Aberdeen Coalition 1852–1855* (Cambridge, 1968), p. 420.
11 Clarendon to Reeve, 14 Feb. 1852, Clarendon Papers, C. 534.
12 *M.E.T.*, ii, no. 205.
13 For an account of these events see Dr R. J. Bullen's forthcoming book, *Palmerston, Guizot and the Collapse of the Entente Cordiale.*

IX 'Non-intervention'

1 Greville, *Memoirs* (London, 1938), vi, p. 443.
2 Hansard, 3, clxxvi, col. 813, 4 July 1864.
3 Cobden to Richard, 14 July 1864, Cobden Papers, B.M. 43,659.
4 Cobden, *England, Ireland and America* (London, 1835), p. 42.
5 Speech at Manchester, 25 Oct. 1862, Cobden, *Speeches* (London, 1870), ii p. 302.
6 Speech at King's Lynn, 19 Oct. 1864, *Times*, 20 Oct. 1864.
7 Cobden to Chevalier, 5 Nov. 1864, Morley, *Cobden*, ii, p. 450.
8 Cobden to Richard, 10 Nov. 1864, Cobden Papers, B.M. 43,659.
9 *Spectator*, 30 June 1866.
10 Queen Victoria to Derby, 30 June 1866, *L.Q.V.*, 2, i, p. 353.
11 Derby to Queen Victoria, 1 July 1866, *L.Q.V.*, 2, i, p. 353.

12 Speech at King's Lynn, 11 July 1866, *Times*, 12 July 1866.
13 For the Luxemburg crisis see M. R. D. Foot, 'Great Britain and Luxemburg 1867', *E.H.R.*, lxvii (1952), p. 352; R. Millman, *British Foreign Policy and the Coming of the Franco-Prussian War* (Oxford, 1965), chs. III–V.
14 Stanley to Cowley, 16 April 1867, Cowley Papers, F.O. 519/182.
15 Stanley to Derby, 17 April 1867, Papers of the 14th Earl of Derby, 161/3.
16 Loftus to Buchanan, 19 April 1867, Buchanan Papers.
17 Stanley to Clarendon, 23 April 1867, Clarendon Papers, C. 525.
18 Stanley to Bloomfield, 23 April 1867, Bloomfield Papers, F.O. 356/33.
19 Buchanan to Stanley, 23 April 1867, F.O. 65/724, no. 139.
20 *M.E.T.*, iii, no. 405.
21 Stanley to Grey, 27 April 1867, *L.Q.V.*, 2, i, p. 423.
22 Stanley to Cowley, 28 April 1867, F.O. 27/1652, no. 192.
23 Hammond to Cowley, 6 May 1867, Cowley Papers, F.O. 519/193.
24 Stanley to Cowley, 3 May 1867, F.O. 27/1653, no. 223.
25 Stanley to Cowley, 3 May 1867, F.O. 27/1653, no. 226.
26 Stanley to Loftus, 4 May 1867, F.O. 64/615, no. 148.
27 King William I to Queen Victoria, 27 April 1867, R.A. I. 71/167; Bismarck to Bernstorff, 3 May 1867, *A.P.P.*, viii, no. 570.
28 Loftus to Stanley, 4 May 1867, F.O. 64/620, no. 272.
29 Loftus to Stanley, 5 May 1867, F.O. 64/620, no. 276.
30 Buchanan to Stanley, 4 May 1867, F.O. 65/725, no. 158.
31 La Tour d'Auvergne to Moustier, 5 May 1867, enclosure, *O.D.*, xvi, no. 4976.
32 La Tour d'Auvergne to Moustier, 6 May 1867, *O.D.*, xvi, no. 4987.
33 La Tour d'Auvergne to Moustier, 6 May 1867, *O.D.*, xvi, no. 4987; Bernstorff to Bismarck, 7 May 1867, *A.P.P.*, viii, no. 592.
34 Hammond to Cowley, 6 May 1867, Cowley Papers, F.O. 519/193.
35 Queen Victoria to Stanley, 5 May 1867 (copy), R.A. I. 71/248.
36 Grey to Stanley, 5 May 1867 (copy), R.A. I. 71/252.
37 Grey to Disraeli, 5 May 1867, Disraeli Papers, Box 85.
38 Bernstorff to Bismarck, 6 May 1867, *A.P.P.*, viii, no. 588.
39 Derby to Stanley, 5 May 1867, Papers of the 15th Earl of Derby, 920, DER 12/3/7.
40 Disraeli to Queen Victoria, 6 May 1867, *L.Q.V.*, 2, i, p. 424.
41 Hammond to Stanley, 6 May 1867, Papers of the 15th Earl of Derby, 920, DER 12/1/14.
42 Ibid.
43 Ibid.
44 Bernstorff to Bismarck, 7 May 1867, *A.P.P.*, viii, no. 593.
45 Stanley to Cowley, 7 May 1867, Cowley Papers, F.O. 519/182. Stanley did not explicitly state in this letter that he was writing before the actual meeting of the conference. That he did so is, however, made clear by Hammond's letter to Cowley, 7 May 1867, Cowley Papers, F.O. 519/193, and by Stanley's own letter to Cowley, 8 May 1867, Cowley Papers, F.O. 519/182.
46 Stanley to Grey, 7 May 1867, R.A. I. 71/261. For the time at which this letter was written, see the previous note.
47 *B.F.S.P.*, lx, p. 497. Italy had expressed a desire to be represented at the conference. See Stanley to Derby, undated, Papers of the 14th Earl of Derby, 161/3. Copy, dated 29 April 1867, in papers of the 15th Earl, 920, DER, 13/2/3.
48 Stanley to Cowley, 8 May 1867, Cowley Papers, F.O. 519/182.
49 Hammond to Cowley, 7 May 1867, Cowley Papers, F.O. 519/193.

50 Bernstorff to Bismarck, 7 May 1867, *A.P.P.*, viii, no. 595.
51 Loftus to Stanley, 7 May 1867, F.O. 64/620, no. 278.
52 'Yesterday a Cabinet', records the entry for 9 May 1867 in Gathorne Hardy's diary, Cranbrook Papers, H.A. 43, T. 501/294.
53 Stanley to Cowley, 8 May 1867, Cowley Papers, F.O. 519/182.
54 Stanley to Loftus, 8 May 1867 (copy), Papers of the 15th Earl of Derby, 920, DER, 13/1/14.
55 *B.F.S.P.*, lx, p. 503.
56 Hammond to Stanley, 9 May 1867, Papers of the 15th Earl of Derby, 920, DER, 12/1/14.
57 Hansard, 3, clxxxvii, cols. 259–60, 9 May 1867.
58 Hammond to Cowley, 9 May 1867, Cowley Papers, F.O. 519/193.
59 Stanley to Grey, 10 May 1867, R.A. B. 23/60.
60 Loftus to Stanley, 10 May 1867, F.O. 64/620, no. 286.
61 Hansard, 3, clxxxvii, cols. 378 and 397, 13 May 1867.
62 Stanley to Bloomfield, 14 May 1867, Bloomfield Papers, F.O. 356/33.
63 Bernstorff to King William I, 15 May 1867, *A.P.P.*, ix, no. 10.
64 Hansard, 3, clxxxvii, col. 1910, 14 June 1867.
65 Ibid., col. 1915.
66 Ibid., cols. 1918–19.
67 Hansard, 3, clxxxviii, cols. 150–7, 20 June 1867.
68 Clarendon to Cowley, 18 May 1867, Cowley Papers, F.O. 519/181.
69 Hansard, 3, clxxxviii, col. 154, 20 June 1867.
70 Bismarck to Bernstorff, 26 April 1867, *A.P.P.*, viii, no. 532.
71 King William I to Queen Victoria, 27 April 1867, R.A. I. 71/167.
72 Van de Weyer to Grey, 4 May 1867, R.A. I. 71/240.
73 Hammond to Stanley, 21 June 1867, Papers of the 15th Earl of Derby, 920, DER, 12/1/14.
74 Hammond to Cowley, 22 June 1867, Cowley Papers, F.O. 519/193.

x   'Moonshine'

1 See above, ch. VI.
2 *M.E.T.*, ii, no. 253.
3 *M.E.T.*, ii, no. 264.
4 *M.E.T.*, ii, no. 270.
5 *M.E.T.*, ii, no. 286.
6 La Tour d'Auvergne to Moustier, 6 May 1867, *O.D.*, xvi, no. 4987.
7 Bernstorff to Bismarck, 6 May 1867, *A.P.P.*, viii, no. 588.
8 Hammond to Stanley, 21 June 1867, Papers of the 15th Earl of Derby, 920, DER, 12/1/14.
9 Ibid.
10 Hammond to Cowley, 22 June 1867, Cowley Papers, F.O. 519/193.
11 *Times*, 11 June 1867.
12 Hansard, 3, clxxxvii, col. 260, 9 May 1867.
13 Hansard, 3, clxxxvii, cols. 1922–3, 14 June 1867.
14 Hansard, 3, clxxxviii, col. 151, 20 June 1867.
15 Ibid., col. 157.
16 Ibid., cols. 147–57.
17 Ibid., col. 154.
18 Ibid., col. 156.

19 Loftus to Stanley, 22 June 1867, F.O. 64/621, no. 363.
20 *Neue preussische Zeitung*, 21 June 1867, enclosed with Loftus to Stanley, 22 June 1867, F.O. 64/621, no. 361.
21 *Norddeutsche allgemeine Zeitung*, 27 June 1867, enclosed with Loftus to Stanley, 29 June 1967, F.O. 64/621, no. 373.
22 Stanley to Loftus, 25 June 1867, F.O. 64/615, no. 200.
23 Stanley to Loftus, 25 June 1867 (copy), Papers of the 15th Earl of Derby, 920, DER, 13/1/14.
24 Stanley to Loftus, 3 July 1867 (copy), Papers of the 15th Earl of Derby, 920, DER, 13/1/14.
25 Hammond to Stanley, 21 June 1867, Papers of the 15th Earl of Derby, 920, DER, 12/1/14.
26 Hammond to Cowley, 22 June 1867, Cowley Papers, F.O. 519/193.
27 Hammond to Cowley, 25 June 1867, Cowley Papers, F.O. 519/193.
28 Hansard, 3, clxxxviii, col. 966, 4 July 1867.
29 Hansard, 3, clxxxviii, col. 973, 4 July 1867.
30 Thile to Bernstorff, 10 July 1867, *A.P.P.*, ix, no. 94.
31 Stanley to Loftus, 12 July 1867, F.O. 64/616, no. 209.
32 Loftus to Stanley, 13 April 1867, F.O. 64/619, no. 205.
33 Stanley to Loftus, 25 June 1867 (copy), Papers of the 15th Earl of Derby, 920, DER, 13/1/14.
34 Hammond to Cowley, 25 June 1867, Cowley Papers, F.O. 519/193.
35 See above, ch. VIII.
36 Speech in Reichstag, 24 Sept. 1867, Bismarck, *Die politischen Reden*, ed. H. Kohl, iii, p. 312.
37 Currie, note of conversations with Bismarck at Friedrichsruh, 28 Sept, 1885, *P.D.I.*, p. 250.
38 A. W. Heffter, *Das europäische Völkerrecht der Gegenwart*, ed. F. H. Geffcken (Berlin, 1881), p. 210; G. Quabbe, *Die völkerrechtliche Garantie* (Breslau, 1911), pp. 101, 159 and 164.
39 Grey to Queen Augusta of Prussia, July 1867, *A.P.P.*, ix, no. 91.
40 Hansard, 3, clxxxvii, col. 1923, 14 June 1867.
41 Hansard, 3, clxxxviii, col. 150, 20 June 1867.
42 Ibid., col. 152.
43 Clarendon to Hammond, 17 June 1867, Hammond Papers, F.O. 391/4.
44 Hansard, 3, clxxxvii, col. 1918, 14 June 1867.
45 See below, ch. XIV.
46 Clarke, 'Treaty Guarantees and the Obligations of Guaranteeing Powers', 1 Aug. 1905, Cab. 38/10, no. 67.
47 Sanderson to Clarke, 10 Aug. 1905, Cab. 17/69.
48 Ibid.

XI 'Engagements to go to war'

1 Hansard, 3, clxxvi, col. 838, 5 July 1864.
2 *Times*, 11 July 1864.
3 Speech at Liverpool, 12 Oct. 1864, *Times*, 13 Oct. 1864.
4 Gladstone to Grey, 17 April 1869, R.A. Q. 3/115.
5 Speech at Edinburgh, 17 March 1880, *P.S.S.*, 2, p. 33.
6 *M.E.T.*, iii, nos. 427–8. See also above, ch. II.
7 Loftus to Stanley, 13 April 1867, F.O. 64/619, no. 205.

8 Loftus to Stanley, 13 April 1867, Papers of the 15th Earl of Derby, 920, DER, 12/1/16; Loftus to Clarendon, 20 Feb., 27 Feb. and 6 March 1869, Clarendon Papers, C. 478.
9 Loftus to Clarendon, 10 July 1869, Clarendon Papers, C. 478.
10 Loftus to Granville, 16 July 1870, Granville Papers, P.R.O. 30/29/90.
11 Granville to Lyons, 25 July 1870, F.O. 27/1792, no. 130.
12 W. A. Fletcher, *The Mission of Vincent Benedetti to Berlin 1864–1870* (The Hague, 1965), p. 265; Millman, op. cit., p. 201.
13 *Times*, 25 July 1870.
14 Hertslet, memorandum, 26 July 1870, Gladstone Papers, B.M. 44,615.
15 Gladstone, memorandum, undated, Gladstone Papers, B.M. 44,638.
16 Gladstone to Queen Victoria, 30 July 1870, *L.Q.V.*, 2, ii, p. 54.
17 Hammond, memorandum, 29 July 1870, Granville Papers, P.R.O. 30/29/104.
18 Lyons to Granville, 3 Aug. 1870, Granville Papers, P.R.O. 30/29/85.
19 G. M. Trevelyan, *John Bright*, p. 406.
20 Gladstone to Bright, 1 Aug. 1870, Bright Papers, B.M. 43,385.
21 Bright to Gladstone, 3 Aug. 1870, Gladstone Papers, B.M. 44,112.
22 Gladstone to Bright, 4 Aug. 1870, Bright Papers, B.M. 43,385. For an account of this correspondence see also Morley, *Gladstone*, ii, p. 341.
23 Hansard, 3, cciii, col. 1788, 10 Aug. 1870.
24 Ibid., col. 1739.
25 Granville to Buchanan, 20 Aug. 1870, Buchanan Papers.
26 Beaconsfield to Marlborough, 8 March 1880, Monypenny and Buckle, *Disraeli* (London, 1929), ii, p. 1387.
27 Speech at Edinburgh, 17 March 1880, *P.S.S.*, 2, p. 30.
28 *P.S.S.*, 2, p. 33.

XII 'Diplomatic liabilities'

1 Hansard, 3, clxxxvii, col. 1917, 14 June 1867.
2 Speech at King's Lynn, 11 July 1866, *Times*, 12 July 1866.
3 For Britain's part in the Savoy incident see A. G. Imlah, *Britain and Switzerland 1845–60* (London, 1966), p. 156; D. Mack Smith, *Victor Emanuel, Cavour, and the Risorgimento* (London, 1971), p. 159.
4 Palmerston to Russell, 5 Feb. 1860, Russell Papers, P.R.O. 30/22/21.
5 Hansard, 3, clvi, col. 2170, 2 March 1860.
6 Russell to Palmerston, 5 March 1860, Palmerston Papers, GC/RU/581.
7 Russell to Palmerston, 12 March 1860, Palmerston Papers, GC/RU/582.
8 *M.E.T.*, ii, no. 307.
9 Russell to Cowley, 17 March 1860, Cowley Papers, F.O. 519/198, pt. 1.
10 Russell to Cowley, 19 March 1860, Cowley Papers, F.O. 519/198, pt. 1.
11 *M.E.T.*, ii, no. 313.
12 Queen Victoria to Russell, 25 March 1860, Russell Papers, P.R.O. 30/22/27.
13 Russell, memorandum, 25 March 1860, Russell Papers, P.R.O. 30/22/27.
14 Palmerston to Russell, 6 Nov. 1862, Russell Papers, P.R.O. 30/22/14D.
15 Ibid.
16 Russell to Palmerston, 8 Nov. 1862, Palmerston Papers, GC/RU/741.
17 *M.E.T.*, ii, no. 347.
18 *M.E.T.*, iii, no. 357.
19 J. du Mont, *Corps universel diplomatique du droit des gens*, viii, 2, p. 33.
20 Hammond to law officers, 11 Feb. 1864, F.O. 83/2261.

21 Hammond to law officers, 14 Feb. 1864, F.O. 83/2261.
22 Russell to Queen Victoria, 14 Feb. 1864, R.A. I. 94/136. Russell actually wrote 'the previous Treaty (of 1718)'. '1718' was, presumably, a slip for '1715'.
23 Phillimore to Hammond, 17 Feb. 1864, F.O. 83/2261.
24 Palmer and Collier to Hammond, 17 Feb. 1864, F.O. 83/2261.
25 See above, ch. xi.
26 Stanley to Disraeli, 23 April 1867, Disraeli Papers, Box 111.
27 See above, ch. x.
28 Gordon A. Craig, War, Politics and Diplomacy (London, 1966), p. 153.
29 Clarendon to Lumley, 6 March 1869 (copy), Clarendon Papers, C. 475.
30 Clarendon to Gladstone, 3 April 1869, Gladstone Papers, B.M. 44,133.
31 Clarendon to Gladstone, 14 April 1869, Gladstone Papers, B.M. 44,133.
32 Clarendon to Queen Victoria, 13 April 1869, L.Q.V., 2, i, p. 589.
33 Queen Victoria to Clarendon, 15 April 1869, L.Q.V., 2, i, p. 589.
34 Clarendon to Queen Victoria, 16 April 1869, L.Q.V., 2, i, p. 590.
35 See above, ch. xi.
36 Hansard, 3, cciii, col. 1787, 10 Aug. 1870.
37 Law officers to Granville, 6 Aug. 1870, B.D., viii, no. 311.
38 Hansard, 3, cciii, col. 1740, 9 Aug. 1870.
39 See above, ch. vi.
40 Hansard, 3, cciii, cols. 1288–9, 1 Aug. 1870.
41 Gathorne Hardy, diary, 3 Aug. 1870, Cranbrook Papers, H.A. 43. T. 501/295.
42 Hansard, 3, cciii, col. 1290, 1 Aug. 1870.
43 Gathorne Hardy, diary, 3 Aug. 1870, Cranbrook Papers, H.A. 43. T. 501/295.
44 Hansard, 3, cciv, col. 102, 9 Feb. 1871.
45 Granville to Gladstone, 10 Dec. 1870, G.G. 1868–76, i, no. 400.
46 Gladstone to Granville, 12 Dec. 1870, G.G. 1868–76, i, no. 406.
47 Granville to Queen Victoria, 2 March 1871, R.A. B. 26/11.
48 Hansard, 3, cciv, cols. 1360–8, 6 March 1871.
49 Hansard, 3, cciv, col. 1368, 6 March 1871.
50 A.P., 1871, lxxii, p. 449.
51 G. W. E. Russell, Sir Wilfrid Lawson (London, 1909), p. 98.
52 Hansard, 3, ccx, col. 1151, 12 April 1872.
53 Hansard, 3, ccx, col. 1164, 12 April 1872.
54 Hansard, 3, ccx, cols. 1176–82, 12 April 1872. See also Times, 13 April 1872.
55 Hansard, 3, ccx, col. 1183, 12 April 1872.
56 Times, 13 April 1872.
57 Spectator, 20 April 1872.

XIII 'The national honour'

1 Derby to Buchanan, 4 March 1874, Buchanan Papers.
2 Hansard, 3, ccxxiv, col. 1099, 31 May 1875.
3 Odo Russell to Derby, 1 Feb. 1876, Papers of the 15th Earl of Derby, 920, DER, 16/1/16.
4 Derby to Odo Russell, 16 Feb. 1876, F.B.F.P., no. 139.
5 Beaconsfield to Queen Victoria, 10 June 1877, R.A. H. 14/74.
6 Beaconsfield to Queen Victoria, 14 June 1877, R.A. H. 14/84.
7 Buchanan to Derby, 7 July 1877, F.O. 7/903, no. 575; Andrassy to Beust, communicated to Derby, 9 July 1877, R.A. H. 15/10.
8 Derby to Buchanan, 10 July 1877, Buchanan Papers.

9 Salisbury to Layard, 2 May 1878, Layard Papers, B.M. 39,137.
10 Cecil, *Salisbury*, ii, p. 263.
11 Salisbury to Layard, 2 May 1878, Layard Papers, B.M. 39,137.
12 Salisbury to Layard, 10 May 1878, Layard Papers, B.M. 39,137.
13 Salisbury to Layard, 24 May 1878, *L.Q.V.*, 2, ii, p. 623.
14 Sandon, cabinet journal, 23 May 1878, Ryder Papers, 407.
15 Ibid.; cf. also Gladstone's speech at Mid-Calder, 20 March 1880, *P.S.S.*, 2, p. 181.
16 C. U. Aitchison, *A Collection of Treaties, Engagements and Sanads relating to India and Neighbouring Countries* (Calcutta, 1909), xi, passim.
17 Salisbury to Cross, 12 July 1878, Cross Papers, B.M. 51,263.
18 Sandon, cabinet journal, 17 July 1878, Ryder Papers, 408.
19 Elliot to Layard, 17 July 1878, Layard Papers, B.M. 39,021.
20 Salisbury to Layard, 2 May 1878, Layard Papers, B.M. 39,137.
21 Salisbury to Layard, 9 May 1878, Layard Papers, B.M. 39,137.
22 Salisbury to Layard, 10 May 1878, Layard Papers, B.M. 39,137.
23 Lytton to Cranbrook, 22 May 1879, Cranbrook Papers, H.A. 43. T. 501/32.
24 Ibid. See also above, ch. II.
25 Beaconsfield to Derby, 13 Sept. 1877, Papers of the 15th Earl of Derby, 920 DER 16/2/3.
26 As reported by Münster to Bülow, 29 March 1878, *G.P.*, ii, no. 375.
27 Speech at Knightsbridge Riding School, 27 July 1878, *Times*, 29 July 1878.
28 Beaconsfield, memorandum, 27 Sept. 1879, R.A. A. 62/50.
29 Beaconsfield to Salisbury, 1 Oct. 1879, Salisbury Papers, Beaconsfield Correspondence.
30 Salisbury to Beaconsfield, 14 Oct. 1879, Hughenden Papers, Box 92.
31 Queen Victoria, journal, 30 Oct. 1879, *L.Q.V.*, 2, iii, p. 53.
32 Northcote to Beaconsfield, 30 Oct. 1879, Hughenden Papers, Box 107.
33 Beaconsfield to Queen Victoria, 5 Nov. 1879, R.A. B. 62/27.
34 Speech at West Calder, 2 April 1880, *P.S.S.*, 2, p. 356.
35 Hansard, 3, ccxlii, col. 509, 29 July 1878.
36 Salisbury to Cranbrook, 17 Sept. 1878, Cranbrook Papers, H.A. 43. T. 501/269.

XIV   'Misty and shadowy guarantees'

1 Hansard, 3, ccxli, col. 1796, 18 July 1878.
2 E.g., by Gladstone, Hansard, 3, ccx, col. 1180, 12 April 1872.
3 E.g., by Harcourt, Hansard, 3, ccxlii, col. 1083, 2 Aug. 1878.
4 *M.E.T.*, iv, no. 530.
5 *B.F.S.P.*, lxxii, p. 900.
6 *B.F.S.P.*, lxxvi, pt. 1, p. 349.
7 *B.F.S.P.*, lxxix, p. 18.
8 *B.D.*, i, no. 118.
9 *M.E.T.*, iii, p. 2057.
10 *Parliamentary History of England*, xv, col. 653, 10 Dec. 1755. See also above, ch. II.
11 Bentham, op. cit., ii, p. 549. See also above, ch. II.
12 *Spectator*, 6 Feb. 1864.
13 Hansard, 3, clxxxvii, col. 1913, 14 June 1867.
14 *Saturday Review*, 22 June 1867.
15 Hansard, 3, clxxxviii, col. 155, 20 June 1867.

16 *Times*, 13 April 1872.
17 Hansard, 3, ccxiv, col. 463, 14 Feb. 1873.
18 Hansard, 3, clxxxviii, col. 151, 20 June 1867.
19 Derby to Lytton, 1 Oct. 1874, Lytton Papers, Box 89.
20 Hansard, 3, ccxl, col. 1412, 13 June 1878.
21 Hansard, 3, ccxlii, col. 509, 29 July 1878.
22 Ibid.
23 Hansard, 3, ccxxxii, col. 41, 8 Feb. 1877.
24 Hansard, 3, ccxlii, col. 509, 29 July 1878.
25 Salisbury, minute, undated, but evidently written in March 1902, Balfour Papers, B.M. 49,727.
26 Derby to Lytton, 1 Oct. 1874, Lytton Papers, Box 89.
27 *D.E.W.H.*, i, p. 205.
28 Report of the Committee appointed to consider certain Questions relating to the future Administration of Egypt, 4 Nov. 1882, Granville Papers, P.R.O. 30/29/194.
29 *B.F.S.P.*, lxxvi, pt. 1, p. 345.
30 Malet to Granville, 8 Oct. 1882, Granville Papers, P.R.O. 30/29/160.
31 Granville, draft dispatch to Malet, 18 Oct. 1882, Joseph Chamberlain Papers, J.C. 7/1/3/8.
32 Chamberlain, memorandum, 18 Oct. 1882, Joseph Chamberlain Papers, J.C. 7/1/3/4.
33 Gladstone to Granville, 19 Oct. 1882, *G.G. 1876–86*, i, no. 871.
34 Gladstone, memorandum, 21 Oct. 1882, Gladstone Papers, B.M. 44,643.
35 Salisbury to Devonshire, 2 March 1896, Devonshire Papers, 340. 2685.
36 D.M.I., memorandum, 15 Oct. 1896, A. J. Marder, *British Naval Policy 1880–1905* (London, 1941), pp. 576–7.
37 D.N.I., memorandum, 28 Oct. 1896, Marder, op. cit., p. 580.
38 J. A. S. Grenville, *Lord Salisbury and Foreign Policy* (London, 1964), p. 185; Z. S. Steiner, *The Foreign Office and Foreign Policy 1898–1914* (Cambridge, 1969), p. 38.
39 Chamberlain, memorandum, 18 June 1897, Joseph Chamberlain Papers, J.C. 7/3/2c/5.
40 Sanderson, memorandum, 21 March 1898, Joseph Chamberlain Papers, J.C. 7/3/20/9.
41 Bertie, memorandum, 1 May 1898, *B.D.*, i, no. 65.
42 Drury to Hopkins, 14 July 1898, F.O. 185/866; Biddulph to War Office, 19 July 1898, Balfour Papers, B.M. 49,746; Ardagh, memoranda on Spanish works in the neighbourhood of Gibraltar, 18 and 24 Aug. and 17 Sept. 1898, Ardagh Papers, P.R.O. 30/40/14, pt. ii.
43 Balfour to Wolff, 11 Aug. 1898, F.O. 185/866, no. 102; 25 Aug. 1898, F.O. 185/867, no. 109.
44 Salisbury to Balfour, 31 Aug. 1898, Balfour Papers, B.M. 49,691.
45 Balfour, draft telegram to Wolff, 1 Sept. 1898, Salisbury Papers, A/96.
46 Gosselin to Wolff, 6 Sept. 1898, F.O. 185/867, no. 384.
47 Wolff to Salisbury, 8 Sept. 1898, Salisbury Papers, A/133.
48 Salisbury to Queen Victoria, 27 Oct. 1898, R.A. J. 42/75.
49 Salisbury to Wolff, 21 Dec. 1898, F.O. 185/868, no. 293a.
50 See below, ch. XVI.

xv 'The Liberal view'

1 Speech at West Calder, 27 Nov. 1879, *P.S.S.*, i, pp. 115–16.
2 Ripon, memorandum, 9 May 1880, Wolf, *Ripon*, ii, p. 20.
3 Hansard, 3, cclxiv, col. 433, 1 Aug. 1881.
4 Chamberlain, minute, 17 March 1885, Joseph Chamberlain, *A Political Memoir* (London, 1953), pp. 180–2.
5 Kimberley, memorandum, 18 March 1885, Joseph Chamberlain Papers, J.C. 7/1/2/2.
6 Chamberlain, minute, 17 March 1885, Chamberlain, op. cit., p. 181.
7 *Lord Carlingford's Journal*, ed. A. B. Cooke and J. R. Vincent (Oxford, 1971), p. 82.
8 For an account of this meeting see Lyall, *Dufferin and Ava*, ii, pp. 89–101.
9 Dufferin to Kimberley, 5 April 1885, Dufferin Collection, I.O.L., MSS. Eur. F. 130/2.
10 Ibid.
11 Dufferin to Kimberley, 11 April 1885, Dufferin Collection, I.O.L. MSS. Eur. F. 130/2.
12 Dufferin to Kimberley, 5 May 1885, Dufferin Collection, I.O.L. MSS. Eur. F. 130/2.
13 Dufferin to Churchill, 28 Sept. 1885, Dufferin Collection, I.O.L. MSS. Eur. F. 130/2.
14 Speech at Rawtenstall, 22 March 1880, *Times*, 23 March 1880.
15 Granville to Lyons, 1 May 1880, F.O. 27/2421, no. 447.
16 Speech at Blackburn, 10 Oct. 1885, *Times*, 12 Oct. 1885.
17 Labouchere to Harcourt, 3 Jan. (1888), Harcourt Papers. Year of letter not stated, but evident from contents.
18 Ibid.
19 Ibid.
20 Hansard, 3, cccxxii, cols. 152, 377 and 557, 10, 14 and 16 Feb. 1888.
21 Hansard, 3, cccxxii, col. 1172, 22 Feb. 1888.
22 Ibid., col. 1187.
23 Hansard, 3, ccclv, cols. 210 and 546, 2 and 7 July 1891.
24 Ibid., col. 546.
25 Labouchere to Harcourt, 7 July (1891), Harcourt Papers. Year of letter not stated, but evident from contents.
26 Hansard, 3, ccclv, col. 771, 9 July 1891.
27 Ibid., cols. 778–80.
28 Ibid., cols. 786–7.
29 Harcourt to Gladstone, 11 July 1891, Gladstone Papers, B.M. 44,202.
30 Ibid.
31 Ibid.
32 Gladstone to Rosebery, 12 July 1891, Rosebery Papers, Box 19.
33 Rosebery to Gladstone, 16 July 1891, Gladstone Papers, B.M. 44,289.
34 Harcourt to Gladstone, 22 July 1891, Gladstone Papers, B.M. 44,202.
35 Waddington to Ribot, 14 July 1891, *D.D.F.*, i, viii, no. 421, enclosure.
36 Salisbury to Hicks Beach, 20 Oct. 1891, St Aldwyn Papers. D. 2455, PCC/69
37 Salisbury to Currie, 18 Aug. 1892, Cecil, *Salisbury*, iv, pp. 404–5.
38 Rosebery to Gladstone, 27 Aug. 1892, Gladstone Papers, B.M. 44,289.
39 Sanderson, memorandum, 22 Jan. 1903, *B.D.*, viii, no. 2.
40 Rosebery, memorandum, 5 Sept. 1892, *B.D.*, viii, no. 1.
41 Rosebery to Malet, 3 Jan. 1894, Malet Papers, F.O. 343/3.

NOTES, PAGES 126–33 191

XVI 'Our popular constitution'

1 E.g., *Quarterly Review*, cxcvi (1902), p. 664. There are many other examples. See below, ch. XVII.
2 Salisbury to Queen Victoria, 12 Jan. 1896, *L.Q.V.*, 3, iii, p. 21.
3 Salisbury to Lascelles, 10 March 1896, F.O. 800/9.
4 Ibid.
5 Currie, copy of paper shown to Count Herbert Bismarck at Königstein, 3 Aug. 1885, *P.D.I.*, pp. 239–41.
6 Currie, notes of conversations with Prince Bismarck at Friedrichsruh, 28 Sept. 1885, *P.D.I.*, p. 250.
7 Malet to Salisbury, 1 Feb. 1887, F.O. 64/1155, no. 33.
8 Salisbury to Queen Victoria, 23 Feb. 1887, R.A. H. 34/41.
9 Salisbury, memorandum, 23 Feb. 1887, R.A. H. 34/42.
10 Salisbury to Paget, 26 Feb. 1887, F.O. 7/1113, no. 39.
11 Odo Russell to Granville, 18 Dec. 1870, Granville Papers, P.R.O. 30/29/92.
12 Pauncefote to Salisbury, 17 March 1898, F.O. 5/2361, no. 70.
13 Hansard, 3, cccxliv, col. 1062, 16 May 1890.
14 Waddington to Spuller, 23 March and 14 Nov. 1889, *D.D.F.*, 1, vii, nos. 353 and 504.
15 Memorandum, 23 Feb. 1887, *G.P.*, iv, no. 894.
16 E. Walters, 'Lord Salisbury's Refusal to Revise and Renew the Mediterranean Agreements', *Slavonic Review*, xxix (1950–51), pp. 276–86.
17 *Spectator*, 6 June 1891.
18 Loftus, op. cit., i, p. 272.
19 *Fortnightly Review*, lix (1896), p. 340.
20 See below, ch. XVII.
21 See below, ch. XVIII.
22 Salisbury to Monson, 4 Feb. 1896, F.O. 120/721, no. 17.
23 See above, ch. XIV.
24 Wolff to Salisbury, 10 and 15 March 1899, F.O. 185/891, nos. 49 and 57, the latter enclosing translation of note from Silvela.
25 Salisbury to Wolff, 16 March 1899, F.O. 185/888, f. 64.
26 Wolff to Salisbury, 17 March 1899, Salisbury Papers, A/134.
27 See above, ch. XIV and below, ch. XIX.
28 Holstein to Chirol, 3 Jan. 1902, *B.D.*, ii, no. 96.
29 Salisbury to Sanderson, 15 Jan. 1902 (copy), Lascelles Papers, F.O. 800/10.
30 Sanderson to Lascelles, 15 Jan. 1902, Lascelles Papers, F.O. 800/10.
31 I. H. Nish, *The Anglo-Japanese Alliance* (London, 1966), p. 209.
32 Salisbury to Lascelles, 10 March 1896, Lascelles Papers, F.O. 800/9.
33 *Contemporary Review*, lxix (1896), p. 165.
34 See above, ch. XV.
35 Salisbury to Queen Victoria, 25 Aug. 1888, *L.Q.V.*, 3, i, p. 437.
36 Salisbury to Queen Victoria, 10 June 1890, *L.Q.V.*, 3, i, p. 614.
37 Salisbury to Dufferin, 16 Jan. 1891, Dufferin Papers, P.R.O. of Northern Ireland, D. 1071/H/NI/1.
38 Salisbury to Lascelles, 10 March 1896, Lascelles Papers, F.O. 800/9.
39 Salisbury to Balfour, 9 April 1898, Balfour Papers, B.M. 49,691.
40 *Speaker*, 18 Jan. 1896.
41 Speech at Eighty Club, 13 April 1897, *Times*, 14 April 1897.
42 Salisbury to Robert Morier, 1 Feb. 1888, Morier Papers.

XVII   'Policy of alliances'

1 *Contemporary Review*, lxvii (1895), p. 845.
2 *Contemporary Review*, lxix (1896), pp. 157-9.
3 *Saturday Review*, 25 Jan. 1896.
4 *Spectator*, 18 Jan. 1896.
5 H. Spenser Wilkinson, *The Nation's Awakening* (London, 1896).
6 Ibid., p. 127.
7 Ibid.
8 Ibid., pp. 129-31.
9 Ibid., pp. 132-49.
10 Ibid., p. xix.
11 Speech at Lewes, 26 Feb. 1896, *Times*, 27 Feb. 1896.
12 See specially the speeches by Rosebery and Harcourt, mentioned below.
13 Speech at Eighty Club, 3 March 1896, *Times*, 4 March 1896.
14 Speech at Ebbw Vale, 5 Oct. 1896, *Times*, 6 Oct. 1896.
15 Speech at Eighty Club, 13 April 1897, *Times*, 14 April 1897. See also above, chs. v and xvi.
16 *Speaker*, 18 Jan. 1896.
17 I have not been able to locate the origin of this term. It may be an adaptation of the phrase 'system of alliances', employed by Rosebery in his Eighty Club speech of 3 March 1896.
18 Grenville, op. cit., pp. 24-147.
19 There was much to this effect. See, e.g., Lloyd George's speeches at Penarth, 28 Nov. 1896, *South Wales Daily News*, 30 Nov. 1896, and at Kettering, 12 Nov. 1897, *Kettering Leader and Observer*, 19 Nov. 1897. I owe these references to Dr M. L. Dockrill.
20 Harcourt to Morley, 1 Oct. 1897 (copy), Harcourt Papers.
21 Hansard, 4, liv, cols. 303-4, 1 March 1898.
22 Balfour to Pauncefote, 7 March 1898, F.O. 5/2364, no. 18.
23 Pauncefote to Salisbury, 17 March 1898, F.O. 5/2361, no. 70. See also above, ch. xvi. Like many other people Pauncefote attributed this 'celebrated warning' to Washington.
24 Wilkinson, op. cit., p. 129.
25 Curzon to Salisbury, 29 Dec. 1897, Salisbury Papers, Curzon Correspondence.
26 Garvin, *Joseph Chamberlain*, iii, p. 249.
27 Nish, op. cit., p. 63.
28 Nish, op. cit., p. 65.
29 Although not explicitly stated, this seems to be implied in Wilkinson's letter to Chamberlain, 12 March 1898, Joseph Chamberlain Papers, J.C. 7/2/1/5, quoted below.
30 Ibid.
31 G. S. Papadopoulos, 'Lord Salisbury and the Projected Anglo-German Alliance of 1898', *B.I.H.R.*, xxvi (1953), p. 214.
32 This conversation marks the beginning of the negotiations for an alliance with Germany, concerning which a great deal has been written. See especially H. W. Koch, 'The Anglo-German Alliance Negotiations: Missed Opportunity or Myth?', *History*, liv (1969), p. 378. Dr P. M. Kennedy has kindly shown me the typescript of his forthcoming article on 'German World Policy and the Alliance Negotiations with England 1897-1900'. I have not myself attempted to describe the negotiations.

33 Chamberlain, memorandum, 29 March 1898, Joseph Chamberlain Papers, J.C. 7/2/2A/3. Chamberlain subsequently deleted the references to Alfred Rothschild. His revised version is printed in Garvin, *Joseph Chamberlain*, iii. pp. 259-60, with a correction of the spelling mistake.
34 Garvin, *Joseph Chamberlain*, iii, pp. 262–77.
35 Hansard, 4, lvi, col. 281, 5 April 1898.
36 Hansard, 4, lvi, col. 286, 5 April 1898.
37 Chamberlain to Salisbury, dated 'April 1898', endorsed '29 April 1898', Salisbury Papers, Chamberlain Correspondence.
38 Salisbury to Chamberlain, 2 May 1898, Joseph Chamberlain Papers, J.C. 5/67/91.
39 Salisbury to Chamberlain, 3 May 1898, Joseph Chamberlain Papers, J.C. 5/67/92.
40 Speech at Albert Hall, 4 May 1898, *Times*, 5 May 1898.
41 Speech at Cambridge, 7 May 1898, *Times*, 9 May 1898.
42 Salisbury to Lascelles, 11 May 1898, F.O. 64/1436, no. 109.
43 Speech at Birmingham, 13 May 1898, *Times*, 14 May 1898.
44 Ibid.
45 Ibid.
46 *Financial Times*, 16 May 1898.
47 *Economist*, 21 May 1898.
48 *City Review* and *Statist*, 21 May 1898. There was much to the same effect in other newspapers and reviews. Some, e.g., the *Financial Times*, 16 May 1898, also blamed Salisbury, who had delivered a speech to a group of bankers.
49 *Times, Morning Post* and *St James's Gazette*, 14 May 1898.
50 *Westminster Gazette*, 17 May 1898.
51 *Speaker*, 21 May 1898.
52 Hansard, 4, lvii, col. 1384, 16 May 1898.
53 John Morley to Harcourt, 16 May 1898, Harcourt Papers.
54 Harcourt to John Morley, 17 May 1898 (copy), Harcourt Papers.
55 Hansard, 4, lvii, cols. 1512-4, 17 May 1898.
56 Ibid., col. 1515.
57 Speech at Leeds, 8 June 1898, *Manchester Guardian*, 9 June 1898.
58 Hansard, 4, lviii, col. 1317, 10 June 1898.
59 Ibid., cols. 1334–8.
60 Ibid., cols. 1347–50.
61 Ibid., col. 1420.
62 Ibid., col. 1430.
63 Curzon to Salisbury, 12 June 1898, Salisbury Papers, Curzon Correspondence.
64 *Fortnightly Review*, lxiv (1898), p. 634.
65 Ibid., p. 317. There was much at this period to similar effect on the subject of Salisbury's conduct of foreign affairs. See also Harcourt's speech at Cambridge, 7 May 1898, quoted above.
66 Harcourt to Morley, 10 Oct. 1898 (copy), Harcourt Papers.
67 Edward Hamilton, diary, 3 Nov. 1898, Hamilton Papers, B.M. 48,673. Misdated 5 Nov. in MS.
68 *Fortnightly Review*, lxiv (1898), p. 1002.
69 Ibid.
70 Robertson, essay, 8 Dec. 1898, Robertson Papers, I/2/1.
71 Edward Hamilton, diary, 28 Nov. 1899, Hamilton Papers, B.M. 48,675.
72 Chamberlain, second speech at Leicester, 30 Nov. 1899, *Times*, 1 Dec. 1899.
73 Ibid.

74 Garvin, *Joseph Chamberlain*, iii, p. 508.
75 Kimberley to Spencer, 7 Dec. 1899, Spencer Papers.
76 Lansdowne to Lascelles, 19 Dec. 1901, *B.D.*, ii, no. 94.

XVIII   'A pretty sudden shock'

1 Salisbury to O'Connor, 25 Jan. 1898, *B.D.*, i, no. 9.
2 L. K. Young, *British Policy in China 1895–1902* (Oxford, 1970), p. 95.
3 *B.F.S.P.*, xci, p. 91.
4 *B.F.S.P.*, xcii, p. 31.
5 Young, op. cit., p. 207.
6 Hermann, Freiherr von Eckardstein, *Lebenserinnerungen und politische Denkwürdig-keiten* (Leipzig, 1919–20), ii, p. 236.
7 Lansdowne to Lascelles, 18 March, 9 and 13 April 1901, *B.D.*, ii, nos. 77, 80 and 81.
8 Lansdowne, memorandum, 24 March 1901, *B.D.*, ii, no. 82.
9 Sanderson, memorandum, 27 May 1901, *B.D.*, ii, no. 85.
10 Salisbury, memorandum, 29 May 1901, *B.D.*, ii, no. 86.
11 Nish, op. cit., p. 147.
12 Lansdowne to Whitehead, 31 July 1901, *B.D.*, ii, no. 102.
13 Selborne, memorandum, 4 Sept. 1901, Z. Steiner, 'Great Britain and the Creation of the Anglo-Japanese Alliance', *J.M.H.*, xxxi (1959), p. 29.
14 Salisbury to King Edward VII, 5 Nov. 1901, R.A. R. 22/57.
15 Salisbury, memorandum, 7 Jan. 1902, Salisbury Papers, Cabinet Papers, Box 5.
16 Balfour, memorandum, 12 Dec. 1901, Balfour Papers, B.M. 49,727.
17 Hicks Beach to Lansdowne, 2 Jan. 1902, Lansdowne Papers, F.O. 800/134.
18 Balfour, memorandum, 12 Dec. 1901, Balfour Papers, B.M. 49,727.
19 Hicks Beach to Lansdowne, 2 Jan. 1902, Lansdowne Papers, F.O. 800/134.
20 Lansdowne to MacDonald, 7 Jan. 1902, *B.D.*, ii, no. 120.
21 *Daily News*, 12 Feb. 1902.
22 *Saturday Review*, 15 Feb. 1902.
23 *Spectator*, 15 Feb. 1902.
24 *Fortnightly Review*, lxxi (1902), p. 365.
25 Hansard, 4, cii, col. 1273, 12 Feb. 1902.
26 Ibid., col. 1311.
27 Ibid., col. 1303.
28 Ibid., col. 1301.
29 Speech at Liverpool, 14 Feb. 1902, *Times*, 15 Feb. 1902.

XIX   'Still in force'

1 See above, ch. XVIII.
2 See above, ch. XVII.
3 As pointed out by Lillian M. Penson, 'Obligations by Treaty', Sarkissian, op cit., p. 76.
4 Hansard, 3, ccxxix, col. 1891, 15 June 1876.
5 See above, ch. XIV.
6 For the failure of the Tripartite Treaty see A. F. Pribram, *The Secret Treaties of Austria-Hungary* (New York, 1967), ii, p. 194; W. E. Mosse, *The Rise and Fall of the Crimean System*, pp. 192–8.

7 Cecil, *Salisbury*, ii, p. 85.
8 Ibid., p. 266.
9 Hansard, 4, xxxix, col. 450, 30 March 1896.
10 There was a great deal said and written to this effect at the time. See, e.g., *Punch*, 18 Jan. 1896.
11 Hansard, 4, xlv, col. 29, 19 Jan. 1897.
12 Hansard, 4, xlviii, col. 993, 12 April 1897.
13 Hansard, 4, lxi, col. 1195, 15 July 1898.
14 *A.P.*, 1899, cix, p. 1.
15 See above, ch. xiv.
16 Hansard, 3, ccxxxii, col. 41, 8 Feb. 1877.
17 Derby to Loftus, 1 May 1877, *M.E.T.*, iv, no. 496.
18 Currie, notes of conversation with Bismarck at Friedrichsruh, 28 Sept. 1885, *P.D.I.*, p. 250.
19 Salisbury, memorandum, 27 Sept. 1896, Cab. 37/42, no. 35.
20 Granville to Goschen, 10 June 1880, *F.B.F.P.*, no. 154.
21 Harcourt to Hartington, 8 Sept. 1879, Devonshire Papers, 340.829.
22 Address to the Electors of North-East Lancashire, *Times*, 11 March 1880.
23 Hansard, 4, xxxix, col. 449, 30 March 1896.
24 Hansard, 3, ccx, col. 1153, 12 April 1872.
25 *B.D.*, viii, no. 103.
26 Granville to Layard, 19 Feb. 1873, and to Murray, 27 Feb. 1973, *B.D.*, i, no. 69.
27 R. J. Hammond, *Portugal and Africa 1815–1910* (Stanford, 1966), pp. 125–47; E. Axelson, *Portugal and the Scramble for Africa 1875–1891* (Johannesburg, 1967), pp. 201–97.
28 Hammond to Currie, 22 Jan. 1890, Hammond Papers, Foxholm, 13.
29 Currie to Hammond, 29 Jan. 1890, Hammond Papers, Foxholm, 13.
30 See P. R. Warhurst, *Anglo-Portuguese Relations in South-Central Africa* (London, 1962), pp. 109–49; Hammond, op. cit., pp. 247–52.
31 Joseph Chamberlain, memorandum, 10 May 1897, Joseph Chamberlain Papers, J.C. 7/3/2A/2.
32 Salisbury to MacDonnell, 22 June 1898, *B.D.*, i, no. 68.
33 *B.D.*, i, nos. 90–2.
34 Salisbury to Balfour, 31 Aug. 1898, Balfour Papers, B.M. 49,691.
35 *A.P.*, 1899, cix, p. 85.
36 Salisbury to Soveral, 8 Oct. 1899 (copy), Salisbury Papers, A/128.
37 *B.D.*, i, no. 118.
38 Robertson, 'Memorandum on our Military responsibilities with regard to Belgium, Holland, Norway, Sweden, and Portugal', 30 Jan. 1902, Balfour Papers, B.M. 49,739. There is a copy of this document at the Public Record Office, W.O. 106/44. See also Valerie Cromwell, 'Great Britain's European Treaty Obligations in March 1902', *H.J.*, vi (1963), p. 272.
39 Nicholson to Sanderson, 5 March 1902, Balfour Papers, B.M. 49,739.
40 Robertson, memorandum, 30 Jan. 1902, Balfour Papers, B.M. 49,739.
41 Sanderson, minute, undated, Balfour Papers, B.M. 49,739.
42 Lansdowne, minute, 19 March 1902, Balfour Papers, B.M. 49,727.
43 *M.E.T.*, iii, nos. 427–8.
44 Lumley to Granville, 5 Aug. 1870, F.O. 10/306, no. 188.
45 Hansard, 3, ccx, col. 1154, 12 April 1872.
46 Derby to Odo Russell, 27 Feb. 1874, *F.B.F.P.*, no. 136.
47 *Fortnightly Review*, xli (1887), pp. 24–8; Charles W. Dilke, *The Present Position of European Politics* (London, 1887), pp. 40–8.

48 *Standard*, 4 Feb. 1887. For Salisbury's relations with Alfred Austin and the *Standard* see Cecil, *Salisbury*, iv, pp. 55–62. Austin's own papers, preserved in the library of the National Liberal Club, do not, unfortunately, shed any light on this particular episode.
49 Dilke, op. cit., p. 374.
50 *Pall Mall Gazette*, 4 Feb. 1887.
51 *Morning Post*, 5 Feb. 1887.
52 Vivian to Iddlesleigh, 7 Jan. 1887, F.O. 10/498, no. 7.
53 Vivian to Salisbury, 18, 28 and 31 Jan. 1887, F.O. 10/498, nos. 17, 26 and 29.
54 Vivian to Salisbury, 1 Feb. 1887, Salisbury Papers, A. 49.
55 Vivian to Salisbury, 5 Feb. 1887, F.O. 10/498, no. 33.
56 Salisbury to Vivian, 11 Feb. 1887, F.O. 10/497, no. 22.
57 Vivian to Salisbury, 26 Feb. 1887, F.O. 10/498, no. 60.
58 See above, ch. VI.
59 See above, ch. X.
60 Loftus, op. cit., i, p. 272.
61 Sanderson to Clarke, 10 Aug. 1905, Cab. 17/69. See also above, ch. X.
62 Derby to Odo Russell, 3 March 1874 (copy), Papers of the 15th Earl of Derby, 920, DER 17/1/6.
63 Robertson, memorandum, 30 Jan. 1902, Balfour Papers, B.M. 49,739.
64 Currie, notes of conversations with Bismarck at Friedrichsruh, 28 Sept. 1885, *P.D.I.*, p. 250.
65 Lansdowne, minute, 17 March 1902, Balfour Papers, B.M. 49,727.
66 Dilke, op. cit., p. 47.
67 *P.D.I.*, p. 22.
68 D.M.I., memorandum, 15 Oct. 1896, Marder, op. cit., p. 575.
69 Hansard, 3, clxxvi, col. 1280, 8 July 1864.

XX   'Semi-detached policy'

1 J. L. Hammond, article on C. P. Scott, *D.N.B. 1931–1940*, p. 795.
2 Bernard, op. cit., p. 96.
3 Speech at Blackburn, 10 October 1885, *Times*, 12 Oct. 1885.
4 Cardwell, memorandum, 24 July 1870, Gladstone Papers, B.M. 44,119.
5 Lyons to Granville, 31 July 1870, Granville Papers, P.R.O. 30/29/85.
6 Dilke, op. cit., p. 277.
7 See, e.g., Richthofen, memorandum, 3 Feb. 1901, Bülow, *Denkwürdigkeiten*, i, p. 510.
8 Hansard, 4, lviii, col. 1338, 10 June 1898.
9 Lascelles to Salisbury, 27 May 1898, Salisbury Papers, A/121. See also Lascelles to Salisbury, 26 May 1898, *B.D.*, i, no. 53.
10 *Nineteenth Century*, xl (1896), p. 684.
11 Sanderson to Clarke, 10 Aug. 1905, Cab. 17/69.
12 Layard to Lytton, 19 June 1878, Lytton Papers, Box 91.
13 R. Robinson, J. Gallagher and A. Denny, *Africa and the Victorians* (London 1961), p. 12.
14 St Aldwyn, memorandum, Jan. 1914, V. Hicks Beach, *Hicks Beach*, ii, p. 362.
15 For a discussion of this term see D. Vital, *The Making of British Foreign Policy* (London, 1968), p. 10.

INDEX

À Court, 29–30, 33–4, 37–8, 45
Abdul Rahman, 17, 117–20, 162
Aberdeen, and France, 19; and Netherlands, 20, 47; and Greece, 36; on guarantees, 40; and Switzerland, 62; mentioned, 44
Admiralty, 115
Afghanistan, 16–17, 105, 107, 117–120, 127, 171
Aix-la-Chapelle, Congress of, 5, 19
Albert, Prince Consort, 23
Alexander I, 23, 35
Algeciras, Bay of, 21, 115, 130, 162, 170
Alliance and friendship, treaties of, 19, 63, 169
Andrássy, 102
Angola, 17, 155
Angoulême, duc d', 32
Apponyi, 71
Ardahan, 16
Argyll, 56, 79
Armenians, 108, 134
Asquith, 143–4
Athens, 62
Austin, Alfred, 157–9
Austria, agreements with (1887), 15, 20, 162; and Tripartite Treaty, 21, 25, 49–52, 112, 151; offer to (1877), 102; and guarantees, 116; Salisbury on, 132–3, 153; mentioned, 14, 19, 25, 55, 67, 88, 90, 92, 114, 133, 163, 173

Bagot, 20, 36, 38, 45
Balearic Islands, 116
Balfour, and Germany, 17, 155; and Gibraltar, 115; and Spain, 115–16; on alliances, 129, 148–9;

and U.S.A., 137–8; and Japan, 148–9; mentioned, 133
Baltic, 54
Banda Oriental, 34–5
Bangkok, 17, 129, 162
Bartlett, 137
Batum, 16
Bavaria, 25, 48
Beaconsfield, see Disraeli
Beernaert, 158–9
Belgium, treaties concerning (1870), 10–11, 86–90, 156, 169; guarantee to (1831), 24–5, 40, 44–8, (1839), 24–5, 28, 43, 47–8, 62, 67, 83, 86–7, 95–8, 156–61; Britain's interest in, 47–8, 97–8, 153; mentioned, 167
Benedetti, 87, 96
Bentham, 7, 110
Bentinck, 68, 71
Beresford, 139
Berlin, Treaty of, 107–8
Bernstorff, 66, 68–74, 77, 80–1, 87
Bertie, 114–15, 140
Birmingham Liberal Unionist Association, 141
Bismarck, Otto von, and Luxemburg, 66–9, 72, 74, 79, 81–2; on guarantees, 81–2, 87; approach to Britain, 100, 106; on treaties with Britain, 127; on Belgium, 87, 160; mentioned, 106, 116, 128
Bismarck, Herbert von, 127
Bloomfield, 67, 73
Boer War (1899), 130, 145, 155, 167
Bourqueney, 50
Brazil, 34, 170
Bright, Jacob, 89